# BEHIND
# THE COVERS

# BEHIND THE COVERS

INTERVIEWS WITH AUTHORS AND ILLUSTRATORS
OF BOOKS FOR CHILDREN AND YOUNG ADULTS

## Jim Roginski

Bibliographies compiled by Muriel Brown
Children's Literature Specialist
Dallas Public Library

1985

Libraries Unlimited, Inc.
Littleton, Colorado

LIBRARIES UNLIMITED, INC.
P.O. Box 263
Littleton, Colorado 80160-0263

The following have graciously granted permission to use extended quotations.
The author thanks Sister Magdalen Mary of Immaculate Heart College, Los Angeles,
for "Without Reservations," and Princeton University Press for Mai-mai Sze,
trans. and ed., *The Mustard Seed Garden Manual of Painting* by Chieh Tzu Yuan
Hua Chuan, 1679-1701. Bollingen Series. Copyright © 1956, 1963 by Princeton
University Press. Excerpt reprinted by permission of Princeton University Press.

**Library of Congress Cataloging in Publication Data**

Roginski, James, 1945-
   Behind the covers.

   Includes bibliographies and index.
   1. Children--Books and reading. 2. Young adults--
Books and reading. 3. Children's literature--Authorship.
4. Young adult literature--Authorship. 5. Authors,
American--20th century--Interviews. 6. Illustrators--
United States--Interviews. I. Title.
Z1037.A1R65   1985   808.06'8   85-18129
ISBN 0-87287-506-7

Libraries Unlimited books are bound with Type II nonwoven material that meets
and exceeds National Association of State Textbook Administrators' Type II nonwoven material specifications Class A through E.

*For H. C.*

# CONTENTS

# PREFACE

*Behind the Covers* is an addition to the growing number of books devoted to the backgrounds of children's authors and illustrators. Students of children's literature are familiar with omnibus directories such as the continuing *Junior Book of Authors* series (H.W. Wilson), *Something about the Author* (Gale Research), and *Illustrators of Children's Books* (Horn Book) which are considered standards on the subject for the information they impart. There are many others also. All of these books offer staff-written critiques and evaluations, or offer author- or illustrator-supplied comments reformatted for directory use. More personal volumes are also available such as Lee Bennett Hopkins's *Books Are by People* and *More Books by More People* (Citation Press), among others. *Behind the Covers* fits more correctly in the scheme of Hopkins's books, in that this volume is uncritical and presents more of the "other side" of the creator—the more personal, the intimate and the working sides.

And yet *Behind the Covers* takes readers one step further—by allowing them to *see* or perhaps *glimpse* into the work habits and creative lives of the twenty-two people here. Through a question-and-answer format, the authors and illustrators are presented here in their own words, not my words, not the words of a critic, not the words of an evaluator.

The people here display a simultaneous mixture of freshness and familiarity, speaking candidly about their work, offering their views and perceptions to the public (many of them for the first time), giving credence to this volume's title, *Behind the Covers.* Here is the opportunity to hear from the creator's side, many of the issues that are discussed in college classrooms, schoolrooms, and professional schools, and, sometimes, in the press. Here are comments on reviewers, on buyers, on bookmaking, and on the creative process. The full scheme of creating children's and young adult books is here, in one form or another.

The broad selection of people here—novelists, poets, folklorists, fine artists, biographers—is intentional; it provides a sampling of the diversity of the activity and opinion of those creating children's and young adult books. There is a balance of well-known award-winners and newcomers; there are authors, illustrators, and author-illustrators, fiction and nonfiction specialists, the known and the soon-to-be-known. This selection of people may well represent the larger creative community of those who develop books for a young audience. As with all work, there are satisfactions and dissatisfactions. These are discussed—as are the frustrations, the good times and the lean times. The wide selection of talents and skills—and opinion—will lead the reader to a more insightful view of the publishing industry and some of the people who begin the process, the creators.

All interviews were compiled throughout 1983 and early 1984. We met in homes, apartments, and restaurants. Once settled in, we turned the tape recorder on and began talking. It was essentially that simple. After the meeting, usually only one which lasted an average of four hours, tapes were transcribed and edited. As often happens in conversations, points were made, dropped, and referred to later. The editing process involved taking these points and formatting them to a complete, instead of a scattered, thought. Deleted were conversational pauses, repetitions, and other material that could be jarring to readers. (That is a difficulty in transcription: keeping the mood, flavor and intensity of the conversation, but at the same time, keeping it interesting and readable.) Final manuscripts were sent to the individuals interviewed to verify names, dates, bibliographies and other pertinent information.

Questions were easy enough to devise. Having worked with authors and illustrators for almost a decade through my work as a librarian and for publishers, and having toured with them at conventions, bookstores, and press parties, I noticed there is a similarity in questions, especially from an admiring public that is meeting a favorite author or illustrator for the first time. "Why do you. . . ?" "How do you. . . ?" "What is your reason for. . . ?" I started with these, using the premise of meeting someone for the "first time." As conversations deepened and broadened, questions developed from the conversations themselves. Each interview is structured to present a complete reference to past and ongoing (through 1984) creative work.

Each presentation has the following:

*Biographical note,* including career and education information.

*Prelude to the interview,* a personal impression of the interviewee at the time of the interview.

*The interview,* in question-and-answer format. (Questions are preceded by my initials, J.R.; answers are preceded by the initials of the interviewees.)

*Bibliography of books,* representing the individual's entire book publication work through 1984.

*Awards and honors* through 1984, a select listing of literary and honorary awards. Most of these awards are presented in the year of publication or the year following publication of a given book. A brief description of the awards and honors cited here appears on pages 240-44 of this book.

*Additional sources,* a selected listing of other volumes which offer more information on the individuals here. A description of these appears on pages 246-47.

If a section is missing, such as awards and honors, that indicates no information was available as of the preparation of this book.

Following the interviews are appendixes and a general bibliography of books used for the development of this book.

Perhaps the best way to approach this book is to read one interview at a time. Then close the book and go away from it for a while. That will give you time to reflect on what has been said and give the interview a chance to breathe naturally. To read all interviews at once may lead to muddled voices and a sort of reader confusion.

This book has been developed for those who are interested in knowing more of the personal sides of authors and illustrators. For librarians, it is another book to hand to patrons needing more information for general background, research papers, or theses. For teachers in the classroom, it allows the opportunity to present "inside" information to their students, leading, perhaps, to classroom simulations developed from the questions here. For the student of children's literature, it offers some inside views from those on the inside.

What must be kept in mind is that these interviews reflect the interviewees' ideas and opinions at the time of the interview. In the eighteen and more months that have passed during the development of this book, ideas and situations may have changed and the statements may now comprise a sort of momentary historical record. The statements reflect the individual only. Each person speaks only for himself or herself and represents no cause, publisher, or outside agency.

# ACKNOWLEDGMENTS

As Lee Bennett Hopkins says in his interview, the acknowledgments page is one of the most important sections of every book. It is a public thank-you for all those who were involved in the development of the book.

For their help and assistance in suggesting or locating authors and illustrators for interviews: Kate Briggs (Holiday House), Dilys Evans (Dilys Evans Fine Illustration), Suzanne Glazer (Random House/Alfred A. Knopf), Donne Forrest (E. P. Dutton), Dagmar Greve (Holt, Rinehart & Winston), Mimi Kayden (E. P. Dutton), Kathleen O'Connor (William Morrow/Lothrop, Lee & Shepard/ Greenwillow Books), Regina Hayes (Viking-Penguin), and Pat Ross (formerly of Random House/ Alfred A. Knopf).

For librarians who tracked down pieces of information: Ann Weeks (Association for Library Service to Children/American Library Association), Karen Nelson Hoyle (Kerlan Collection/University of Minnesota), Dolores Jones (de Grummond Collection/University of Southern Mississippi), Edward Kemp (Library/ University of Oregon), Edward Skipworth and Kevin Mulcahy (Rutgers Universty), and Patricia Hennessey (Brooklyn Public Library).

For their general background help: Steve Mooser of the Society for Children's Book Writers; Kay Markey for her midnight stoop sittings; Marilyn Kaye for brainstorming; John Donovan and Paula Quint of the Children's Book Council; and Ann Hartman for her three-thousand-mile (and continuing) encouragement. And also to Kathy Wisch for coming in at the eleventh hour and performing necessary editorial duties.

Muriel Brown, Children's Literature Specialist of the Dallas Public Library, receives a special acknowledgment. It fell to her to research and confirm the complete bibliographies of the people here. She tackled the problem well and in the process discovered she is a bibliographer as well as a bibliophile.

Acknowledgment is also due to W. Geiger Ellis and Charlie Reed for their help in tracking down material from *The ALAN Review,* and to Diana Green for locating material in *Parents' Choice.*

Acknowledgments must be made, too, to the twenty-two people here who gave so freely of their time to make this book possible. Without them, there would have been no book.

Betty Washabaugh and Hannah L. Kelminson of Libraries Unlimited must also be recognized. They kept the manuscript intact when I could not. Heather Cameron must be congratulated again for her editorial foresightedness.

And, of course, and most of all, to Jackie who kept the boys at bay and everything else together when most everything else was not. Thank you.

*Martha Alexander*

**Martha Alexander**

## BIOGRAPHICAL NOTE

Martha Alexander is an author and illustrator who was born in Augusta, Georgia, on May 25, 1920. She attended the Cincinnati Academy of Fine Arts in Ohio from 1938 through 1942. Her marriage to Willson Stamper ended in divorce in 1959. Ms. Alexander, the creator of so many humorous children in literature, is the mother of two—a girl, Kim, and a boy, Allen.

## PRELUDE TO THE INTERVIEW

Martha Alexander is the embodiment of the person who marches to the beat of a different drummer.

On first impression, she is a quiet, almost unassuming person. It is when she speaks that the forceful, independent and determined person she is comes forward.

At the time of this interview, she was in the process of moving to Homer, Alaska from Manhattan's Upper East Side. She discovered the state while on a speaking tour and fell in love with it and immediately made preparations for a move there.

What is unusual about this move is that Martha is at a point in her life when other people in her age group opt for Florida condominiums or trailer parks; a time to relax and enjoy the euphemistic 'golden years.' This move, of course, made people wonder about her. But there is nothing to wonder about. This is Martha. She has always done what she feels she must do.

It is this same determination that has made her so successful in publishing. Her first published illustrative work was not for children, but for adults, drawing cosmetics for magazines. When she made the discovery that she was not going to get rich by drawing makeup, she decided she may as well draw something she would like to. And if she became rich in the process, so much the better. Her economic status aside, Martha has decidedly enriched the children's book field with her characteristically small-format books such as the *Blackboard Bear* series, among others.

1

## THE INTERVIEW

J.R.      You've lived all over the world, from Hawaii to Alaska, where you live now. What's it like?

M.A.      As you say, I've lived many places. But when I found Alaska I had a strange feeling of home. It felt like the place I've been looking for without even knowing it. This was *IT!* And I really love living here.

It is called "the last frontier," which it is. Homer, where I live, is a very special place. It attracts most interesting people, too. That is a good part of it.

Perhaps I needed new challenges, too, and Alaska offers these. I have a rather restless side. I need to make changes from time to time, often drastic changes. This was one of them.

J.R.      Let's start chronologically. You moved from Hawaii to New York after training as an illustrator?

M.A.      No. I had gone to a fine arts school. After school I did many related things, but I had had no commercial training. While living in Hawaii I did several murals for pediatricians' offices and I was drawn to doing work relating to children. I also did mosaics and pottery, collages, silk screening, and paintings for children, which I sold through a gallery.

After my divorce I moved to New York. I had two teenagers and I needed to get out of Hawaii. I needed to start a new life in a new place.

I received a letter from an old friend from art school days, Ginnie Hofmann, when she heard I was divorced. She invited me to visit her in New York. My plan had been to go to San Francisco to work for decorators and architects as I felt that I had many skills that I could use to survive. My friend, who is a very successful illustrator, encouraged me to consider New York instead of San Francisco. New York? Me in New York? It seemed like an impossible thing for me to do. She suggested I send her samples of work I had done over the years to see if she felt that I could make it in New York. So I did that and she continued urging me to make the leap. "I'll help you find an apartment, I'll help you get started," she said, and she did. What a friend!

So, in 1960 I moved to New York and free-lanced for magazines for five years. And it was touch and go the whole time. I survived, but with difficulty. It was *hard.*

Ginnie advised me not to try books at first as I needed an immediate income and books were long range and by reputation seldom provided an adequate income. She suggested that I start with magazines as the income was more immediate.

The first thing I had to do was make up a portfolio. This was much more difficult than I had expected it to be. Ginnie's advice was to just do drawings that I enjoyed and that could be possibly used in magazines. I drew flowers and bottles and shoes and spoons, et cetera, et cetera, et cetera.

After several months I mustered the nerve to call *Harper's Bazaar.* I thought I would never forget that wonderful man's name who gave me my first crack at the magazine world, but I have.

The job was a half-page illustration for some eye makeup article. I was to do a large, sexy, watery eye with fluttery lashes that was called the "Moth Eye." They gave me a week to do this. I must have done twenty-five drawings and chose two to show them. They liked what I did and said to bill them for twenty-five dollars.

I was thrilled. I would have done it for nothing, of course, to have something published. But twenty-five dollars was next to nothing. They explained that they had spent a fortune on a color photo for the article, which they hadn't used for some reason.

I had begun! A job on my first try! But the magazine field was not satisfying to me. Though I worked for all the top magazines, I did mostly editorial drawings that did not pay at all well, and I found myself running all the time just to keep going.

(I remember the man's name I referred to above, Marvin Israel! Thanks, Marvin.)

J.R.    Did your magazine background make things a bit easier for you?

M.A.    Yes. Having worked for magazines helped me become a little familiar with production problems. My work was so delicate and it was always a struggle to get good reproduction because of this.

J.R.    Where did the first book come from then?

M.A.    The turning point came one day when I felt so tired of the struggle. I was frustrated and angry that I was working so hard and getting nowhere. I took the day off. I sat down and did many playful drawings of children doing nonsensical things. It was for myself. I had fun! I put the drawings away and forgot about them.

Several weeks later I looked at the drawings and made a big decision. I concluded that I wanted to illustrate children's books more than anything in the world. If I was going to be poor, I was going to be poor doing something I *liked* doing. And I knew I would like illustrating children's books.

I stuck the drawings in a book and took them to Harper & Row. Within a short time they called me to try a story.

Laying out the dummy was easy for me. It was accepted—a book! I had a book to illustrate!

I was working with Charlotte Zolotow[1] and Ursula Nordstrom[2] and they must have liked my illustrations as they offered me one book after another.

Financially I had a struggle for a long time. The advance for that first book was five hundred dollars. I work very slowly and five hundred dollars didn't go very far, even in 1965.

My complaints about poverty were met with, "But wait until you start earning royalties!" I didn't believe for a moment that I would ever see a royalty check, but I did! There was a light at the end of the tunnel.

J.R.      What was that first book?

M.A.      *Come and See Me,* by Mary Kennedy.

J.R.      When did you start writing your own books?

M.A.      As I worked on illustrating books I began having ideas for stories inspired by my grandchild, Lisa. I chatted with Charlotte and Ursula about my ideas and they encouraged me to try to write them. I did, over and over with no luck until finally I discovered the way for me to approach a book was to start with a dummy and draw and write together, doing pictures wherever I could convey my ideas and resorting to words when pictures were inadequate. That worked for me, as it does to this day.

J.R.      You mentioned Harper as your publisher, but isn't Dial your current publisher?

M.A.      Yes. I was illustrating for Harper when I came up with five little dummies all at once. I submitted three to Harper and two to Dial. Dial called me almost immediately and said they were going to publish one of my books. I could hardly believe it. I had a publisher!

Harper showed an interest in the dummies I had submitted to them, but they were slow moving so I retrieved them and stuck with Dial. This was a real beginning for me as an author.

J.R.      Let's discuss some specific books. How about *Nobody Asked Me If I Wanted a Baby Sister?*

M.A.      Oh, Phyllis[3] was wonderful! When I asked her if I could do a book about the older child giving the baby away she gulped and said, "If you can make it work."

My daughter, Kim, had called me from Hawaii to tell me that Christina, who was two years old, said "Leslie (six months) wants to go live with Grandma." I thought, "Ah-ha!" She wants to get rid of the new baby? The story began spinning around in my head, getting rid of the new baby . . . getting rid of the new baby. If Phyllis had not left the door open, I wouldn't have tried that story.

That book was very hard for me but I was determined to do it. I *had* to.

J.R.      What was the problem?

M.A.      I was directing it toward parents at first. Then I just couldn't make sense of the baby being given away. I finally resolved it when I realized that giving the baby away was not the important thing. What was important was that she wanted to give the baby away. Then I was able to complete the story.

J.R.      What about your little jewel, *Blackboard Bear?*

M.A.      *Blackboard Bear* was my first big success. That book was born as the result of a trip to visit my sister and her grandson, Christopher, who was then four years old. Christopher lived in the country with no one to play with and spent his days racing around the yard as though playing the parts of all the actors of a play—first a cowboy, then an Indian, a cop, a robber. When I returned home I couldn't get him off my mind. One night I couldn't sleep for thinking of him and got up and made a dummy and that story just seemed to happen to me. It just came out page after page without my having any idea what was coming. All I know is that it was inspired by a little boy named Christopher who had a wild imagination.

J.R.      What about *How My Library Grew?*

M.A.      Bruce Carrick[4] called me one day and asked if I would be interested in writing and illustrating a book to interest small children in using libraries. I loved the idea. Bruce gave me all of his thoughts and ideas and turned me loose. I certainly enjoyed the project and I also enjoyed working with Bruce.

It was different than any other book I had done and it was full color, too. A treat after so many color-separated books.

J.R.      And your flip books?

M.A.      I felt a real need to do something different, a new format. When I become restless I need change of some kind. Anyway I worked a long time on ideas for the flip books. They evolved from simple nature growth flips such as egg to chicken to rather involved stories. I love doing the unexpected, the surprise ending.

Those books are 3 1/4 x 3 7/8 inches. I like working small!

J.R.      You must have very sharp pencils when you work.

M.A.      Yes, I do. I sharpen my pencil about every three seconds! I really do.

J.R.      What kind of a work schedule do you keep?

M.A.      I don't have a schedule for work. That's the joy of free-lancing. I like to do what I do; I do it and I like to get it done. I like to work a few hours and then do something else for a while and come back to my work. I like to break it up. I do work many hours. I'm pretty good about deadlines. The one problem I have never solved is that I think I can do more in a given time than I can—always, always. I still can't judge time.

J.R.      You work primarily with the pre-separated art, don't you?

M.A.      Yes, I do, though I've done many full-color books. My three-color books have become so complex that I have found people to do the separations for the last few years. It takes someone with endless patience and skill.

J.R.    Outside of moving around the country a lot, you must have some hobbies or other interests besides books?

M.A.    Yes, I enjoy doing pottery. For the last two years I have concentrated on making pottery whistles and small musical instruments.

My burning interest is in the world of metaphysics, including dowsing, reincarnation, past lives, soul regression, walk-ins, UFO's, space and time travel and more.

Egypt holds a great fascination for me. My first trip there was in 1981. It was that trip that opened the doors so wide into my current interest in the world of metaphysics. Perhaps my three Magic flip books are also a result of this trip. At sixty-four I do feel that the best and most interesting part of my life has only just begun.

## Notes

[1] Charlotte Zolotow, editorial consultant and editor of Charlotte Zolotow Books for Harper & Row, also a children's book writer.

[2] Ursula Nordstrom, then publisher of children's books at Harper & Row.

[3] Phyllis Fogelman, editor-in-chief of Dial Books for Young Readers.

[4] Bruce Carrick, head of general publications for H.W. Wilson Company.

## BIBLIOGRAPHY

### As Author/Illustrator

*And My Mean Old Mother Will Be Sorry, Blackboard Bear.* New York: Dial, 1972.

*Babies Are Like That.* New York: Western, 1967.

*Bad Thad.* By Judy Malloy. New York: Dutton, 1980.

*Big Sister and Little Sister.* By Charlotte Zolotow. New York: Harper & Row, 1966.

*Blackboard Bear.* New York: Dial, 1969.

*Bobo's Dream.* New York: Dial, 1970.

*Charles.* By Liesel Moak Skorpen. New York: Harper & Row, 1971.

*Come and See Me.* By Mary Kennedy. New York: Harper & Row, 1966.

*Elizabeth.* By Liesel Moak Skorpen. New York: Harper & Row, 1970.

*Emily and the Klunky Baby and the Next-Door Dog.* By Joan M. Lexau. New York: Dial, 1972.

*The Everyday Train.* By Amy Ehrlich. New York: Dial, 1977.

*Forget Me Not.* By Louis Untermeyer. New York: Western, 1967.

*Four Bears in a Box.* New York: Dial, 1981.

*Grandfathers Are to Love.* By Lois Wyse. New York: Parents Magazine, 1967.

*Grandmothers Are to Love.* By Lois Wyse. New York: Parents Magazine, 1967.

*How My Library Grew.* By Dinah. Bronx, N.Y.: H.W. Wilson, 1983.

*I Have a Tree.* By Lillie D. Chaffin. New York: D. White, 1969.

*I Sure Am Glad to See You, Blackboard Bear.* New York: Dial, 1976.

*I'll Be the Horse If You'll Play with Me.* New York: Dial, 1975.

*I'll Protect You from the Jungle Beasts.* New York: Dial, 1973; new ed., 1983.

*Jeremy Isn't Hungry.* By Barbara Williams. New York: Dutton, 1978.

*Maggie's Moon.* New York: Dial, 1982.

*The Magic Box.* New York: Dial, 1984.

*The Magic Hat.* New York: Dial, 1984.

*The Magic Picture.* New York: Dial, 1984.

*Mandy's Grandmother.* By Liesel Moak Skorpen. New York: Dial, 1975.

*Marty McGee's Space Lab, No Girls Allowed.* New York: Dial, 1981.

*Mary Ann's Mud Day.* By Janice Udry. New York: Harper & Row, 1967.

*Maybe a Monster.* New York: Dial, 1968; new ed., 1983.

*Move Over, Twerp.* New York: Dial, 1981.

*Night Noises.* By LaVerne Johnson. New York: Parents Magazine, 1968.

*No Ducks in Our Bathtub.* New York: Dial, 1973.

*Nobody Asked Me If I Wanted a Baby Sister.* New York: Dial, 1971.

*Out! Out! Out!* New York: Dial, 1968.

*Poems and Prayers for the Very Young.* New York: Random House, 1973.

*Sabrina.* New York: Dial, 1971.

*The Story Grandmother Told.* New York: Dial, 1969.

*Too Hot for Ice Cream.* By Jean Van Leeuwen. New York: Dial, 1974.

*Understood Betsy.* By Dorothy Canfield Fisher. New York: Holt, 1972.

*We Never Get to Do Anything.* New York: Dial, 1970.

*We're in Big Trouble, Blackboard Bear.* New York: Dial, 1980.

*What Is a Whispery Secret?* By Lois Hobart. New York: Parents Magazine, 1968.

*When the New Baby Comes, I'm Moving Out.* New York: Dial, 1979.

*Whose Turtle?* By Doris Orgel. Cleveland: World, 1968.

*The Wizard of Walnut Street.* By Carol K. Scism. New York: Dial, 1973.

*You: A Poem.* By Louis Untermeyer. New York: Golden, 1969.

### As Compiler

*Pigs Say Oink: A First Book of Sounds.* New York: Random House, 1978.

## AWARDS AND HONORS

*Blackboard Bear*
> Best Illustrated Children's Book
> Library of Congress list

*Bobo's Dream*
> Best Book of the Year
> Library of Congress list

*Charles*
> Library of Congress list

*The Everyday Train*
> Children's Choice Book

*I Sure Am Glad to See You, Blackboard Bear*
> Children's Choice Book

*I'll Protect You from the Jungle Beasts*
> Christopher Award

*Move Over, Twerp*
> Bluegrass Award
> Children's Choice Book

*Nobody Asked Me If I Wanted a Baby Sister*
> Book Show
> Library of Congress list
> Showcase Book

*Sabrina*
> Spring Book Festival
> Book World

## ADDITIONAL SOURCES

Commire. *Something about the Author.*
*Contemporary Authors.*
de Montreville and Crawford. *Fourth Book of Junior Authors and Illustrators.*
Kingman. *Illustrators of Children's Books: 1967-1976.*
Ward. *Illustrators of Books for Young People.*

_Isaac Asimov_ (signature)

**Isaac Asimov**

## BIOGRAPHICAL NOTE

Born in the U.S.S.R. on January 20, 1920, this well-known and prolific writer is also a noted scientist. He received his Ph.D. from Columbia University in 1948 and since 1949 has been on the faculty of the Boston University School of Medicine, where he is currently a professor of biochemistry. Mr. Asimov, who is also published under the pseudonyms Dr. A and Paul French, is married to Janet Jeppson. His first marriage, in 1942 to Gertrude Blugerman, ended in divorce. He has two children, David and Robyn. His original manuscripts are held at the Boston University Library.

Among the innumerable awards and honors accorded to him are five Hugo Awards for lifetime achievement in science fiction writing and fourteen honorary doctorates.

## PRELUDE TO THE INTERVIEW

Isaac Asimov, though I didn't know it beforehand, is an extremely easy person to be with. I had incorrectly reasoned that if I was going to meet with one of the world's most prolific writers he probably didn't want to be bothered with yet another interview.

I imagined he would be fidgety and unsettled, searching for a quick exit to get back to his writing to channel his seemingly inexhaustible energy to a work in progress.

I was happy to discover that nothing could be further from the truth.

Isaac, I discovered, is an expansive and ready talker. He is willing to speak of his craft and work. His familiarity and in-depth knowledge of many subjects is as impressive as his list of books. And he is also a great wit, but it's a droll one. If you are not listening carefully, the joke may go right past you.

Generally perceived as a writer of books for adults, he has produced an impressive list of children's nonfiction books. His is the ability to distill the most complicated scientific and mathematical concepts, simultaneously making them interesting and comprehensible for young children.

His writing talent is such that it is possible for any child born today to spend a lifetime reading Asimov; he is literally a childhood-to-adulthood writer.

A child can move from Asimov's simple, but scientifically accurate, science books on to his multivolume science fiction novels as an adult.

Asimov's name has become synonymous with prodigious output. What is even more astonishing than the 326 books listed in his bibliography, is that more than half are in print at the time of the preparation of this book. That, in itself, is a singular feat attesting to Asimov's abilities and loyal readers.

## THE INTERVIEW

J.R.    You are one of the world's most prolific writers. Do you have any count of how many books you currently have in print?

I.A.    Oh, gee. I'd have to count it up in *Books in Print.* I imagine it's something like 150. I believe I have more books in print than anybody else in the world. There may be one or two people who have written more than I have, but they do not have more books in print.

J.R.    Who would they be?

I.A.    Georges Simenon. John Creasey. And maybe Barbara Cartland.

J.R.    But, for the most part, they're category writers in that they tend to write the same type of book each time.

I.A.    Well, I like to think that nobody in the world writes as many books on so many different subjects so well. There are those who write well in one or another of those categories I write in, but no one can match me.

You'll notice of course that I'm extremely modest!

J.R.    Along with books, you do a number of magazine articles and editorials each year. What do you estimate is your average weekly output?

I.A.    I suppose I publish something like three-quarters to a million words a year. That would be like two thousand words a day of published material. That'll be like seven or eight pages a day.

J.R.    You're right. That's a lot. I would think keeping up with that would be a terrible strain.

I.A.    Yeah, especially if I have to put everything through my typewriter twice.

But that's not what gives me a feeling of strain. What gives me a feeling of strain is when I'm not writing. I saw *All the President's Men*[2] on television once and that set a fire under me. I reread *Blind Ambition*[3] and *The Final Days*[4] because of it. It wastes a lot of time, but I figure if I want to do something I should do it. So, I do it. And every once in a while I get in a sneaky mood and I figure it's time to reread *The Lord of the Rings.*[5]

My wife and I are both like that. That is, we don't feel an extreme necessity to read only new books. We would just as soon reread a book that has caught our lives.

Every once in a while we reread our Agatha Christie mysteries or some of the collections of mysteries we have. Or a Wodehouse book.

You might feel with life so short and so many books, that to read an old book means you miss the chance to read a new book that you may never read as a result. But that's all right.

J.R.   Who are some of your favorites that you do reread?

I.A.   Agatha Christie. P. G. Wodehouse. Mark Twain. Charles Dickens.

My wife gave away our copy of *Our Mutual Friend* [6] because I said so casually, "I don't like it very much." So I asked her why she didn't ask me first. She said, "Because you said you didn't like it very much." I said, "You don't give away Dickens just because I said that!" So she bought me a new copy and I now have to reread it.

J.R.   So when you're not reading, you're producing an enormous number of words for other people to read.

I.A.   Yeah. I've averaged about 8.3 books a year since 1950. In the last thirteen years I've published a little over a book a month.

J.R.   But that's not all original work.

I.A.   It includes fifty-three, fifty-four anthologies of other people's stories. I count them as full-fledged books. And I've done a significant number of children's books. But also a significant number of "big" books.

On the whole, I guess I can do it because I don't do anything else.

J.R.   How many articles are you doing each year?

I.A.   Well, I do thirteen editorials for the *Isaac Asimov's Science Fiction Magazine,* twelve articles for *Fantasy and Science Fiction,* twelve for *American Way.* I imagine I must do about ninety a year altogether.

I would say it's now been over twenty-five years that an article by me hasn't appeared somewhere each individual month. And generally it is an unusual week when something doesn't appear somewhere.

J.R.   You must be able to do things quickly and well the first time by now.

I.A.   I used to say everything goes through my typewriter twice . . .

J.R.   As a matter of fact you just said that a few minutes ago . . .

I.A.   . . . Now that I have a word processor my shorter pieces are done directly on it. They go through once with editing. The longer pieces I do in a typewriter first. In the old days I would do them, edit them in ink, and type them again. This time I do them on the typewriter and type them out a second time in the word processor, editing as I go along, and then print it out. I don't save much time that way, but I do have cleaner copy!

J.R.    In looking over your books there are very few collaborations, except those with your wife, Janet. Why is that?

I.A.    Well, I'm used to working on my own. I don't look for collaborations. I don't particularly enjoy them.

The way we worked on the *Norby* books was she sat down and wrote the book in the first draft and I put the thing in front of me in my word processor and edited as I went along.

In hindsight, the books are ninety per cent her and ten per cent me. I just helped polish them.

J.R.    I'm about to ask a standard question, one I'm sure you hear continually: Where do you get your ideas from?

I.A.    A lot of pepole may think you can sit around till inspiration strikes. Or, you have to do something physical to yourself.

The only answer in my case is very dull, not exciting. I just sit down and think and think and think until something comes to me. I've always got a number of projects on hand. If one isn't working, I switch to another.

I usually have six, seven, possibly eight, things I'm working on. Janet sometimes makes speeches about being a desperate wife. And my answer is, "Yes, but you knew that when you married me, didn't you?"

J.R.    With your tremendous output you must keep your agent happy.

I.A.    Nope. I have no secretary. I have no agent. No business manager. I do it all myself with difficulty.

I have a set of books, so to speak, that I don't think anyone could possibly understand but me. Sometimes I dread the thought of dying. Not so much for dying, but what the devil is my wife going to do? She'll never understand my system!

J.R.    What do you mean?

I.A.    I have a complete library of everything I have written in English that we've gotten hold of. I presume there is a possibility that something I wrote appeared in some small magazine and that I never received a copy of it. I used to save my foreign editions, too, but I gave that up. It's too much. There isn't enough room.

Anyway, publishers will call me to say they have a request for such-and-such story and where does it appear? I refer to my card catalog and can find them in a matter of half a minute. That's for stories in books.

On the other hand, magazines frequently change titles of my articles. I keep my own titles on the cards. But people who know only the magazine's title ask me for permission to reprint. And I am forced to have to try and remember and usually say, "I'm sorry, but I can no longer keep track of my articles by magazine alone. Can you please tell me which issue of the magazine this piece appeared in?"

If I know about when it appeared, I can look in some of my bound volumes. I can't just look through them indiscriminately because I have over three hundred of them with various tearsheets of my stories, articles, and reprints.

J.R.     Since you don't have an agent, aren't you fearful that some of your publishers may try to take advantage of you? Agents could at least look over your contracts for you.

I.A.     No, I don't worry about it. I never read contracts. To this day, I don't. God knows what these companies are doing to me. I've had hundreds of contracts and not one have I read.

You see, each year I make more money than the year before. And I say, what the heck. I figure no one's out to cheat me. After I discovered that money came in every half year, I discovered that the more books I'd write, the more money I'd earn.

J.R.     But what about the publishing theory that dictates you don't publish too much at one time because you'll sell against yourself and reduce sales on the new books?

I.A.     That *was* a theory.

An editor told me early on not to write so much because I would compete with myself. And I said, "Well, I would like to write less but I can't bear it even if it ends up me making less money per book."

Some years later he asked me if I'd write him a book on something. And I said, "Well, I already did X number of books this year. And you said I would compete with myself." He said, "Oh, but that's changed!"

In fact, people now *expect* me to be prolific. If I didn't publish lots of books they'd feel vaguely disappointed and hurt. Once you're known to be prolific, it's a plus. People who like your books are grateful because the books are interesting to them. And they're going to keep looking for them. As my wife says, "Too much of a good thing can be wonderful."

J.R.     Well, at least you keep collectors happy. I assume there are collectors of Asimoviana?

I.A.     There are several. Some write to me periodically and ask for a complete list of my books. They have a compulsion to have every book I've ever done.

There's a young man who gets not only every book I did in hard or soft covers or special editions, but foreign editions as well. If he has a book that is not a first edition he goes to a certain amount of trouble to try to get one that is.

I called up his mother when this first came to my attention and said, "I don't think it's wise for your son to spend all this money on my books. I don't want you to think I'm encouraging him." "Oh, no!" she says.

*"We* are. We are as interested as he is." So now he's getting started in college and every once in awhile he comes visiting with books he wants signed. And if there are books he's having problems getting, I get it for him. He's my number one collector.

But there are others like him. I suppose it makes it fun because collecting books is a very complicated process and you have definite feelings of achievement and triumph. "Oh, here's another one! I've been looking for it for years." You know.

J.R.     It goes without saying your bibliography is a lengthy one. Do you attempt to keep it up to date?

I.A.     Not really. In my autobiographies I divided up my books into different categories. But they're out of date already.

I do keep a list of dedications. It sounds silly but I have to know if I've dedicated a book to somebody a million times, how often did I dedicate a book to my wife, things like that.

I've even dedicated books to my curator, Howard Gottlieb, at Boston University. One thing about writing a lot of books is that you can dedicate them to everybody you know. Even people passing you in the street or girls I've glanced at from afar.

It seems that Douglas Jarrell, an eighteenth-century wit, had a friend who was a prolific writer of mediocre books. Douglas was told by someone, "So-and-so is dedicating his most recent book to you." Douglas shook his head saying, "That's a fearful weapon that man has."

J.R.     Did you say you have a curator at Boston University?

I.A.     Yes, Howard Gottlieb. Since 1966 Boston University has been collecting my papers. They get everything.

I send them a copy of every book in every edition. If it's one foreign edition I send it to them. If it's English, I send it provided I get two. I need one for my own library. I'm sure my wife will want the whole library after I've gone on. And perhaps my daughter might want it, too. But I can't see it going any further than that. I'll just give it all to Boston.

J.R.     How large is your library?

I.A.     Well, it has everything of mine, both books and articles. In addition, I have a useful library of non-Asimov books, a working library. It hasn't got great literature and it doesn't have stuff I don't use. Every book there is a reference for me.

I've reached the stage where people send me books constantly so I've kept up to date that way. I'm sent more books than I can possibly use. A great many of them, though, are useful.

I get lots of magazines, too. Some I subscribe to and some are sent to me. And magazines, one way or another, keep me up to date with science. And people write me letters every time they catch a mistake. They keep me up-to-date, too.

J.R.    So Boston University gets *everything*?

I.A.    *Everything.* They have all my correspondence, my first drafts, my carbons, my galley proofs, my page proofs. Everything. If I happen to get a mention in a newspaper, that too. Anything that mentions me. Everything. I just put it all into a box and every couple of weeks or so, it gets mailed off to them.

Every once in a while I write to them saying, "This is getting ridiculous. You want me to stop? Why don't I just send you copies of my books?" And they write back very excitedly, "No, no, no! Send us everything!" They're thinking in terms of centuries and of the time Boston University will be primarily known for having the most complete collection of Asimoviana in the world! And people will come from all over the world to see it, to look at it, and handle with care the most precious items under helium! Things like that. And I always feel bad because I think of it as my junk.

When they first started collecting, I said I'd give everything I got. And I did. And they said, "But you've been writing for so long, is this all you've got?" And I said, "Yes, this is all I've got now since the last time I burned it." "You *burned* it?" they asked. "Yeah," I said. "Well, what am I going to do with it? I can't keep it in the house. Every once in a while I collect a whole bag of junk and I fling it out." Gee, I never saw anyone come so close to apoplexy in my whole life.

So then they compelled me to send them *everything.* One time they were looking at one of my manuscripts and it had a holographic correction. And I said, "You should see the first drafts. Too bad I burned it." He said, "You are to send everything to me." And I said, "Everything?" "*Everything!*" he screamed at me. "Including scrap paper!"

So after that I always scribble something on the back of one of the first drafts or calculate something just so he has something to look at.

J.R.    Certainly when you first started writing you didn't have the idea you would rise quite so high. Or did you intentionally set out to do it?

I.A.    No! When I first began I didn't think I would sell my stories. What would give me the idea that I could sell my stories? Then when I did, I assumed that I would simply write stories for magazines and they'd appear each month, go off the stands, and never be heard of again. And I would receive one payment and that would be it. That was the way life was for us pulp writers and that was all we expected.

There were no science fiction hardcover books then. A number had been published by semiprofessional outfits. But Doubleday was the first of the major publishers to set up a science fiction line as a regular hardcover adult line.

In 1949 their first book was *The Big Eye*[7] by Max Ehrlich. Their second book was *Pebble in the Sky* by Isaac Asimov. That was my first book. Their second, my first. Their third book was *The Martian Chronicles*[8] by Ray Bradbury. That got them off and running.

In 1949 I had been writing for eleven years. Doubleday asked to see one of my books. All I had was a forty-thousand-word story that had been rejected by the magazines. And they wanted something that possibly hadn't been published. So I showed that to them and they said if I would expand it to seventy thousand words they'd take it.

They gave me two hundred fifty bucks. I thought I was rich! And they published it.

And then I sold them another novel. After I rewrote it a couple of times, they took it. Then I made the discovery that the money keeps coming, that it's not a one-time payment such as I was used to with magazines. I didn't know anything about royalties then.

J.R.    Were you still teaching at that point?

I.A.    Yeah. I got my Ph.D. when I was twenty-eight and joined the faculty of the Boston University School of Medicine. I had already been a professional writer for eleven years. I remained a professor for nine years and realized I had to make a choice. So in 1958 I chose writing and have been a full-time writer since, but I kept my title.

My son was born in '51, my daughter '55, and I became a full-time writer in '58. At the time I quit full-time teaching I was associate professor. I had become that in '55. And in 1979, after I had been an associate professor for twenty-four years, I was promoted to full professor! They said it was embarrassing to have the best-known member of the school's faculty only as an associate professor. So. Here I am, full professor of biochemistry. But they don't pay me.

J.R.    What was the impetus to enter biochemistry?

I.A.    My father wanted me to be a doctor, M.D. I just took it for granted that's what I'd be. It never occurred to me to go against anything my father said.

By the time I was finishing college and getting ready to apply to medical school I was no longer interested. But I applied dutifully. I did my best for two years, was rejected everywhere, and chucked it all in. My father was intensely disappointed, but I was relieved and went on for my Ph.D. in chemistry and eventually got it.

I don't think I would have finished medical school anyway. I'm a queasy guy. I was sickened by it the way Charles Darwin was sickened by it.

Once I stopped into the anatomy lab. I leaned against the table and realized what I had thought was a wax model was not. I never returned. I routinely walked out of my lab whenever anyone brought in animals. I couldn't stay in the same room with animal experimentation. On paper I wrote in defense of animal experimentation, as being essential and necessary, but, please, not in my presence.

Even if I had stayed with medical school, I would have been the world's rottenest doctor. Even if I had been a good doctor, I'm sure that in the end I'd have been a writer. But I would have lost years during which I wouldn't have written.

J.R.    How did all this begin?

I.A.        Oh, that's not hard to say. When I was very young we were an immigrant family and had no money. Zero. And there was nothing to read in the house except schoolbooks, which I got at the beginning of the term and read all the way through the first week. When I was six, my parents got me into a library, but I couldn't go often enough. Once a week. Once every two weeks. And they'd only let me have two books at a time.

        So when I was eleven years old, maybe I was younger I don't remember, I had a bright idea. If I copied a book, I'd still have it after I returned it to the library. So I got a little notebook and started copying. After one page I realized it was impractical.

        Then I got another bright idea; I would write my own book from scratch. So I started. I wrote about eight chapters. And I don't even have it anymore. But I would cheerfully pay someone five hundred dollars if they find it!

        And when I was seventeen it suddenly occurred to me to write a story and submit it to a magazine. Since I was a big reader of science fiction I wrote a science fiction story, and finished it a year later.

        I brought it in in June, 1938, and the magazine promptly rejected it. The editor wrote such a nice long letter that I was inspired to write another story. And I kept on writing and sending, writing and sending, and eventually I sold something. It took exactly four months. My first visit to an editor was on June 21 and the first check I got, not from that editor, was on October 21.

        That was 1938. It was twelve years since the first science fiction magazine had been published. I suppose it was a genre by then if you look at it from the present viewpoint. But to me, at the age of seventeen, I'd been reading science fiction for eight years. At seventeen, eight years is a long time. I didn't think of science fiction as a new form. I thought it was an old established thing.

        And from that first sale I continued to make sales.

J.R.    Of all your science fiction books, would you agree that the "Foundation" books are the best-known?

I.A.        Yes, and the most profitable. I sold the most copies and made the most money on them.

        The series started in 1942. The stories first appeared as individual stories in magazines, eight of them between 1942 and the beginning of 1950. Then I added a ninth one, which never did come out in a magazine.

        They came out in three books in 1951, 1952, and 1953. The last bit of writing I did on them was in 1950. Then *Foundation's Edge* was written as a continuation in 1982, thirty-two years later! Now it's a tetrology, but it's easier to call it a series.

        I also had two books published in 1954 and 1957 called *The Caves of Steel* and *The Naked Sun,* respectively, about a detective named Elizah Baley. I promised a third book, which was *The Robots of Dawn.* That came out in 1983.

I'm always anxious to see how my books do, because on each one publishers give me larger advances. And they want me to do a new one. But I won't write until I'm sure the one before is going to pay back its advance. Otherwise I'll return the new advance.

J.R.    Who are your major publishers, irrespective of the various types of books you do?

I.A.    Doubleday, Walker, and Houghton Mifflin. The three together have done more than half my books. The remainder is divided among thirty-seven other publishers.

J.R.    Do you follow the new science fiction and mystery writers?

I.A.    No, I don't, as a matter of fact. I'm quite out of touch.

Both my science fiction and mysteries are distinctly old-fashioned. My mysteries are strictly the classic puzzle story of the thirties. When I did *Murder at the ABA* Doubleday gave up the struggle. In the blurb they said, "an old-fashioned mystery." When I read that I turned pale. I thought it was the kiss of death. But it sold pretty well, pretty well. I can't do that hard, brittle dialogue. I tried to get a little close to it in *ABA*, but people still know it's me. In all my mysteries there's only one dead body. Really. And that's the opening, with the murder already committed. No murder. No violence. It's just ratiocination.

In my science fiction I allow myself a little violence, but for the most part there's no action, no sex, no sensationalism. But an awful lot of dialogue, what one reviewer called "the flow and interplay of ideas."

When I reread the *Foundation* trilogy before I did the fourth book I was horrified to find out how little action there was. My goodness. People just talked. And I decided that was what some readers must want. So I wrote *Foundation's Edge* with hardly any action, all talk. Some reviewers noticed that, so they thought the book was slow-moving. One reviewer actually started off with, "This book is unreadable," and he went downhill from there. The book still sold 230,000 copies at full price. That doesn't count book club sales, foreign editions, or the paperback. The heck with it. I can live with his comments! I figure what I please my readers with is the "interplay of ideas."

J.R.    Do your readers send you ideas for books?

I.A.    Oh, yeah, all the time. Publishers too. Many of my books are written at publishers' requests.

Readers generally manage to suggest a subject I know nothing about but they've been looking for it. As you know, I have written on many subjects. I've never written books on art, on economics, and on psychology. These are all subjects that don't interest me. And I haven't done a cookbook.

I *can't* write a cookbook. I can barely boil water to make coffee. You'd be surprised how often I'm asked for a recipe for a cookbook. I always say, "I have no recipes." They don't believe me and think I have totally wonderful recipes I don't want other people to know about!

J.R.    By way of my curiosity, do people send you unsolicited manuscripts in the mail, hoping you'll be able to do something with them?

I.A.    Well, I tell you. I get a great deal of that in the mail. It's also embarrassing, because I have to refuse it. I *have* to. I'm no judge of what's good and what's not. I can't judge if something is written well or not. I don't have any in with publishers in the sense I can get something unpublishable published just because I order them to. So these people don't get any more chance of being published if I bring it than if they send it in themselves.

People who are amateurs feel that when they send out their manuscripts and they come back, there must be something they don't know; some button that's supposed to be pushed; some trick they're supposed to use. They think a guy like me would know and he could just tell them.

Generally I never hear from those people again. I imagine they feel that I do know something and I'm just too rotten to tell them because I want to save all the money, fame, et cetera, for myself.

And I get lots of mail, generally. In the old days I used to answer all of it. These days I'm forced to be slightly selective. I look for excuses not to write. If I do, it's minimal, like a postcard or something like that. There are probably about twenty-five items a day I guess that require an answer from me.

J.R.    Have you had any problems being associated with your magazine?

I.A.    That magazine started in 1977. What happened was one of the people at Davis Publications[9] attended a Star Trek convention. He was taken by the enthusiasm and the numbers of those who attended and thought it might be a good idea for Davis to put out a science fiction magazine.

Davis had two fiction magazines at the time. Both had famous names attached—Ellery Queen and Alfred Hitchcock. And to make the new one sell they wanted another famous name in the magazine. And the only science fiction writer he knew was me, because I was periodically submitting stories for *Ellery Queen,* one of his detective magazines. So he asked me what I thought of the idea of lending my name to the magazine. I hesitated for a long time, because there's never been a science fiction magazine named for a living writer. And I thought it would be resented by the readers, even more so by the writers.

I had visions of writers *en masse* refusing to write for the magazine that would serve as an apotheosis of one of their own peers. So I presented all this stuff to Davis and he said "nonsense." Finally, I let him talk me into it.

It hasn't been bad. I write an editorial for every issue. I read the letters and answer them. If there are any problems that have to be faced,

I'm there to give it my bit. But I'm not the editor and I don't do the day-to-day work.

J.R.    Well, among your own ideas, your readers', and your publishers', you certainly don't have to worry about running out of book or magazine article possibilities.

I.A.    I don't have that problem because I never work on one thing only. I've been trying to outstrip my powers of invention. Invariably something comes up that simply must be done. A monthly column, something I've promised, a book I'm trying to do. You can only write a novel so fast. Then you have to remove yourself and let the well fill up again.

J.R.    Of your books, which type sells the best?

I.A.    I'm afraid my fiction sells considerably better than my nonfiction. But I'm afraid I like writing nonfiction more. I've reached the stage where my income is high enough so I don't have to write something just to make money. So I balance it.

Some things I write to make myself happy, even though I know it's not going to make me a cent. And some pieces I write because I know it's going to make my publishers or my readers happy.

And I don't write anything that's not going to make anybody happy. At least I try not to.

## Notes

[1] As of September, 1983, when this interview took place.

[2] Carl Bernstein and Bob Woodward, *All the President's Men* (New York: Simon & Schuster, 1974).

[3] John Dean, *Blind Ambition: The White House Years* (New York: Simon & Schuster, 1976).

[4] Carl Bernstein and Bob Woodward, *The Final Days* (New York: Simon & Schuster, 1976).

[5] J. R. R. Tolkien, *The Lord of the Rings* (Boston: Houghton Mifflin, 1954).

[6] Charles Dickens, *Our Mutual Friend.* il. Marcus Stone (London: Chapman and Hall, 1865). Originally published May, 1864-November, 1865, and issued as twenty volumes in nineteen.

[7] Max Ehrlich, *The Big Eye* (Garden City, N.Y.: Doubleday & Company, 1949).

[8] Ray Bradbury, *The Martian Chronicles* (Garden City, N.Y.: Doubleday, 1950).

[9] Davis Publications, Inc., publisher of *Isaac Asimov's Science Fiction Magazine.*

# BIBLIOGRAPHY
## As Isaac Asimov:
### As Author:

*ABC's of Ecology.* New York: Walker, 1972.

*ABC's of Space.* New York: Walker, 1969.

*ABC's of the Earth.* New York: Walker, 1971.

*ABC's of the Ocean.* New York: Walker, 1970.

*Adding a Dimension: Seventeen Essays on the History of Science.* Garden City, N.Y.: Doubleday, 1964.

*Alpha Centauri: The Nearest Star.* New York: Lothrop, Lee & Shepard, 1976.

*Animals of the Bible.* il. Howard Berelson. Garden City, N.Y.: Doubleday, 1978.

*The Annotated Gulliver's Travels.* Text by Jonathan Swift. New York: Crown, 1980.

*Asimov on Astronomy.* Garden City, N.Y.: Doubleday, 1974.

*Asimov on Chemistry.* Garden City, N.Y.: Doubleday, 1974.

*Asimov on Numbers.* Garden City, N.Y.: Doubleday, 1977.

*Asimov on Physics.* Garden City, N.Y.: Doubleday, 1976.

*Asimov on Science Fiction.* Garden City, N.Y.: Doubleday, 1981.

*Asimov's Annotated Don Juan.* Text by Lord Byron. il. Milton Glaser. Garden City, N.Y.: Doubleday, 1972.

*Asimov's Annotated Paradise Lost.* Text by John Milton. Garden City, N.Y.: Doubleday, 1974.

*Asimov's Biographical Encyclopedia of Science and Technology: The Lives and Achievements of 1195 Great Scientists from Ancient Times to the Present, Chronologically Arranged,* new rev. ed. Garden City, N.Y.: Doubleday, 1972.

*Asimov's Biographical Encyclopedia of Science and Technology: The Lives and Achievements of 1510 Great Scientists from Ancient Times to the Present, Chronologically Arranged,* 2d rev. ed. Garden City, N.Y.: Doubleday, 1982.

*Asimov's Biographical Encyclopedia of Science and Technology: The Living Stories of More than 1000 Great Scientists from the Age of Greece to the Space Age, Chronologically Arranged.* Garden City, N.Y.: Doubleday, 1964.

*Asimov's Choice: Black Holes to Bug-eyed Monsters.* ed. George Scithers. New York: Davis, 1977.

*Asimov's Choice: Comets and Computers.* ed. George Scithers. New York: Dale, 1978.

*Asimov's Choice: Dark Stars and Dragons.* ed. George Scithers. New York: Dale, 1978.

*Asimov's Guide to Science.* New York: Basic Books, 1972.

*Asimov's Guide to Shakespeare.* il. Rafael Palacios. 2 vols. Garden City, N.Y.: Doubleday, 1970.

*Asimov's Guide to the Bible.* Maps by Rafael Palacios. Garden City, N.Y.: Doubleday, 1968; Vol. 2, 1969.

*Asimov's Mysteries.* Garden City, N.Y.: Doubleday, 1968.

*Asimov's Sherlockian Limericks.* frontis. by Gahan Wilson. New York: Mysterious, 1978.

*Atomic Weights. Energy. Electricity.* Washington, D.C.: U.S. Atomic Energy Commission, Office of Information Services, 1972.

*The Beginning and the End.* Garden City, N.Y.: Doubleday, 1977.

*The Best Thing.* il. Symeon Shimin. New York: World, 1971.

*The Best of Isaac Asimov.* ed. Angus Wells. London: Sidgwick and Jackson, 1973.

*Bicentennial Man and Other Stories.* Garden City, N.Y.: Doubleday, 1976.

*Biochemistry and Human Metabolism.* with Burnham S. Walker and others. Baltimore: Williams & Wilkins, 1952.

*The Birth of the United States, 1763-1816.* Boston: Houghton Mifflin, 1974.

*Breakthroughs in Science.* il. Karoly and Szanto. Boston: Houghton Mifflin, 1960.

*Building Blocks of the Universe.* New York: Abelard-Schuman, 1957; rev. ed. 1964.

*Buy Jupiter, and Other Stories.* Garden City, N.Y.: Doubleday, 1975.

*Casebook of the Black Widowers.* Garden City, N.Y.: Doubleday, 1980.

*The Caves of Steel.* Garden City, N.Y.: Doubleday, 1954.

*Change! 71 Glimpses of the Future.* Boston: Houghton Mifflin, 1981.

*The Chemicals of Life: Enzymes, Vitamins, Hormones.* New York: Abelard-Schuman, 1954.

*Chemistry and Human Health.* New York: McGraw-Hill, 1956.

*A Choice of Catastrophes: The Disasters That Threaten Our World.* New York: Simon & Schuster, 1979.

*The Clock We Live On.* il. John Bradford. New York: Abelard-Schuman, 1959; rev. eds. 1962, 1965.

*The Collapsing Universe.* New York: Walker, 1977.

*The Collected Fiction of Isaac Asimov.* Garden City, N.Y.: Doubleday, 1979.

*Comets and Meteors.* il. Raul Mina Mora. Chicago: Follett, 1972.

*The Complete Robot.* Garden City, N.Y.: Doubleday, 1982.

*Constantinople: The Forgotten Empire.* Boston: Houghton Mifflin, 1970.

*Counting the Eons.* Garden City, N.Y.: Doubleday, 1983.

*The Currents of Space.* Garden City, N.Y.: Doubleday, 1952.

*The Dark Ages.* Boston: Houghton Mifflin, 1968.

*Death Dealers.* New York: Avon, 1958.

*The Double Planet.* il. John Bradford. New York: Abelard-Schuman, 1960; rev. ed. 1966.

*The Dream, Benjamin's Dream, and Benjamin's Bicentennial Blast: Three Short Stories.* New York: Printing Week in New York, 1976. (Privately Printed)

*The Early Asimov: Or, Eleven Years of Trying.* Garden City, N.Y.: Doubleday, 1972.

*Earth Is Room Enough: Science Fiction Tales of Our Own Planet.* Garden City, N.Y.: Doubleday, 1957.

*Earth: Our Crowded Spaceship.* New York: John Day, 1974.

*An Easy Introduction to the Slide Rule.* il. William Barss. Boston: Houghton Mifflin, 1965.

*The Egyptians.* Boston: Houghton Mifflin, 1967.

*Electricity and Man.* Oak Ridge, Tenn.: U.S. Atomic Energy Commission, Office of Information Services, 1972.

*The End of Eternity.* Garden City, N.Y.: Doubleday, 1955.

*The Ends of the Earth: The Polar Regions of the World.* il. Bob Hines. New York: Weybright and Talley, 1975.

*Environments Out There.* foreword by Tad Harvey. New York: Abelard-Schuman, 1967.

*Exploring the Earth and the Cosmos: The Growth and Future of Human Knowledge.* New York: Crown, 1982.

*Extraterrestrial Civilizations.* New York: Crown, 1979.

*Eyes on the Universe: A History of the Telescope.* Boston: Houghton Mifflin, 1975.

*Fact and Fancy.* Garden City, N.Y.: Doubleday, 1962.

*Fantastic Voyage: A Novel.* Based on the screenplay by Harry Kleiner, adapted by David Duncan from the original story by Otto Klement and Jay Lewis Bixby. Boston: Houghton Mifflin, 1966.

*The Far Ends of Time and Earth: The Collected Fiction of Isaac Asimov.* Garden City, N.Y.: Doubleday, 1979.

*Foundation.* Garden City, N.Y.: Doubleday, 1951.

*Foundation and Empire.* Garden City, N.Y.: Doubleday, 1952.

*The Foundation Trilogy: Three Classics of Science Fiction.* Garden City, N.Y.: Doubleday, 1953.

*Foundation's Edge.* Garden City, N.Y.: Doubleday, 1982.

*From Earth to Heaven.* Garden City, N.Y.: Doubleday, 1966.

*Galaxies.* il. Alex Ebel and Denny McMains. Chicago: Follett, 1968.

*The Genetic Code.* New York: Orion, 1962.

*The Genetic Effects of Radiation.* With Theodosius Dobzhansky. Washington, D.C.: U.S. Atomic Energy Commission, Division of Technical Information, 1966.

*Ginn Science Program: Advanced Level A, B.* 2 vols. Boston: Ginn, 1973.

*Ginn Science Program—Intermediate Level A, B, C.* 3 vols. Boston: Ginn, 1972.

*The Gods Themselves.* Garden City, N.Y.: Doubleday, 1972.

*The Golden Door: The United States from 1865 to 1918.* Boston: Houghton Mifflin, 1977.

*Good Taste: A Story.* il. Brent Garrett. Topeka, Kans.: Apocalypse, 1976.

*Great Ideas of Science.* il. Lee Ames. Boston: Houghton Mifflin, 1969.

*The Greeks: A Great Adventure.* Boston: Houghton Mifflin, 1965.

*A Grossery of Limericks.* With John Ciardi. New York: Norton, 1981.

*Have You Seen These?* Boston: NESFA Press, 1974.

*The Heavenly Host.* il. Bernard Colonna. New York: Walker, 1975.

*The History of Physics.* New York: Walker, 1984.

*How Did We Find Out about Antarctica?* il. David Wool. New York: Walker, 1979.

*How Did We Find Out about Atoms?* il. David Wool. New York: Walker, 1976.

*How Did We Find Out about Black Holes?* il. David Wool. New York: Walker, 1978.

*How Did We Find Out about Coal?* il. David Wool. New York: Walker, 1980.

*How Did We Find Out about Comets?* il. David Wool. New York: Walker, 1975.

*How Did We Find Out about Computers?* il. David Wool. New York: Walker, 1984.

*How Did We Find Out about Dinosaurs?* il. David Wool. New York: Walker, 1973.

*How Did We Find Out about Earthquakes?* il. David. Wool. New York: Walker, 1978.

*How Did We Find Out about Electricity?* il. Matthew Kalmenoff. New York: Walker, 1973.

*How Did We Find Out about Energy?* il. David Wool. New York: Walker, 1975.

*How Did We Find Out about Genes?* il. David Wool. New York: Walker, 1983.

*How Did We Find Out about Germs?* il. David Wool. New York: Walker, 1974.

*How Did We Find Out about Life in the Deep Sea?* il. David Wool. New York: Walker, 1982.

*How Did We Find Out about Nuclear Power?* il. David Wool. New York: Walker, 1976.

*How Did We Find Out about Numbers?* il. Daniel Nevins. New York: Walker, 1973.

*How Did We Find Out about Oil?* il. David Wool. New York: Walker, 1980.

*How Did We Find Out about Our Human Roots?* il. David Wool. New York: Walker, 1979.

*How Did We Find Out about Outer Space?* il. David Wool. New York: Walker, 1977.

*How Did We Find Out about Robots?* il. David Wool. New York: Walker, 1984.

*How Did We Find Out about Solar Power?* il. David Wool. New York: Walker, 1981.

*How Did We Find Out about the Beginning of Life?* il. David Wool. New York: Walker, 1982.

*How Did We Find Out about the Universe?* il. David Wool. New York: Walker, 1983.

*How Did We Find Out about Vitamins?* il. David Wool. New York: Walker, 1974.

*How Did We Find Out about Volcanoes?* il. David Wool. New York: Walker, 1981.

*How Did We Find Out the Earth is Round?* il. Matthew Kalmenoff. New York: Walker, 1973.

*The Hugo Winners.* Garden City, N.Y.: Doubleday, 1962; Vol. 2, 1971; Vol. 3, 1977.

*The Human Body: Its Structure and Operation.* il. Anthony Ravielli. Boston: Houghton Mifflin, 1963.

*The Human Brain: Its Capacities and Functions.* il. Anthony Ravielli. Boston: Houghton Mifflin, 1963.

*I, Robot.* Garden City, N.Y.: Doubleday, 1950.

*In Joy Still Felt: Autobiography, 1954-1978.* Garden City, N.Y.: Doubleday, 1980.

*In Memory Yet Green: The Autobiography of Isaac Asimov, 1920-1954.* Garden City, N.Y.: Doubleday, 1979.

*In the Beginning: Science Faces God in the Book of Genesis.* New York: Crown, 1981.

*Inside the Atom.* il. John Bradford. New York: Abelard-Schuman, 1956; rev. ed. 1958, 1961, 1966, 1974.

*The Intelligent Man's Guide to Science.* New York: Basic Books, 1960.

*The Intelligent Man's Guide to the Physical Sciences.* New York: Washington Square, 1964.

*Is Anyone There?* Garden City, N.Y.: Doubleday, 1967.

*An Isaac Asimov Double: "Space Ranger" and "Pirates of the Asteroids."* London: New English Library, 1972.

*An Isaac Asimov Omnibus.* London: Sidgwick and Jackson, 1966.

*Isaac Asimov's Aliens and Outworlders.* ed. Shawna McCarthy. New York: Dial, 1983.

*Isaac Asimov's Book of Facts.* New York: Grosset & Dunlap, 1979.

*Isaac Asimov's Masters of Science Fiction.* ed. George Scithers. New York: Davis, 1978.

*Isaac Asimov's Masters of Science Fiction,* Vol. 2. ed. George Scithers. New York: Davis, 1979.

*Isaac Asimov's Space of Her Own.* ed. Shawna McCarthy. New York: Dial, 1983.

*Isaac Asimov's Wonderful World of Science Fiction #1: Intergalactic Empires.* New York: Signet, 1983.

*Isaac Asimov's Wonderful World of Science Fiction #2: The Science Fictional Olympics.* New York: Signet, 1984.

*Isaac Asimov's Wonders of the World.* ed. Kathleen Moloney and Shawna McCarthy. New York: Dial, 1982.

*Isaac Asimov's Worlds of Science Fiction.* ed. George Scithers. New York: Dial, 1980.

*Jupiter, the Largest Planet.* New York: Lothrop, Lee & Shepard, 1973; rev. ed. 1976.

*The Key Word and Other Mysteries.* il. Rod Burke. New York: Walker, 1977.

*The Kingdom of the Sun.* New York: Abelard-Schuman, 1960; rev. ed. 1963.

*The Kite That Won the Revolution.* il. Victor Mays. Boston: Houghton Mifflin, 1963.

*The Land of Canaan.* Boston: Houghton Mifflin, 1971.

*Lecherous Limericks.* il. Julien Dedman. New York: Walker, 1975.

*The Left Hand of the Electron.* Garden City, N.Y.: Doubleday, 1972.

*Life and Energy.* Garden City, N.Y.: Doubleday, 1962.

*Life and Time.* Garden City, N.Y.: Doubleday, 1978.

*Light.* photogs. by Allen Carr. Chicago: Follett, 1970.

*Limericks: Too Gross.* With John Ciardi. New York: Norton, 1978.

*The Living River.* London: Abelard-Schuman, 1959.

*Mars.* il. Herb Herrick. Chicago: Follett, 1967.

*Mars, the Red Planet.* New York: Lothrop, Lee & Shepard, 1977.

*The Martian Way, and Other Stories.* Garden City, N.Y.: Doubleday, 1955.

*Mass and Energy. The Neutron. The Structure of the Nucleus.* Washington, D.C.: U.S. Atomic Energy Commission, Office of Information Services, 1972.

*The Measure of the Universe: Our Foremost Science Writer Looks at the World Large and Small.* il. Roger Jones. New York: Harper & Row, 1983.

*The Moon.* il. Alex Ebel. Chicago: Follett, 1966.

*More Lecherous Limericks.* il. Julien Dedman. New York: Walker, 1976.

*More Tales of the Black Widowers.* Garden City, N.Y.: Doubleday, 1976.

*More Words of Science.* il. William Barss. Boston: Houghton Mifflin, 1972.

*More—Would You Believe?* il. Pat Schories. New York: Grosset & Dunlap, 1982.

*Murder at the ABA: A Puzzle in Four Days and Sixty Scenes.* Garden City, N.Y.: Doubleday, 1976.

*The Naked Sun.* Garden City, N.Y.: Doubleday, 1957.

*The Near East: 10,000 Years of History.* Boston: Houghton Mifflin, 1968.

*The Neutrino, Ghost Particle of the Atom.* Garden City, N.Y.: Doubleday, 1966.

*The New Intelligent Man's Guide to Science.* foreword by George W. Beadle. New York: Basic Books, 1965.

*The New Testament.* maps by Rafael Palacios. Garden City, N.Y.: Doubleday, 1969.

*Nightfall, and Other Stories.* Garden City, N.Y.: Doubleday, 1969.

*Nine Tomorrows: Tales of the Near Future.* Garden City, N.Y.: Doubleday, 1959.

*The Noble Gases.* New York: Basic Books, 1966.

*Norby, the Mixed-Up Robot.* With Janet Asimov. New York: Walker, 1983.

*Norby's Other Secret.* With Janet Asimov. New York: Walker, 1984.

*Nuclear Fission. Nuclear Fusion. Beyond Fusion.* Washington, D.C.: U.S. Atomic Energy Commission, Office of Information Services, 1972.

*Of Matters Great and Small.* Garden City, N.Y.: Doubleday, 1975.

*Of Time and Space and Other Things.* Garden City, N.Y.: Doubleday, 1965.

*Only a Trillion.* New York: Abelard-Schuman, 1958.

*Opus 100.* Boston: Houghton Mifflin, 1969.

*Opus 200.* Boston: Houghton Mifflin, 1979.

*Our Federal Union: The United States from 1816 to 1865.* Boston: Houghton Mifflin, 1975.

*Our World in Space.* foreword by Edwin Aldrin, Jr. il. Robert McCall. Greenwich, Conn.: New York Graphic Society, 1974.

*Pebble in the Sky.* Garden City, N.Y.: Doubleday, 1950.

*Photosynthesis.* New York: Basic Books, 1968.

*The Planet That Wasn't.* Garden City, N.Y.: Doubleday, 1976.

*Planets for Man.* With Stephen H. Dole. New York: Random House, 1964.

*Please Explain.* il. Michael McCurdy. Boston: Houghton Mifflin, 1973.

*Prisoners of the Stars.* 2 vols. Garden City, N.Y.: Doubleday, 1979.

*Quasar, Quasar, Burning Bright: Essays.* Garden City, N.Y.: Doubleday, 1978.

*Quick and Easy Math.* Boston: Houghton Mifflin, 1964.

*Races and People.* With William Clouser Boyd. il. John Bradford. New York: Abelard-Schuman, 1955.

*Realm of Algebra.* il. Robert Belmore. Boston: Houghton Mifflin, 1961.

*Realm of Measure.* il. Robert Belmore. Boston: Houghton Mifflin, 1960.

*Realm of Numbers.* il. Robert Belmore. Boston: Houghton Mifflin, 1959.

*The Rest of the Robots.* Garden City, N.Y.: Doubleday, 1964.

*The Road to Infinity.* Garden City, N.Y.: Doubleday, 1979.

*The Robots of Dawn.* Garden City, N.Y.: Doubleday, 1983.

*The Roman Empire.* Boston: Houghton Mifflin, 1967.

*The Roman Republic.* Boston: Houghton Mifflin, 1966.

*The Roving Mind.* Buffalo, N.Y.: 1983.

*Satellites in Outer Space.* il. John Polgreen. New York: Random House, 1960; rev. ed. 1964, 1966.

*Saturn and Beyond.* il. Giulio Maestro. New York: Lothrop, Lee & Shepard, 1979.

*Science, Numbers, and I.* Garden City, N.Y.: Doubleday, 1968.

*Science Past, Science Future.* Garden City, N.Y.: Doubleday, 1975.

*The Search for the Elements.* New York: Basic Books, 1962.

*Second Foundation.* New York: Gnome, 1953.

*The Shaping of England.* Boston: Houghton Mifflin, 1969.

*The Shaping of France.* Boston: Houghton Mifflin, 1972.

*The Shaping of North America from Earliest Times to 1763.* Boston: Houghton Mifflin, 1973.

*A Short History of Biology.* Garden City, N.Y.: Doubleday, 1964.

*A Short History of Chemistry.* Garden City, N.Y.: Anchor, 1965.

*The Solar System.* il. David Cunningham. Chicago: Follett, 1975.

*The Solar System and Back.* Garden City, N.Y.: Doubleday, 1970.

*Stars.* il. Herb Herrick. Chicago: Follett, 1968.

*The Stars in Their Courses.* Garden City, N.Y.: Doubleday, 1971.

*The Stars, Like Dust.* Garden City, N.Y.: Doubleday, 1951.

*Still More Lecherous Limericks.* New York: Walker, 1977.

*Stories from the Hugo Winners.* New York: Fawcett, 1972.

*The Story of Ruth.* Garden City, N.Y.: Doubleday, 1972.

*The Sun.* il. Alex Ebel. Chicago: Follett, 1972.

*The Sun Shines Bright.* Garden City, N.Y.: Doubleday, 1981.

*Tales of the Black Widowers.* Garden City, N.Y.: Doubleday, 1974.

*The Third Isaac Asimov Double: The Rings of Saturn and The Moons of Jupiter.* London: New English Library, 1973.

*Through a Glass, Clearly.* London: New English Library, 1975.

*To the Ends of the Universe.* New York: Walker, 1967; rev. ed. 1976.

*Today and Tomorrow and. . . .* Garden City, N.Y.: Doubleday, 1973.

*The Tragedy of the Moon.* Garden City, N.Y.: Doubleday, 1973.

*Travels through Time.* Milwaukee: Raintree, 1981.

*Treasury of Humor: A Lifetime Collection of Favorite Jokes, Anecdotes, and Limericks with Copious Notes on How to Tell Them and Why.* Boston: Houghton Mifflin, 1971.

*Triangle: The Currents of Space. Pebble in the Sky. The Stars, Like Dust.* Garden City, N.Y.: Doubleday, 1961.

*Twentieth Century Discovery.* Garden City, N.Y.: Doubleday, 1969.

*Understanding Physics: Light, Magnetism and Electricity.* New York: Walker, 1966.

*Understanding Physics, Vol. 2: Motion, Sound and Heat.* New York: Walker, 1966.

*Understanding Physics, Vol. 3: Electron, Proton and Neutron.* New York: Walker, 1966.

*The Union Club Mysteries.* Garden City, N.Y.: Doubleday, 1983.

*The Universe: From Flat Earth to Quasar.* New York: Walker, 1966; rev. ed. 1971.

*The Universe: From Flat Earth to Black Holes—and Beyond.* 3d ed. New York: Walker, 1980. (Revision of *The Universe: From Flat Earth to Quasar.*)

*Venus, Near Neighbor of the Sun.* il. Yukio Kondo. New York: Lothrop, Lee & Shepard, 1981.

*View from a Height.* Garden City, N.Y.: Doubleday, 1963.

*The Wellsprings of Life.* London: Abelard-Schuman, 1960.

*What Makes the Sun Shine?* il. Mark Brown. Boston: Little, Brown, 1971.

*Where Do We Go from Here?* Garden City, N.Y.: Doubleday, 1971.

*The Winds of Change and Other Stories.* Garden City, N.Y.: Doubleday, 1983.

*Wizards: Isaac Asimov's Magical Worlds of Fantasy#1;* with Martin H. Greenberg and Charles G. Waugh. New York: New American Library, 1983.

*Words from History.* il. William Barss. Boston: Houghton Mifflin, 1968.

*Words from the Exodus.* il. William Barss. Boston: Houghton Mifflin, 1963.

*Words from the Myths.* il. William Barss. Boston: Houghton Mifflin, 1961.

*Words in Genesis.* il. William Barss. Boston: Houghton Mifflin, 1962.

*Words of Science, and the History Behind Them.* il. William Barss. Boston: Houghton Mifflin, 1959; rev. ed. Harrap, 1974.

*Words on the Map.* il. William Barss. Boston: Houghton Mifflin, 1962.

*The World of Carbon.* New York: Abelard-Schuman, 1958; rev. ed. 1962.

*The World of Nitrogen.* New York: Abelard-Schuman, 1958; rev. ed. 1962.

*Worlds within Worlds: The Story of Nuclear Energy.* Washington, D.C.: U.S. Atomic Energy Commission, Office of Information Services, 1972.

*Would You Believe?* il. Sam Sirdofsky Haffner. New York: Grosset & Dunlap, 1981.

*X Stands for the Unknown.* Garden City, N.Y.: Doubleday, 1984.

*As Editor:*

*After the End.* With Charles Waugh and Paul Vaccarello. Milwaukee: Raintree, 1981.

*Before the Golden Age: A Science Fiction Anthology of the 1930s.* Garden City, N.Y.: Doubleday, 1974.

*Catastrophes!* With Martin Harry Greenberg and Charles Waugh. New York: Ballantine, 1981.

*Caught in the Organ Draft: Biology in Science Fiction.* With Martin H. Greenberg and Charles G. Waugh. New York: Farrar, Straus & Giroux, 1983.

*Creations: The Quest for Origins in Story and Science.* With others. New York: Crown, 1983.

*Earth Invaded.* With Harry Greenberg and Charles Waugh. il. Yoshi Miyake. Milwaukee: Raintree, 1982.

*Familiar Poems, Annotated.* Garden City, N.Y.: Doubleday, 1977.

*Fantastic Creatures: An Anthology of Fantasy and Science Fiction.* With others. New York: Watts, 1981.

*Fifty Short Science Fiction Tales.* With Groff Conklin. New York: Collier, 1963.

*Flying Saucers.* With Martin Greenberg and Charles Waugh. New York: Fawcett, 1982.

*The Future in Question.* With others. New York: Fawcett, 1980.

*Hallucination Orbit: Psychology in Science Fiction.* With Charles G. Waugh and Martin H. Greenberg. New York: Farrar, Straus & Giroux, 1983.

*Isaac Asimov Presents the Best Fantasy of the 19th Century.* With Charles G. Waugh and Martin Harry Greenberg. New York: Beaufort, 1982.

*Isaac Asimov Presents the Best Horror and Supernatural Fiction of the 19th Century.* With Charles G. Waugh and Martin H. Greenberg. New York: Beaufort, 1983.

*Isaac Asimov Presents the Best Science Fiction Firsts.* With Charles G. Waugh and Martin H. Greenberg. New York: Beaufort, 1984.

*Isaac Asimov Presents the Golden Years of Science Fiction: 28 Stories and Novellas.* With Martin H. Greenberg. New York: Bonanza, 1983; series 2, 1983.

*Isaac Asimov Presents the Great Science Fiction Stories.* With Martin H. Greenberg. New York: DAW. Vol. 1, *1939,* 1979; Vol. 2, *1940,* 1980; Vol. 3, *1941,* 1980; Vol. 4, *1942,* 1980; Vol. 5, *1943,* 1981; Vol. 6, *1944,* 1981; Vol. 7, *1945,* 1982; Vol. 8, *1946,* 1982; Vol. 9, *1947,* 1983; Vol. 10, *1948,* 1983; Vol. 11, *1949,* 1984.

*Isaac Asimov's Near Futures and Far.* With George Scithers. New York: Davis, 1981.

*The Last Man on Earth.* With Martin H. Greenberg. New York: Fawcett, 1982.

*Laughing Space. Funny Science Fiction. Chuckled Over.* With J.O. Jepson. Boston: Houghton Mifflin, 1982.

*Machines That Think: The Best Science Fiction Stories about Robots and Computers.* With Patricia S. Warrick and Martin H. Greenberg. New York: Holt, 1984.

*Mad Scientists.* With Martin Harry Greenberg and Charles Waugh. il. Joel Naprstek. Milwaukee: Raintree, 1982.

*Microcosmic Tales: 100 Wondrous Science Fiction Short-Short Stories.* With Martin Harry Greenberg and Charles G. Waugh. New York: Taplinger, 1980.

*Miniature Mysteries: 100 Malicious Little Mystery Stories.* With Martin Harry Greenberg and Joseph D. Olander. New York: Taplinger, 1981.

*More Stories from the Hugo Winners.* New York: Fawcett, 1973.

*Mutants.* With Martin Harry Greenberg and Charles Waugh. il. William Ersland. Milwaukee: Raintree, 1982.

*Nebula Award Stories 8.* New York: Harper & Row, 1973.

*100 Great Science Fiction Short-Short Stories.* With Martin H. Greenberg and Joseph D. Olander. Garden City, N.Y.: Doubleday, 1978.

*Science Fiction A to Z: A Dictionary of the Great Science Fiction Themes.* With Martin H. Greenberg and Charles G. Waugh. Boston: Houghton Mifflin, 1982.

*The Science-Fiction Weight-Loss Book.* With George R. R. Martin and Martin H. Greenberg. New York: Crown, 1983.

*The Science Fictional Solar System.* With Martin Harry Greenberg and Charles Waugh. New York: Harper & Row, 1979.

*The Seven Cardinal Virtues of Science Fiction.* With others. New York: Fawcett, 1981.

*The Seven Deadly Sins of Science Fiction.* With others. New York: Fawcett, 1980.

*Space Mail.* New York: Fawcett, 1980.

*Speculations.* With Alice Laurence. Boston: Houghton Mifflin, 1982.

*Starships: Stories Beyond the Boundaries of the Universe.* With Martin H. Greenberg and Charles Waugh. New York: Ballantine, 1983.

*Tantalizing Locked Room Mysteries.* With Charles G. Waugh and Martin Harry Greenberg. New York: Walker, 1982.

*Thinking Machines.* With Martin Harry Greenberg and Charles Waugh. il. Bruce Bond. Milwaukee: Raintree, 1981.

*The 13 Crimes of Science Fiction.* With Martin Harry Greenberg and Charles Waugh. Garden City, N.Y.: Doubleday, 1979.

*Those Amazing Electronic Thinking Machines: An Anthology of Robot and Computer Stories.* With Martin Greenberg and Charles Waugh. New York: Watts, 1983.

*Time Untamed.* With others. New York: Belmont, 1967.

*Tomorrow's Children: 18 Tales of Fantasy and Science Fiction.* il. Emanuel Schongut. Garden City, N.Y.: Doubleday, 1966.

*Tomorrow's TV.* With Martin Harry Greenberg and Greg Hargreaves. Milwaukee: Raintree, 1982.

*TV: Two Thousand.* With others. New York: Fawcett, 1982.

*The Untamed.* With others. New York: Belmont, 1967.

*Wild Inventions.* With others. Milwaukee: Raintree, 1981.

*Young Extraterrestrials.* With Martin Greenberg and Charles Waugh. New York: Harper & Row, 1984.

*Young Mutants.* With Martin Greenberg and Charles Waugh. New York: Harper & Row, 1984.

### As Consultant:

*Concepts in Physics.* Del Mar, Calif.: CRM Books, 1973.

### As Contributor:

*Frontiers of Knowledge.* With others. Garden City, N.Y.: Doubleday, 1975.

### As Introducer:

*Soviet Science Fiction.* tr. Violet L. Dutt. New York: Collier, 1962.

## As Dr. "A":

*The Sensuous Dirty Old Man.* New York: Walker, 1971.

## As Paul French:

*David Starr, Space Ranger.* Garden City, N.Y.: Doubleday, 1952.

*Lucky Starr and the Big Sun of Mercury.* Garden City, N.Y.: Doubleday, 1956.

*Lucky Starr and the Moons of Jupiter.* Garden City, N.Y.: Doubleday, 1957.

*Lucky Starr and the Oceans of Venus.* Garden City, N.Y.: Doubleday, 1954.

*Lucky Starr and the Pirates of the Asteroids.* il. Richard Powers. Garden City, N.Y.: Doubleday, 1953.

*Lucky Starr and the Rings of Saturn.* Garden City, N.Y.: Doubleday, 1958.

## ADDITIONAL SOURCES

Bleiler. *Science Fiction Writers.*
Commire. *Something about the Author.*
*Contemporary Authors.*
*Contemporary Literary Criticism.*
de Montreville and Hill. *Third Book of Junior Authors.*
Nicholls. *The Encyclopedia of Science Fiction.*
Reginald. *Contemporary Science Fiction Authors.*
*Science Fiction and Fantasy Literature.*
Smith. *Twentieth-Century Science Fiction Writers.*
Steinbrunner. *Encyclopedia of Mystery and Detection.*
Vinson. *Contemporary Novelists.* 1972, 1976 and 1982.
Wakeman. *World Authors, 1950-1970.*

## BIOGRAPHICAL NOTE

Avi (Wortis) was born in New York City on December 23, 1937. He has master's degrees from the University of Wisconsin and Columbia University. From 1962 to 1970 he was a librarian in the theater collection of the New York Public Library and is presently a humanities librarian at Trenton State College in New Jersey. Avi is divorced from Joan Gabriner, whom he married in 1963, and has two sons, Shaun and Kevin.

## PRELUDE TO THE INTERVIEW

Avi* and I sandwich his interview between one of his New York City editorial meetings and an inflexible commuter train schedule he must meet if he is to return home that evening.

His novels for middle-grade children are careful ones and the ones for which he is best-known. With richly recorded and researched details, they require attentive and careful reading to uncover their full meaning and their implications. His are not easy novels. They are tense, are full of excitement, and bring fictionalized history to life in a way that causes it to remain in the memory.

His interest in storytelling and in American history perhaps stems from his own family. Avi is a second-generation American, not all that far removed from his family's Western European origins and traditions. As with many second-generation children, Avi was raised with an undivided bias for the "new" country with all its promise while maintaining a close tie with the "old" country and its colorful and meaningful past. In these families a sense of the past is paramount: a sense of family is a sense of self. That sense is very often transmitted through storytelling.

Avi is a thoughtful speaker in that he will question questions, seeking clarity before answering. It is when he is discussing the reasons for his writing that he comes truly animated. His intensity deepens; he involves himself further in the

---

*Pronounced AH-vee.

question until he gets to the essence of the question; he answers confidently because he has been thinking about the answer for some time, quite possibly long before the interview.

## THE INTERVIEW

J.R.     Many of your books deal with historical subjects. Why is this?

A.       Well, I have a history degree but there are two sides to that.

One side is I hated being a student and I hated to study. The way I learned to study history was to read novels as a way to immerse myself in the subject.

But the other side comes from another place. When I was a kid, my parents were, I'd say, liberal left people. And during the whole McCarthy period they felt very much under attack philosophically. Their defense was that they were supporters of the true historical traditions of this country.

I was constantly imbued with a sense of American history right off. I had a grandfather who came to this country from Russia as a poor boy, and who, as is often the case, developed this great love for America and would tell me a great deal about American history, how wonderful the country was, recounting all the traditions.

And somewhere along the line, I can't explain where, I developed an understanding of history not as fact but as story. That you could look at a field and, with only a slight shift of your imagination, suddenly watch the battle that took place there.

I'm the kind of person who stops to read road markers by the side of the road. They fascinate me.

I find a knowledge of history creates living shadows of what you see. You know what's what. You can see what really is. And then you can depict what could be or will be.

J.R.     What do you mean by you can "see"?

A.       You have to have a willingness to look beyond *things.* And listen to stories.

I remember my father's mother who was French and raised in the Alsace-Lorraine. I remember with great vividness her describing when she was a little girl of six or seven the Germans marching into the Alsace during the Franco-Prussian war of 1870. She would recount all the stories.

Or my wife's father, living on the border between Poland and Russia. There's a wonderful story about when he was a kid: He collected old military buttons. One week the White Russian army was in, the next the Polish army, the next week the Germans. The soldiers would commandeer the women to wash their uniforms and the kids would sneak in and cut off the buttons from the underwear and then swap the buttons the way we do with baseball cards.

There are a lot of wonderful little stories inside the grander stories.

I remember reading about World War One from a book a British military historian had written, *The Face of Battle.*[1] He described not the grand war, but the stories in the war. There was one in which he recounted the story of a regiment of soccer players. There were thirty or forty of them and the captain of the team led them, not carrying a rifle but kicking a soccer ball. That's an incredible story.

When you read history like that, it's *full!*

Or take the Battle of Bunker Hill during the Revolution. The leader of the American troops was Dr. Warren, who was killed during the battle. His body had been so dismembered and disemboweled, the only way he could be identified was by the nature of his teeth. And it was Paul Revere who did it. When you tell the story of war that way, a much stronger statement about how ghastly war really is, is made.

J.R.   Since you work as a librarian full-time, do you take job time to research books?

A.     No! Turn that tape recorder off!

Actually, I steal a lunch hour, steal a half hour, work at night and on the weekends. I'm a compulsive writer in the sense I'm not happy if I'm not writing. It's just part of my existence and I do it when I can.

I'm not a fast writer. I rewrite my books ten, fifteen times before they're finished. I constantly rewrite and rewrite and rewrite. I've taught myself how to set very limited goals, five pages a day sort of thing. Not three hundred pages a summer. But, bit by bit, I'll have three hundred pages at the end of the summer.

When I finish a book I have to force myself not to start something else. I'll wait a couple of days. I have a list of fourteen, fifteen books that are sitting around. Not that I'll ever do them. It's just nice to have them around.

That's it. It's just part of my existence. I don't block out my time. I just steal it by staying an extra hour at work, getting in early. But constant, constant, constant.

If you look at my books you'll notice the nature of them is episodic. That's because I write them in short bits.

J.R.   But you also travel a lot promoting your books. Doesn't this interfere with your daily work?

A.     The library I work in is extremely flexible. There are times I need to work fifteen hours a day, then I get the compensatory time to travel. And my supervisors see this as an extension of my work as a librarian. It works out well.

And I feel traveling is part of my job as a writer. I enjoy doing it, and I love working with kids.

Those trips sort of always refuel me. And you can create situations with kids that are fun because they're unpredictable. The trips give me a lot of feedback I don't get in any other way.

J.R.  What do you mean?

A.  I don't have major recognition as a writer. My reviews are often mixed on some level because my books, I think, are not easy. They don't always tie up easily at the end. There's not always a happy resolution. There's always a kind of ambiguity to them. So I need all the positive reinforcement I can get!

And it's also hard to find anyone who has an overall view of my work. I don't get it from anywhere because of the nature of my writing, which varies from book to book. I'm often still—from time to time—reviewed as a new writer, so I don't have a sense at all of where I'm at. Even reviewers have difficulty staying with me! It's very frustrating, as you can imagine.

J.R.  Why do you think there's little carryover from book to book with reviewers?

A.  And kids, too. What happens is, I know this because I've been told this, when a kid picks up one of my books and really likes it he asks what else is around by me? And he gets a book, but it's a different kind of book. And that's not always what he wants. What it is, I skip all over the place. Reviewers have stylistic, subject, et cetera, expectations. I don't conform.

But I go through moods. There was a time when I was writing a lot of historical fiction. I really liked it. Then I stopped. Then I wrote some contemporary things. Then I didn't do it anymore and went back to historical books.

And I have a certain compulsion to publish a book a year. It's stupid, I know. But I really enjoy writing and I love being published!

J.R.  What do you do with kids in schools?

A.  Discuss my writing process in depth. Writing workshops and so on. Sometimes I read them books before they're done. I love the experience of reading aloud. And I think of my books as very oral and on some levels they are meant to be read aloud. I love the words, the phrasing, the music and the power of story.

I remember when I first read *Captain Grey* in a school. The teacher asked me if I minded if the kids drew while I was reading. That doesn't bother me.

So I started to read and there was one kid in the back who was obviously not going to pay any attention at all. So I started reading and realized he wasn't drawing like the other kids. Just stared at me, intent on the story.

The second time I went back I wondered if I was still going to be able to hold him. He didn't draw again. By the third and fourth times I was ready for that kid! I read right to him. Just to see if I could keep him from drawing at all. He never did.

Kids hear. When I start to read to the kids I say, "I want you to be relaxed. Don't feel like you have to stay in a frozen position. If you need to get up to sharpen a pencil or do anything, do it." I feel the kid who just sits there, uptight, is ultimately more distracting to me than the kid who is scratching or whatever. The only thing I ask of them is not to talk. They can even pass notes. I don't care. If I have thirty-six kids in front of me and two are turned off, I've still got the thirty-four and that's OK.

J.R.      Why children's books?

A.          I used to write for adults, but I wasn't very good at it. I think one of the things I've learned is, I've always loved the form of a novella, a short novel. I love the book you can swallow in one long drink.

When I wrote for adults I started with novellas and they didn't work. And I like the form. There was interest, lots of it, but nothing ever came of it. Then I went to writing very long novels. But I don't feel I was able to control the story in four hundred, five hundred pages. It got to be too complicated.

The young adult novel and the children's novel are basically novellas for me. I love it. I have a wonderful sense of control. When I'm working on a book one of my constant processes is to read the book through to make sure the timing, the style, and all that is there. I like the length. I can move with it, manipulate it as I go along.

J.R.      What about TV or magazines?

A.          Actually, my first writing was for the theater. Then some guy once got interested in doing a television series with the *Captain Grey* saga. He was going to do a five-part, multimillion-dollar prime-time thing. It was wonderful. But the bigger it got the more sure I was that it was never going to occur.

This guy would write and say, "I spoke with John Wayne and he said if only. . . ." They were funny letters but had nothing to do with reality.

J.R.      What do you ultimately want your books to do?

A.          I'd like kids to put down my books, feeling they've had an experience, whatever that means. And I would like to have the reputation of writing exciting books.

There are times, and I'm sure it's true of a lot of other writers, that you write stuff and you just bloody well know that it's good. Or you work all night on a chapter, and all of a sudden you get it right. You rewrite fifty times and all of a sudden it works.

There's an enormous satisfaction in putting together words and emotions and situations, having the sense of pride of doing something worthy of being called writing. That's very exciting.

J.R.     What happens after the excitement?

A.       I get depressed. "What am I going to do next week? I'll never be able to do it again."

When it gets hard on that level I find I use my inner self, wherever that might be, more and more to comfort myself. But sometimes you dont't like what you dredge up!

I think the nicest compliment I ever got was from a kid who wrote me a letter saying this and that and the last line was "thank you for putting another book in the world."

That says it all, doesn't it? "Thank you."

J.R.     What other kind of letters do you get?

A.       A lot of it is Gee, whiz, you're my favorite writer stuff. I get enough of it to know what the kids like, what their perceptions are, and what comes across in the books. And there are a corps of kids who like the hard questions that are sometimes raised, the ironies, the dilemmas and contradictions. It's good to know there are kids who respond and relate to that.

It's really funny how many requests I get for sequels to my books. All the time. It's rare for me not to. At first it puzzled me. Because on the one hand the book is brought to a satisfactory conclusion, but not so satisfactory I don't leave something human to it.

I did a sequel once but I'm reluctant to do it again. Partly because if the book is a good one I'm not sure I can equal it in a sequel. I don't want to write something inferior for the sake of doing a sequel. And very often, too, I'm off onto some other idea.

J.R.     What's the one with the sequel?

A.       *Night Journeys.* The boy who was predominant in *Encounter at Easton* appears briefly in *Night Journeys.* At the end of *Easton* I make reference to the fact that he's going to be adopted by this tavern owner named Mr. Grey. Well, that boy becomes Captain Grey in the second edition reprint. I changed the story slightly from the first edition, so that *Night Journeys, Encounter at Easton,* and *Captain Grey* could be part of one story. There are, in addition, two parts outlined, but as yet, never written. I love writing books which I think are exciting page-turners whether they are sequels or not.

When I used to read to my kids the greatest compliment I could get was when I reached the end of the chapter and they'd say, simply, "More." It was the most, the best, positive criticism I could get. Don't stop! Go on! What more could one ask for?

J.R.     Any theories on writing?

A.       I've got lots of them!

The main one is that for creative people it's very crucial not to stay where you were raised because for better—and for worse—it's better to be an outsider. You see much more. You're more conscious of what's around you.

When you look at my books, you'll see I rarely write about cities. That's because I was raised in Brooklyn and moved to the country. I revel in the country. I think my perceptions are sharper in it because I keep seeing things, feeling things, all the time. Whereas in New York City, I just glaze over.

I love writing for kids. There's nothing I can't write about. I think being able to write for young people is a very free way to write. Yet I think the audience is more demanding than a comparable adult audience. The book has to be a powerful experience for them. You have to get that grunt to go on, go on. If you don't get that with the story, you don't have anything. For me that's fundamental.

J.R.     How about artists for your books? Do you have input there?

A.     Yes, I've been in the position to request, and the request has been met. But I'm not the best judge for that kind of thing. And I don't want to be in that situation. There are so many good artists around and if the editor doesn't know them, then they're in the wrong business. I'm willing to talk, but I don't want to make the final decisions.

J.R.     What else do you expect from an editor?

A.     A good editor leaves you with the feeling of, If I do this, I can expand the character. Or, that's an interesting possibility, I never thought of that. Or, I blew it! What did I do wrong? They raise questions that deepen the book. Laura[2] does that and Fabio[3] did it.

My first book with Fabio was *Snail's Tale.* When I went to his office I said, "Do you feel it needs work?" He said, "Well, maybe eight words." I said, "What are you talking about, eight words?" He really didn't mean eight words, of course. What he meant was if I just strengthen an aspect of one character that would enhance the book. But it was wonderful, "eight words"! Incredibly enough, he was right.

He used to turn books of mine down and I would come away with the feeling that he was right, the book should not be published. It wasn't as good as I thought it was.

That's a wonderful gift. It wasn't that he disappointed me, I was disappointed with myself. It was, Yeah, now let's do something really good and not waste any more time.

And I never sent the rejected manuscript anywhere else. It's not that he demolished them, but he would point out the problems. To me that's a good editor. Or, he would never say to me, Why do you write this stuff? It's good, but unsaleable. He'd say, "You've written a good book and I'm obligated to do it," making me feel like *I* had to make my books saleable.

*Shadrach's Crossing* is dedicated to him. He was wonderful, a great editor.

It also helps to be smart to be an editor. Which means they know what you're trying to do. And that they are willing to go along with it, push you toward it.

J.R.     What would you ultimately like from the entire scheme of things?

A.     To move somebody, to touch somebody. And, I guess I'd like to be known as a good writer. That's what it really comes down to.

You know I almost flunked out of school because my writing was so bad. I was the world's worst writer. There's a sense of satisfaction that I've come as far as I have.

Do you know Edward Gorey's *The Unstrung Harp?*[4] To me that's the quintessential manual of writing. When any aspiring writer comes to ask for a book on writing I say, "Read that and you'll know the mysteries of writing." Writing is work.

You know, I'm a reader, I'm a librarian, I'm a writer. There's a real privilege in being part of all of this.

J.R.     How so?

A.     To be a writer, especially to be published. To be part of that small crowd. That's very meaningful to me. You have to have a certain ego to think that anything you write can justify the energy, time, and effort to be with all the other books on library shelves.

I'm not Hemingway, but we're both writers. I appreciate the fact that I can include myself in the same room as him! And I'd much rather be across the room than outside in the hall.

It's a nice place to be. I don't think there's anything better than writing.

## Notes

[1] John Keegan, *The Face of Battle* (New York: Viking Press, 1976).

[2] Laura Geringer is an editor of children's books for Harper & Row.

[3] Fabio Coen is former editorial director of children's books for Alfred A. Knopf and Pantheon Books.

[4] Edward Gorey, *The Unstrung Harp: Or Mr. Earbrass Writes a Novel* (New York: Duell, Sloan and Pearce, 1953).

## BIBLIOGRAPHY

*Captain Grey.* il. Charles Mikolaycak. New York: Pantheon, 1977.

*Devil's Race.* New York: Lippincott, 1984.

*Emily Upham's Revenge: Or, How Deadwood Dick Saved the Banker's Niece: A Massachusetts Adventure.* il. Paul O. Zelinsky. New York: Pantheon, 1978.

*Encounter at Easton.* New York: Pantheon, 1980.

*The Fighting Ground.* New York: Lippincott, 1984.

*The History of Helpless Harry; to Which Is Added a Variety of Amusing and Entertaining Adventures.* il. Paul O. Zelinsky. New York: Pantheon, 1980.

*Man from the Sky.* il. David Wiesner. New York: Knopf, 1980.

*Night Journeys.* New York: Pantheon, 1979.

*No More Magic.* New York: Pantheon, 1975.

*A Place Called Ugly.* New York: Pantheon, 1981.

*Shadrach's Crossing.* New York: Pantheon, 1983.

*Snail's Tale: The Adventures of a Rather Small Snail.* il. Tom Kindron. New York: Pantheon, 1972.

*Sometimes I Think I Hear My Name.* New York: Pantheon, 1982.

*S.O.R. Losers.* New York: Bradbury, 1984.

*Things That Sometimes Happen.* il. Jodi Robbin. Garden City, N.Y.: Doubleday, 1970.

*Who Stole the Wizard of Oz?* il. Derek James. New York: Knopf, 1981.

## AWARDS AND HONORS

*Encounter at Easton*
      Christopher Award

*Man from the Sky*
      Children's Choice Book

*Night Journeys*
      Best Book of the Year

## ADDITIONAL SOURCES

Commire. *Something about the Author.*
*Contemporary Authors.*

Donald Crews

## BIOGRAPHICAL NOTE

The popular author-illustrator of *Harbor* and *Freight Train* was born in Newark, New Jersey, on August 30, 1938. He completed his studies at the Cooper Union for the Advancement of Science and Art in New York City in 1959, and married Ann Jonas in 1963. His artistic career began as an assistant art director at *Dance Magazine* in 1959 and then as a designer at the Will Burtin Studio, both in New York, through 1962. Since 1964 he has been a free-lance designer. Mr. Crews has two daughters, Nina and Amy.

## PRELUDE TO THE INTERVIEW

Donald Crews is a circuitous talker. He touches on a subject and comes back to it later, remembering that another point must be made and something just said made him think of the previous question. Thus, his conversation expands and contracts simultaneously, widening the conversational base. I note that his voice has just the touch of a New York City accent, but it is softer, slower, and far more elegant than one usually hears from a New Yorker.

He says it took him about ten years to become known as "Donald Crews, artist." It was *Freight Train* that brought him to international prominence in the children's book field. It was that book, with a four-color train whizzing through artful white space, that helped him discover his wider audience. Since then, all of his books are eagerly anticipated, each bringing its own new visual surprise that is his uniquely expressive way of approaching the ordinary and making it new again.

Donald, as with the others here, is slightly bemused by our session, neither of us sure where it's going to go. His first answers are simple and direct. Both of us feel our way around the other. After the first half-hour, he is totally relaxed, increasingly more expansive, talking more intensely about his art and his books for children.

# THE INTERVIEW

**J.R.**   Your books have a very studied, crafted, and designed look about them. Are you by training a designer?

**D.C.**   Yes. I was trained as a designer and started working at a magazine in the sixties. After military service, a couple of short-term jobs eventually led me into free-lance work. I did work for the 1964 World's Fair, started picking up book jackets and book design projects.

**J.R.**   How did you find your way into children's books?

**D.C.**   That began when I was in the army in Germany. I was away from any kind of work at all for eighteen months. I began to work on a portfolio so I could have something new, fresh to build on. Something to show prospective employers and clients.

Portfolios are such a brief experience for art directors. They're looked at, judged, in short order. I needed something to slow down the experience. So I designed a children's book as a "freshener" and a "pacer."

The people we lived with in Germany liked the book as it was being developed. They suggested I show it to German publishers. I got lots of friendly rejections! It was an American primer and they rightfully rejected it for that reason.

So when I got back to the United States I showed it only as often as it was useful to get free-lance work and then I put it away.

Eventually I was asked by Harper & Row if I had ever designed a children's book. Libby Shub[1] asked me to bring it in at some point and said she'd like to look at it.

**J.R.**   That book was . . .?

**D.C.**   *We Read: A to Z.* Then Libby moved to Scribner's and so the next book I did was with them because Libby was the one I knew, she was the one I worked with. In the meantime I was doing free-lance design, book jackets, book illustration, technical illustration, anything that gave us a source of income.

We worked, myself and my wife, hard. We have always worked out of our living space. Our operation in the West Village[2] wasn't a very big one. But then we were doing small projects!

**J.R.**   I think it's fair to say that you received national prominence with the Caldecott Honor Book Medal for *Freight Train.*

**D.C.**   Yeah, when I first heard of it I didn't even know what it was! But I found out fast!

**J.R.**   Did you get the feeling that once you had achieved it, you had to do it again?

D.C.        No. But the next book, *Truck,* also won as unexpectedly as the first.

Awards are terrific. I was at a librarians' conference in the Midwest and introduced as being a Caldecott Honor Medalist and on and on and on. I was asked what I thought about it. I said, "I think if you want to give me an award, I'll take it. It's out of my control!"

The whole thing is terrific. You have this committee and they vote and talk about it, *your* book, discuss it, choose sides. Even if you don't win, just to have your book as a point of discussion means something. I am flattered to have people talking about my work.

J.R.       Do you believe the flattery when you hear it?

D.C.        Oh, no, no. You can't. You hear everything and you can't believe it. They tell you you're the best thing since *The Wizard of Oz.* Let it stay there.

People always ask, "What do your books mean to you? How do you do it?" Well, I don't know what they mean. But I do know if you buy this book, I'll do another one!

*Freight Train* was good for me, yes, because it made me aware that people knew who I was.

But it is very hard for me to get across that my books don't have deeper meanings. For a long time I worked on short projects like book jackets. You rarely see the finished book. You imagine somebody is kind of pulling you along, giving you a few hundred dollars to design a jacket, and you never see it. A book gives you the opportunity to stretch out, develop an idea.

It has come to light that work I did has come to be something special. But it took ten years for it to become viable for me. I have been told that when some people hear I have a new book, that it's automatically purchased. They don't have to look at it. It's a great position to be in. They assume whatever you're doing they're going to be interested in. That carries a responsibility so you begin to think you can't do things haphazardly. It has to be something that appeals to that audience out there.

J.R.       What is another common question asked of you?

D.C.        How I deal with publishers! "How are you sure they're not going to steal one of your ideas?"

What I tell them is that publishers are after a product. If you have something good, they're going to be there. They're not going to try to steal an idea. Authors and illustrators are suppliers. And without them there is no product. One should look at who publishes the books you like and send your books to them. Don't worry about it. You've got to trust somebody. Just don't deal with people you think are nefarious.

Publishers want books to sell. When people tell me they can't find a book in a bookstore I tell them to buy it directly from the publisher. And the more the better. Buy one, buy two.

J.R.    Now you're getting to the subject of distribution, a sore subject among everyone involved in the industry. What are your views?

D.C.    You learn, from talking to people around the country, that most school systems and library systems are slow in the way their books are distributed.

As a designer, as an artist, when I have a copy of the book in my hand, I think everybody else has a copy in their hands, too. But that's far from the truth. It's a year or more after you, the artist, have a physical book in hand when librarians get a chance to consider it in a lot of places. I hear all the time, "I know you've done a new book but we haven't had a chance to review it yet. It'll take a few months." *A few months!* All they have to do is ask me and I'll send them a copy!*

The mechanism seems slow and cumbersome. Librarians have to be able to buy books faster. By the time many get around to ordering, the book can already be out of print, already gone before it gets a chance to get going. Libraries are in the service of making books available to the public. And if they don't have the book to promote, they're not going to be effective. And I know it doesn't help when publishers remainder early. Librarians should be able to find a book five years from when it's published. It's not a simple matter.

One of my tag lines in my talks is to tell audiences that we are in concert. "If you don't buy my book, I don't get published anymore." It's a real symbiotic relationship that we have. We all feed each other. Publishers look at what we create and see its worth, sometimes not. Librarians submit the books to kids to see if they accept them or not.

We're in concert, the buyers and myself. We're both after the same thing, an exciting book. That's the reason I guess I continue to do things that are in a way difficult. They don't know me and I don't know what it is they enjoy in the books. Sales tell me that what I'm doing, whatever it is, however I arrive at the decision to do it, has some value for them, has some value to the kids who read the books. That inspires me to go on. It makes what I do worth something.

J.R.    As an artist, as a freelancer, your success speaks for itself. And it must be gratifying. Many people would have great difficulty leading a freelancer's life.

D.C.    I can go through a week without having a check in the mail. It doesn't frighten me the way it does a lot of people. It doesn't bother me.

There are a lot of areas in art, design, graphics, commercial graphics, advertising, where I can use the abilities I've developed over the years that would probably make some money. But it's much more of a kick to think you're significantly contributing to an area that's special. That's the real

---

*Interviewer's note: This is said more in a joking manner than a serious one. Readers, please do not inundate Don with requests for books!

thing about being a painter, a sculptor, any kind of artist, that you have a point of view, that point of view being a value of its own. I like the fact that people tell me that what I do is special. That charges me. That makes me want to be good and that they feel I give them value for their dollar. I hope so. That's what I'm trying to do.

J.R.   Did you ever think of getting a "real job"?

D.C.   Oh, for awhile. Then everything started slowing down. So I stopped pressing.

Besides I didn't want to have to go to work for somebody. I wanted to find something that made me special. You get a better kick from doing things you initiate. And it's exciting to see if you can carry it out. So I tried art. If that didn't work out, I would have gone and found some other kind of work. Carpentry, some sort of hands-on work, I suppose. I don't know.

As a free-lancer you always think you can accomplish more. It seems to work and there seems to be a future in it. There always is a thought in the back of your head that it would be nice to be able to somehow foresee what you're going to do for the rest of your life, what your backup is going to be.

If you're working for a company, for instance, you're building some kind of pension plan. You have some sort of thing going, some sort of in, with plans for yourself. And if there's anything I've had since I left school that's the training I've had that enables me to continue to do this. That's what I've been doing in children's books, building a future.

I listen a lot to the other guys. They're either working for someone or they're not. People are continually changing jobs. Going from one place to another. It's always fascinating. In free-lancing you're always where you are. You're making some kind of mark in an area by presenting something you can do, something that has a value.

I'm a freelance "book designer," "book creator." I'm committed to it. To see how far, how significant this thing I'm doing is. I really want to do something that adds to the main line, to public view, to public scrutiny. Something that extends my worth, on my terms. Something that fits. Something that shows signs of growth. What I can do. What I'm capable of and what the next possibility is.

J.R.   Did you ever think you would have people lining up to see you and to get your autograph?

D.C.   Ha! It's phenomenal!

I like signing books, especially those dog-eared copies. Those are real diamonds, true testimonials.

I don't understand why people stand in line to get books signed. Why not give them all to me at one time? I'd take them to my hotel room and sit up all night and sign them. That way people could go have a drink, do whatever they want to do, and get the books the next day.

J.R.     Do you draw in your books, too?

D.C.         No, I don't and can't. What I've done is design a stamp based on the book, a truck, a train, a carousel, et cetera. People don't seem to mind. I add something to each one. Sometimes people think I'm going to stamp my name, but I don't, of course.

         I watched an illustrator one time draw in each and every book. It was phenomenal. I can't do that. I don't mind signing because it makes the book more personal. But if you have a long line and people have a lot of books, it's an imposition to other people in line to have to wait very long. Most really want to be in there and get out. They have other things to do, too, than stand in line all day.

J.R.     Characterize your books.

D.C.         They're usable. I think that's the key.

         As a designer, as an artist, I'm doing the book out of my abilities, my attitudes, my point of view. But if librarians or parents can use it, that's *excitement! Excitement!*

         And its good if kids get excited reading them. I've watched kids with several of my books laid out in front of them and a parent wanting to choose *Freight Train* or *Rain* or a choice other than that of the child. And I've seen it become a tug-of-war! There's nothing a librarian or parent can do to make a child take a book unless they respond to it.

J.R.     Do you test your ideas in advance?

D.C.         People ask that a lot; if there is a way to test the book, test the concept, test the design. My response is that for a book to be successful it has to appeal to a lot of people. There is no way for me to test a book on all the various levels. I've never thought about doing that with my books. I just say, "This is what I want to happen." It's rewarding to have the public respond in the way you anticipate.

J.R.     What else do you think about when you sit down to work on a book?

D.C.         There are a lot of things. What you're going to lose in the gutter, how the fold of a book will affect the art, how it's all going to look when it's done.

         You sit there with a story to tell. The thought that goes through your mind is how are you going to work this two-dimensional area you have to work with, to enliven it and make it come to life. How do you do it? How do you start? What do you use?

         What I do is jot down someplace all the possibilities and then choose the most likely for development. I mean, you're anxious to see it, too!

         When you flip through the pages and go through them, one after another, does it make a statement? Is it fleshed out? Is the idea whole? That's what it has to do. It has to begin and it has to end at some point.

In *Parade* I really was interested in the watchers in the crowd, as much as the objects in the parade. There's a lot of activity that happens in a crowd when you're watching it from the opposite side of the street as a spectator. That book is a spectator looking at spectators. The only thing I'm disappointed about the book is that there wasn't any room to watch a crowd build and wane more, as it does in reality.

It gets down to, no matter what subject you work with, what is the central importance, the attitude, the idea? The idea should be a continuous loop. You've got to start, you've got to get back. One has to make a circle out of it. That's really important to me. In essence I think that's what I've done in most of my books. The need to go back again. To start over again.

I don't want to do anything frivolous. I can't. I work only with serious ideas.

J.R.     "Serious ideas"?

D.C.     Something that means something. Some real thing; some tangible thing. When you walk down the street and see a truck or fire engine, what's the importance of that natural event? Can you make a statement about that experience? What's special about it? It's taking a piece of something and seeing if it's special and making it important through a visual medium that can excite you and the children you're working for.

Looking at the carousels on Coney Island I kept thinking, "What is it? What makes it exciting?" It was just that moment of exhilaration that excited me, that ride.

You have to find something that interests you, and create a visual interpretation that will excite people. It's so open. There's so much you can do. With what books cost, they should each be something different and filled with your full creative range.

I always work from the same lack of confidence with each book. "I could be better; I could be different; I could work harder; I could do more research." When you stop working on the book, you stop the struggle. And it's the best you can do. It's pointless to go on with it forever. That's a great point when you can let it go. I try to establish a relationship between reality and a creative interpretation of a moment from that reality, and present it as a concise statement.

It's a gamble. But it's a good gamble.

## Notes

[1] Elizabeth Shub, senior editor of children's books for Greenwillow Books, formerly associated with Macmillan Publishing Company and Charles Scribner's Sons, and also an author and translator of children's books.

[2] The West Village is a neighborhood outside of Manhattan's Greenwich Village.

# BIBLIOGRAPHY

*ABC of Ecology.* By Harry Milgrom. New York: Macmillan, 1972.

*ABC Science Experiements.* By Harry Milgrom. New York: Crowell-Collier, 1970.

*Blue Sea.* By Robert Kalan. New York: Greenwillow, 1979.

*Carousel.* New York: Greenwillow, 1982.

*Eclipse: Darkness in Daytime.* By Franklyn M. Branley. New York: Crowell, 1973.

*Fractions Are Parts of Things.* By J. Richard Dennis. New York: Crowell, 1971.

*Freight Train.* New York: Greenwillow, 1978.

*Harbor.* New York: Greenwillow, 1982.

*Light.* New York: Greenwillow, 1981.

*Parade.* New York: Greenwillow, 1983.

*Rain.* By Robert Kalan. New York: Greenwillow, 1978.

*School Bus.* New York: Greenwillow, 1984.

*The Talking Stone: An Anthology of Native American Tales and Legends.* ed. Dorothy de Wit. New York: Greenwillow, 1979.

*Ten Black Dots.* New York: Scribner, 1968.

*Truck.* New York: Greenwillow, 1980.

*We Read: A to Z.* New York: Harper & Row, 1967; new ed., Greenwillow, 1984.

# AWARDS AND HONORS

*ABC Science Experiments*
  Book Show

*Blue Sea*
  Library of Congress list
  Notable Children's Book

*Carousel*
  Library of Congress list
  Notable Children's Book

*Eclipse*
  Showcase Book

*Freight Train*
  Best Book of the Year
  Best Book of the Best Book
  Book Show
  Brooklyn Art Book for Children
  Caldecott Medal honor book
  Children's Choice Book
  Library of Congress list
  Notable Children's Book

*Harbor*
  Library of Congress list

*Light*
  Children's Choice Book
  Library of Congress list

*Rain*
  Book Show

*School Bus*
  Best Book of the Year

*The Talking Stone*
  Library of Congress list
  Notable Children's Book
  Notable Children's Trade Book
    in the Field of Social Studies

*Truck*
  Best Book of the Year
  Caldecott Medal honor book
  Library of Congress list
  Notable Children's Book

*We Read: A to Z*
        Book Show

## ADDITIONAL SOURCES

Commire. *Something about the Author.*
Kingman. *Illustrators of Children's Books: 1967-1976.*
Ward. *Illustrators of Books for Young People.*

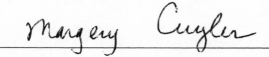

**Margery Cuyler**

## BIOGRAPHICAL NOTE

Born in Princeton, New Jersey, on December 31, 1948, Margery Cuyler graduated from Sarah Lawrence College in Bronxville, New York, in 1970. Her years in publishing began at the Atlantic Monthly Press in Boston, and continued through 1974 as the editor of children's books at Walker & Company in New York. At present Ms. Cuyler, who has written under the name "Daisy Wallace," is the editor-in-chief at Holiday House. She married John Perkins in 1979.

## PRELUDE TO THE INTERVIEW

Margery Cuyler is a textbook example of a Type-A personality. That is the personality that is classified as being most susceptible to heart attacks, ulcers, breakdowns, and other nervous disorders.

She moves, thinks, and talks at an extraordinarily fast pace. For the uninitiated she can be difficult to keep up with. Her long association with children's books as an editor  and as an author gives her a close-up view of all aspects of children's book creation, from editing and production to distribution.

Because of her dual-role and her in-depth knowledge of the subject she is able to provide insights here into children's books as few can. It is a role she moves in and out of easily during an interview, clarifying from which side she is speaking, whether that of editor or creator as she goes along. It can be difficult for an editor of children's books to also be an author at the same time. But there is an axiom in publishing that every author needs an editor, including editors who are authors. Margery has no problem moving in and out of her many roles in the children's book world.

If the Type-A personality theory holds, she will have to slow down or something will slow her down. That "something," whatever it may be, will have one problem: it will have to catch her first!

## THE INTERVIEW

J.R.    You're in that slightly difficult dual role of editor and author. How do you take being edited by someone else?

M.C.    I've been lucky to have good editors. On all counts I haven't had any problems.

I think authors and illustrators should listen to editors. Some are good, some are bad. If editors say something is wrong with your work, there is often a reason. For example, an editor might say, "Rewrite this section because it's too sophisticated for the age level." Or, "This remark is sexist and could cost you some sales." This type of comment is helpful. In the final analysis, however, I don't think an editor should be inflexible. I don't support the idea of an editor saying, "We're going to take these words out and if you don't agree, we're not going to publish the book."

I don't have any problems with being edited. I change personalities. I become a chameleon. When I'm an editor I feel one way and when I'm an author, I feel another. I forget about being an editor. I really do.

That's why when you wrote me at Holiday House and asked for an interview I assumed you wanted to interview me as an editor. When I reread your letter and realized you wanted to interview me as an author, I completely switched roles.

J.R.    Don't your own editorial sensibilities and abilities come into play in your own writing?

M.C.    No. I feel confident as an editor, but when I write, I feel insecure. My insecurity takes over and I leave my editor personality behind.

J.R.    How can that be?

M.C.    I think it's partly because I was raised by parents who didn't recognize the importance of art. I grew up thinking that if you were an artist you were irresponsible or an orphan. My grandfather was an artist and he lost a lot of money. My father had to live on charity from the church because of it. So he went into business and as an adult made a lot of money.

He also had five kids; I'm the youngest. He conveyed the message we should never go into art as a career because he grew up thinking artists ruined his life.

Editing is considered a "legitimate" profession in his eyes, as is architecture. You know, *stable*. It's interesting because all of my siblings have turned out to be artists of one sort or another.

So I feel partly unconfident because I grew up in a family that was not supportive of art. But I also feel unconfident because the books I edit are so much better than the ones I write. I mean that.

J.R.     If you mean that, why do it?

M.C.         When you're an editor you give everything you've got away to bring out other people's creativity. It's like being a midwife. You're helping someone else give birth.

     When you're a writer, you're doing something just for yourself. No one else is involved. And it's important for everybody to experience that private corner in their lives.

J.R.     But as an author-editor don't you find it difficult not to interject your own writing style onto authors you edit?

M.C.         No, as an editor I'm there to catalyze. I learned that from Emilie.[1] She actually trained me when I first started out so I suppose I've been influenced by some of her ideas. For example, she would write in the margin of a manuscript, "no transition," "more possibilities here for character development," or "maybe you should rethink this ending." She was very tactful.

     She was being a good psychologist, really. She didn't rewrite, she *led* her authors to it. I give her a lot of credit for the success of *The Trouble with Soap.*

J.R.     Being an editor is almost a full-time job, as is being a writer. Where do you find the time for the two?

M.C.         I don't need much sleep. I have insomnia so I work in the middle of the night.

     And when I do sleep I sleep really hard for about four hours and then I get up and work again.

J.R.     When you used the name "Daisy Wallace," you served as author-editor to yourself. Didn't that put you in a precarious situation with reviewers and buyers?

M.C.         That was a peculiar situation because the books were anthologies and Holiday House ordinarily doesn't publish books by anyone on its staff.

     The real reason I did those books was to get certain artists that I was interested in at the time onto the Holiday House list. I also felt there was more room for poetry books aimed at ages five to eight.

     I thought if I anthologized some poetry into a thirty-two page picture book and selected very visual poetry, the artists would be stimulated to illustrate the books.

     I used the name "Daisy Wallace" partly so reviewers wouldn't respond to the book according to what they thought of Margery Cuyler because most of them know me and partly because I wanted to separate my role as anthologist from my role as editor. And I did the books on my own time, without royalty.

     After anthologizing five books I realized I liked creating books. So I wrote several using my own name.

J.R.　　What was your first book as Margery Cuyler?

M.C.　　　*Jewish Holidays.* I had the most trouble with that book. It was my first book and I made a lot of mistakes. Miriam Chaikin[2] was my editor. The things she pointed out as weak in the manuscript because I'm not Jewish were absolutely correct.

　　　When I first finished that book, I had a psychological accident. I threw the manuscript in the fire and burned it up!

J.R.　　Please explain that one.

M.C.　　　What happened was I had cleaned my apartment and decided to work on the book. I was working on the chapter on Passover then and couldn't find the manuscript, only the note cards.

　　　I've never found it so I imagine I must have thrown it into the fire. That's the only explanation I can think of for its disappearance. It means I was *very* hesitant about acknowledging myself as an author. It's very significant that I got rid of that manuscript.

J.R.　　So what did you do?

M.C.　　　I sat down and rewrote the entire book from the note cards.

　　　The reason I wrote the book at all was because I was dating a rabbi at the time and he inspired me to do the book. And separately I thought there's nothing in print on Jewish holidays that's of any quality. And I was very interested in Judaism so I just went out and started the research.

　　　When I finished the manuscript, the second time, I had to rewrite it again because of all the mistakes in it.

J.R.　　Mistakes?

M.C.　　　Well, I was inaccurate!

　　　I made glaring errors in my research. When I first turned the book in to Miriam, for example, she said, "On Yom Kippur you don't eat." And I said, "Oh yeah? Really? Why? Is it a fast day?"

　　　After that rewrite I had a rabbi read it, some Jewish friends read it, you know. It was a totally inappropriate book for me to write but it did open the door for me.

J.R.　　Don't you find it difficult sorting out those ideas you'd like to develop as an editor as opposed to those you'd like to develop as an author?

M.C.　　　The advantage of being an editor is you know what holes need to be filled in the market. I knew, for example, there should be a book for ages eight to twelve on Jewish holidays. My editor side could feed the idea to my author side.

　　　The same experience applies to *The All-Around Pumpkin Book.* As an editor, I knew that pumpkins were used at Halloween in schools. You could always find a pumpkin in the classroom. And I thought, why not write a whole book on what you can do with a pumpkin? That's how that book came to be.

No. It's not difficult to sort out ideas. I have far more than I can write about, and most of them are better suited to other authors' talents, anyway.

J.R.     What's the cutoff point?

M.C.     I'm most interested in writing and publishing stuff that comes from my own experience, and passing on to others ideas I know nothing about. For example, I'd rather ask someone on Holiday House's list to write about farm animals, instead of doing so myself.

The novel I'm working on now is coming out of my experience with my stepdaughter. I'm doing the book from her point of view. I'm trying to focus on a problem that modern kids come up against at some point or another, and I'm trying to provide some insight into the problem.

The theme of the book is that you can't control everything in your life. You have to trust fate to a certain extent.

J.R.     Talk about *The Trouble with Soap*. That was your first novel, wasn't it?

M.C.     Yes. It evolved from the Bread Loaf Conference.[3] I had gone there to find authors for Holiday House. I sat around for two weeks and listened to people read their stuff. Then I started writing.

The book just started coming out of my fingers. It was then that I realized I could write a novel if I really wanted to.

It was based on experiences I had as a kid. I was very bad. I got kicked out of several schools, that sort of thing. I was like Soap. But the main character in the book, Laurie, wants to be part of the status quo. She's a goody-goody.

I wanted to write about what it is that makes twelve- and thirteen-year-old kids so sensitive to peer pressure. Why do they care so much about what other kids think of them? They're really imprisoned by collective values—how they think, how they dress, how they look at the world. It's a very conformist way of living. It's hard to be outside the collective spirit at that age and yet my character Soap is. That fascinates me because the whole key to life is to break through the walls that parents and society build around you, to be an individual, to express yourself.

So I wrote about one kid who is a nonconformist and one who is a conformist. I think the whole thing works, but the idea has been explored in many other books.

J.R.     And your picture book . . . because of your editorial connections are you in a position to be a little choosier than most authors about who will illustrate your books?

M.C.     I love writing picture books because I think visually. I always have specific pictures in mind.

The picture book that was published by Holt was written in three nights. I had this dream which was the plot for the whole book. So I woke up as usual at two in the morning and I started writing. It's a Halloween story and I saw all the pictures in my mind. I even made a dummy, roughed out the illustrations and just added the words.

But to answer your question, no, I'm not choosy. I always think it's great to use brand-new artists. I think the children's book field continually needs fresh talent. In fact, I told my editor at Holt, "Don't think because I'm an editor and have been published that you have to go after some big shot." They said, "Hey, terrific." So they got a new talent.

Of all the books I write, picture books are my favorite because I love art. But they're hard to write because each word is naked.

J.R.     What about nonfiction? That's how you got into all of this.

M.C.     Boring to write, but it's a challenge.

It's difficult to work on because you have to get hard ideas across simply, and you have to do an enormous amount of research using primary sources, if possible.

Like, how do you explain the virgin birth to an eight-year-old? I ran into that problem while working on *The All-Around Christmas Book.*

Nonfiction is fascinating because you learn a lot about a subject as you go along. I learned something new about geography, for example, while working on the pumpkin book. There's one theory that pumpkins came to America from Asia across the Bering Straits.

A lot of time is involved in writing nonfiction because you have to travel to research libraries, and then take copious notes. You can't use just your local library. With a full-time job, it's hard for me to map out the time a subject really deserves. I spend more time on the research than the actual writing. Even when writing introductory books for young children you have to do a lot of research, just so you can figure out what material to include.

But all my research has enriched me as a person. I don't want to stop writing nonfiction, ever.

J.R.     And your fiction?

M.C.     One reason I write fiction is a practical one. I don't need to travel to any research libraries!

Fiction is the hardest thing for me to write. Nonfiction takes a certain skill but it doesn't make me feel vulnerable. And with a picture-book text, I don't have to get heavily involved with the motivations of the characters. But with fiction, I'm opening myself wide up. I'm facing problems in myself as I face those in my characters.

J.R.     Expand on that, please.

M.C.     Creating anything is an isolating experience. You don't have people to shore you up. When you're working in the dark hours of the night, you think, "Why is anyone going to want to read this? I'll never publish this."

There is something with writing and illustrating, I suppose, that has nothing to do with whether somebody buys it or not. It has to do with finding a language for your imagination.

I think wholeness comes from living your life consciously during the day and then exploring your inner life or unconscious at night. The whole inner thing comes out in your dreams. Or when you begin to write. That's what's vulnerable about it. You're sharing a private part of yourself, your imagination, with the world. It's a humbling experience.

I'm practical enough to hope to sell what I write. I can always use the money. But I also think writing helps you ventilate your inner life. You need to do it somehow—through religion, art, or going to a shrink.

The Western world doesn't take this seriously enough. I think if you have any artistic inclination at all, you have a duty to honor it. Maybe that's why I started to write.

J.R.    Is it a duty or need?

M.C.    No, you're right. It's a *need*.

But it's a need that's mostly ignored by a lot of people. "It's flaky. I can't spend time just writing and doing this and that. It doesn't lead to anything. It's a luxury."

J.R.    For everyone?

M.C.    No, not for everyone.

I think everyone has some sort of artistic gift. Those people who acknowledge it are in better shape than those who don't. But it doesn't necessarily have to be expressed through writing. Talent is easy to deny, though. Is art more important or is earning money to eat more important? Or both? It bothers me that dollars for art are slashed from school budgets because I think art is a food of life. I may be idealistic, elitist, and all that, but I'm a real believer in artistic expression. Everybody has *something* they can offer. And it requires discipline to make it work. Luckily, I'm very disciplined. I've had many people come into my office with their portfolios. They're talented but they don't have discipline. Some people are born with it. Others see it as a curse.

J.R.    Where do you go from here?

M.C.    I don't know.

I'm always 'on.' I don't know if I'll be like this when I'm sixty. I'm sure I'll get tired at some point!

## Notes

[1] Emilie McLeod, former editor-in-chief of children's books for Atlantic Monthly Press, was also an author of children's books.

[2] Miriam Chaikin, former editorial director of children's books for Holt, Rinehart & Winston, and also an author of children's books.

[3] Bread Loaf Writers' Conference for published and aspiring writers takes place annually at Middlebury College in Middlebury, Vermont.

## BIBLIOGRAPHY

### As Margery Cuyler:

*The All-Around Christmas Book.* il. Corbett Jones. New York: Holt, 1982.

*The All-Around Pumpkin Book.* il. Corbett Jones. New York: Holt, 1980.

*Jewish Holidays.* il. Lisa C. Wesson. New York: Holt, 1978.

*Sir William and the Pumpkin Monster.* il. Marsha Winborn. New York: Holt, 1984.

*The Trouble with Soap.* New York: Dutton, 1982.

### As Daisy Wallace:

#### *As Editor:*

*Fairy Poems.* il. Trina Schart Hyman. New York: Holiday House, 1980.

*Ghost Poems.* il. Tomie dePaola. New York: Holiday House, 1979.

*Giant Poems.* il. Margot Tomes. New York: Holiday House, 1978.

*Monster Poems.* il. Kay Chorao. New York: Holiday House, 1976.

*Witch Poems.* il. Trina Schart Hyman. New York: Holiday House, 1976.


## AWARDS AND HONORS

*The Trouble with Soap*
    Children's Choice Book

*Witch Poems*
    Children's Choice Book

*Demi*

## BIOGRAPHICAL NOTE

Demi is a free-lance artist who was born on September 2, 1942, in Cambridge, Massachusetts. She has a bachelor of arts degree from Immaculate Heart College in Los Angeles, and has also studied around the world in Guanajuato, Mexico, at the Rhode Island School of Design, at the China Institute in New York City, and as a Fulbright scholar in Gujarat, India. She has a son, John.

## PRELUDE TO THE INTERVIEW

Demi, a childhood nickname retained as a professional name by Charlotte Dumaresq Hunt, is most accurately portrayed as a moveable-book maker. Her trade picture books are wonderfully colored and intricately detailed fine-line renderings based on her Far Eastern art and philosophical interests, but it is her toy books that bring her to my attention.

When I met Demi at her apartment, I walked into a virtual toy-shop-in-progress studio. There are neat layers of multicolored papers in various folded configurations about; there are mechanisms that squawk, squeak, and talk; there are bits and pieces of found objects—toothpicks, miniature books, fans, balloons, small-scale diplomas, prisms—and the requisite brushes, palettes, ends of paint tubes, and drawing boards, all which provide grist for one of her ongoing explorations in a wonder-full land.

Demi is an almost reticent speaker. She prefers not to talk about herself or her many accomplishments. It is her work that gives her day a certain meaning. And it is when she is talking about a work-in-progress that she jumps up, commanding me to a bank of file cabinets, thrusting its contents into my hands with, "Here, look at this." or "What do you think of this?" or "Isn't this fun?"

She wants to create surprises for children, and she does. The first requisite, however, is that she must also be surprised. As she says, "I don't want to grow up," meaning she doesn't want to lose her sense of awe. It is in this spirit that her toy books for children are created to amuse and entertain—as much as her four-color books impart a far more artistic and philosophical experience.

## THE INTERVIEW

J.R.    You come from a family of artists, don't you?

D.        Yes. There have been artists and architects in my family for ages.

My great-grandfather is William Morris Hunt, the great American painter and teacher. His paintings are in museums all over the world. He was a visionary and a great spirit. He was one of the first people to appreciate Turner, Corot, and Delacroix. Millet was his best friend.

His brother, my great-grand uncle, Richard Morris Hunt, attended The Ecole des Beaux-Arts in Paris and was regarded by his contemporaries as the dean of American architects. He founded and was president of The American Institute of Architects. His most famous edifices are The Breakers in Newport, Rhode Island, Biltmore House in North Carolina, The Metropolitan Museum of Art in New York City and the base for the Statue of Liberty.

J.R.    Your mother, wasn't she involved in art also?

D.        Oh, yes. She studied with a lot of people in this country and in Italy, and got an early reputation as being a very fine watercolorist. She mastered all the techniques but said that was nothing. She wanted to get away from techniques and work with spirit.

Then she met Sister Corita. When Sister Corita saw my mother lay a wash, she told her to immediately unlearn it because all she was doing was exercising a formula and formulas are too easy.

J.R.    This is Sister Corita, the famous nun-artist of the 1960s?

D.        Yes. And it was because of my mother's involvement with Sister Corita that I studied with her.

J.R.    How did you manage that?

D.        When I was younger I was in Milton Academy in Massachusetts and ended up painting everything.

My mother was very careful about the teachers who taught formulas that killed the spirit of everything. A lot of the time she wouldn't let me take art courses because of that. She mainly kept me away from them. She wanted it to be right or nothing at all. She was my teacher and avoidance director!

She heard The Instituto Allende in San Miguel de Allende had you do everything—murals, silk screen, jewelry, ceramics. She thought that was free, vivid, and alive enough for me. So I went there.

My mother had also taken a course at Immaculate Heart College with Sister Corita and immediately discovered the magic there. It was the next place for me. And it was magic for me, too!

J.R.     In what way?

D.          In every way! There were two nuns. Sister Magdalen Mary began the art department. Then she heard of a tiny extraordinary nun in Canada who was teaching sewing, named Sister Corita, and brought her back to Immaculate Heart College to teach silk screen printing, which she never had done before. Together they created a unique art department and also made the largest folk art collection in the country. They undid any preconceptions one had and kept everyone alive. I have no idea how they undid us, or how they began us new again, but they did and we produced enormous amounts.

          I always like to read Sister Magdalen Mary's words. That explains the experience best.[1]

J.R.     What were some of the things that went on?

D.          A drawing class ended up being banner-making for the World's Fair Vatican Pavilion. This was drawing! It was incredible.

          I had a huge exhibit at the Los Angeles Museum of Science and Industry, which I think came under a painting class. Somebody asked Corita if she'd make curtains for the Museum, but she didn't have any time to do them. When students became seniors they'd get all of Corita's plum assignments. So I did all these huge curtains. They were *huge!* I stretched them on three ping-pong tables and painted them. I'd never done anything like that before.

          People like Henry Miller, Buckminster Fuller, Charles Ives, Fellini, John Cage, and Harry Parch would visit Corita's classes. She would just sit them down and that would be your art class. Incredible. They'd come in and wander around the art department.

          The whole thing was so different from anything you ever heard of!

J.R.     Can you describe what else it was like?

D.          The college is hard to describe. It was madly imaginative. And the girls were mostly isolated Catholics, never having been out of Los Angeles, and Corita got out of them the most unbelievable things. She really proved there is plenty inside all of us. She just brought it out.

          There is no way to describe that place. It was like magic, like a jewel. That was the peak of the college when I was able to go there. It was incredible.

J.R.     What else did Sister Corita do?

D.          Corita became a superstar and the Pope said what she was doing was not religious art because it didn't conservatively depict Mary and Jesus as you're supposed to. Corita beautifully refuted that statement, but she got the ire of the college and California Catholics against her.

          By that time she was exhibiting in all the major museums in the country and in Europe, and by rebelling against the Pope she got on the covers of *Time* and *Life* magazines.

Corita used to go to U.C.L.A. to give speeches. She'd tell everyone who came to bring a copy of *Life* magazine. The whole audience would be sitting there with their magazines. She'd give one of her three-minute magic speeches and then unroll one hundred and fifty yards of paper out into the audience. Then she would say, "We're going to make a collage from *Life.*" The whole audience would begin ripping up their magazines, pasting and working in unison. The result was truly amazing!

J.R.    Between your family and Sister Corita, you've had some extraordinary experiences and influences. You are very, very fortunate.

D.    I have no idea how Sister Magdalen Mary and Corita worked or got out of people what they got.

There's this word, imprevisibility, by Etienne Gilson in *Painting and Reality.*[2] It's like beginning before you know what you're beginning with. That was the same with the nuns. They were a tremendous influence.

And my family life was truly unbelievable. My father, being in theater, founded and was executive producer of the Cambridge Drama Festival. He was the first recipient of the Rodgers and Hammerstein Award,[3] and won the Award of Chevalier des Belles Arts et Lettres[4] from Andre Maurois. He was also on President Nixon's Advisory Committee on the Arts for the Kennedy Center in Washington, D.C. Our house was frequented by such people as Sir John Gielgud, Marcel Marceau, and Emelyn Williams. It was absolutely exciting. Anything was possible.

So to work with nuns was all part of what I was used to, being brought up as a Unitarian.

J.R.    What other big projects did you get involved with besides the curtains?

D.    I painted and gold-leafed a dome in the church of Saint Peter and Paul in Wilmington, California. I needed a car and Corita said she knew of a dome that needed painting. So I painted the dome, got a car and credit for my painting class, too! It worked out nicely. I liked working on scaffolds sixty feet up in the air with Bach in the background.

But after my son was born in Sao Paulo, Brazil, I started drawing books because it was something I could stop and go back to easily.

And I once spent a year in India where Hindus and Buddhists draw a million of everything, repetition of patterns, you know. After you've seen that kind of drawing you think you'll never draw enough.

J.R.    Where does your first book fit in all of this?

D.    That was done when I came back from India and Brazil. Harcourt, Brace asked me if I would illustrate *The Surangini Tales* by Partap Sharma of Bombay, some Indian folk tales. My second book happened while I was visiting the China Trade Museum outside of Boston where Francis Ross Carpenter was the associate director and wizard. He asked me if I would illustrate his new and first translation of *The Classic of Tea* by Lu Yu of the Tang Dynasty. I said I didn't know anything about Chinese art, but he said that was fine, I could start learning. So I began drawing Tang Dynasty tea utensils, which was the beginning of my Chinese studies.

J.R.    You have become quite a force in the toy book field for children. Each season there is at least one new book being published by you. Why the interest in toy books?

D.    I love toys! I never hope to grow up. And I love to play with paper.

*Where Is Willie Worm?* began as a head and no words. It was a green piece of yarn running through the center of a book. I did it for my son who was sick. I felt there was something really there. I showed it to Knopf[5] first and they loved it, but it was too expensive for them, so an editor took it down the hall and showed it to Ole.[6] He costed it out. It took a year! But then he bought it.

I think I ended up doing about twenty versions of *Willie* for Ole. Then when I made a smaller format to follow, that made it easier. I didn't mind doing so many versions because I was learning. I love to keep my dummies because I can see how things progress that way.

The first spin-the-wheel book I did was with Fabio Coen of Knopf. The books are based on the origins of moving pictures, a device called the phenakistascope. The first one I did happened by chance and surprise.

In the Metropolitan Museum I had seen a tiny little pamphlet called *The Origins of the Moving Pictures,*[7] from Her Majesty's Stationery Office in London. They had just one picture of these wheels and I thought them extremely beautiful, particularly the repetition of pattern.

I just started playing with it, with many mirrors. It became fun and I wanted to make more and more. I also did one book for Holt in 1982 of Cinderella spinning on twelve discs with the story on the back of the disc.

J.R.    I would think you would tire of drawing the same image over and over?

D.    Oh, no. It gets better over and over.

J.R.    Your *Peek-a-Boo ABC* has always struck me as a complicated book to produce. Was it?

D.    Oh, yes!

With almost every one of those pictures I had to draw each one three or four times or a million! All the objects had to be a common denominator that appealed to everybody in the world.[8] For instance, a mailbox is not the same to everyone. It was very hard to do.

And because of the flaps and cutouts I had to draw two sides at one time. I had eight drawings superimposed on each other to make things work. Everything was quite mathematical, being backed up one-half inch from the other and at least one-half inch from the center of the book.

The inside of the book was done on separate sheets. The flaps in the book are die-cut. It drives you crazy because you're working back-to-back and on top all the time.

J.R.    How long did it take to produce a book like that?

D.    That one took about three months. But the whole thing was really so joyful. It just came out like a burst.

When I get lit up, the whole thing just comes. I think the first wheel book took about three months, too.

J.R.    Because you work so intensely and intricately, you must be exhausted when you finish a project?

D.    Why?

J.R.    Doesn't the pressure of it get to you?

D.    Not really. I just love all of it.

I get a little uneasy if a book takes longer than it should. I think a book has a life of its own. There is something really natural about when you get the idea, who you take it to, their response, and your mutual response in working it out together. And if it takes too long on one part, even technical things, it becomes unnatural. It just seems that if it's going to happen at all, it should flow at the pace inherent to its own process.

J.R.    Do you try to keep the child reader in mind?

D.    Yes. Somebody who made me think a lot about all that is Ole. I think he really does look at things like that. He just knows, he's had so much experience. Because of him I think about that all the time now.

I think in my first books I just wanted to make something beautiful. Now I'm more aware of the child, the business, the sales, the total.

J.R.    Have you ever been invited to go on press to watch your books being printed?

D.    I love to go on press. In the Indian book I did for Harcourt I was working in a new medium, cel-vinyl, and painting on acetate. I was in touch with them all the time about technical things.

Unless you know what's going to happen to your art and what you do, you could be in for some unpleasant surprises.

J.R.    Has this ever happened to you?

D.    I've often wondered why thick black lines became fuzzy. It's because that black line is made up from four colors. Not wanting that effect, I learned how to separate the color from my line with overlays, blue boards, or whatever. Now I like the way it looks.

I'm learning as much as I can about the printing process. I'd love to go to Singapore and see printing of *Willie Worm* editions. It's quite a thing. There are three pieces of folded paper stuck together, then the gluing and then the folding. I'd love to see it all.

J.R.    Of all the various forms of children's books you've done, which do you find the most enjoyable?

D.    Oh. All of them.

J.R.    Do you spend roughly the same amount of time on each book?

D.    It depends.

Something like the Indian book took me quite awhile. It was an interesting experience because I had never worked on a picture book quite like that one. It was really an honor to work with Anna Bier.[9]

I had one idea that I wanted to do when I read the manuscript. When I went to Anna, I could see she had something else in mind. But not exactly what I wanted to do. She expanded it, almost like Corita, in some invisible way. Instead of making it static, flat art, she opened up the book. She really had a full concept of what she wanted as a whole and of the impact on the reader and buyer.

A lot of the time I couldn't see what she was doing or really understand what she wanted to bring out. And when you see the printed book you can see what she was building up to. I think she is an amazing person.

J.R.    What do you do when you're not working on your books?

D.    I travel. I've been to China and found it the most incredible place. Physically, I've never seen anything so beautiful. Everything there is inexplicably beautiful. The Chinese sense of things is unbelievable. You really feel things in certain places because of the earth's magnetism. You can feel it in Peking and Sian and Chunking.

I sensed certain things there that I've never sensed anywhere else in the world.

The sensitivities, even to tools, like the brush I use, is an example. The Chinese brush can do the thickest or finest point. You paint with it from the shoulder. It's a matter of how you hold it.

J.R.    Do you have a strong sense of the Eastern in your art? Have you been strongly influenced both by India and China?

D.    Oh, yes. I guess I think there's nothing higher than Chinese painting. It's such a standard of excellence. It's hard to reach that standard. It's totally different from the Western art approach.

Want to hear my speech on Chinese art? [She reaches in a drawer, pulls out a scroll, and begins reading from it.]

It comes from the greatest book written on Chinese painting called *The Mustard Seed Garden Manual of Painting*,[10] written in the seventeenth century.

It all has to do, too, with being part of the whole system. I think I've always been a Taoist. I have always proceeded backwards, like opening books backwards. I don't know how to methodically go forward. It's very difficult to talk about.

J.R.    What other types of things have you created for kids?

D.    I did some play sheets for West Point Pepperell. It was fun, a game that went around the sheet. And I periodically perform my Chinese Magic Box Act, which is a box a yard high, octagon-shaped and stuffed with every kind of folded and exploding paper-made object imaginable. There is a forty foot, yard high, red paper collapsible dragon in the very bottom!

J.R.    You have published with a number of publishers over the years. Doesn't this interrupt your freedom to do the kind of books you want to do? By moving around, you begin a new relationship with a publisher each time?

D.    One reason, I think, I have a lot of freedom is because I really have been doing what I've wanted to ever since I began. And partly because I've been jumping from one house to another. My agent is Marilyn Marlow and she's fine. She keeps the business part of publishing straight for me because it gets so complicated.

J.R.    Ever think about winning any of the children's book awards?

D.    No, not really.
    But every year I give the Editor of the Year Award. It's equal to the Newbery or Caldecott!
    What I do is make a marionette that can be manipulated by pulling the strings, to represent the editor. And I get all these microscopic books, tiny yardsticks, and pencils and sew them all over the body. I give it to the editor who has had the most ingenuity and packaging prowess.

J.R.    Such as?

D.    Fabio Coen was the first. I've also given it to Janet Chenery,[11] Ellen Roberts,[12] and Ole Risom, among others.

J.R.    What other types of books would you like to do?

D.    I think my best things have never been produced. Everyone tells me they're too expensive. But that's what I want to do, and I've got drawers full of them. If publishers printed at least a *million* of each, the costs would come down!

## Notes

[1] Demi requested that the following excerpt, "Without Reservations," by Sister Magdalen Mary from *The Irregular Bulletin,* published in 1961, be inserted here. Demi feels this conveys more of the spirit of Immaculate Heart College than anything she could ever say:

We at Immaculate Heart College do not call student explorations and investigations by the name of Art. It is not that we do not prize the results of some of these student investigations. Some of them "wear well" and continue to have a certain "presence" through the years. Even a Picasso can not ask more than that of many of his experiments.

Perhaps here is the difference between *the great* painters of both the early and mid-twentieth century and those painters that are *less than great.* The difference might be called one of orientation. *The great* painters have pursued, like their contemporaries in the field of science, the solutions to new problems along strange, untravelled paths. They have pursued these solutions with such intensity that their recordings of their searchings have great impact even for many who are unable to follow through the pathway cleared for them by *the greats;* have impact even for a few of those who do not see the sense of all this non-sense. The impact is not made on the logical level—it is made on the supralogical level.

The recordings of the searchings of *the great* ones are called "paintings" by the rest of us. But *the great* ones themselves do not have time to call them by that or any other name. There are countless miles still of uncharted, magnetic paths calling to *the greats*—and life is short.

But the *less than great* ones, those who follow in the pathways opened up for them by *the greats*, have a dignity and a validity, also. Their worth lies in their ability to clarify the already achieved objectives of *the greats*, in their ability to develop the discoveries and inventions of *the greats* to their highest potentials, in their ability to make more fruitful the original contributions of *the greats.*

There is another and very large group of people who are responsible for at least a small part of the unrest outside the world of great artists (the unrest inside that world is desirable, for it is basic to the searchings for the unknown.) Let us call these the *wishful thinkers,* or rather the *wishful brush-wielders.* These also have a certain dignity stemming from their sincerity, but they lack validity. These *wishfuls* look at the recordings of *the greats* (frequently once or twice removed through poor reproductions in books and magazines). They miss the essentials. They see only the accidentals; blue and green are being used this year; black lines on stark white; large and larger canvases; mixed media; mixed techniques; disguised subject matter; etc., etc. They sincerely *wish* their work to be valid, but they make no contribution. *The greats* continue to make headway into the unknown; the *less than great* continue to develop and present these discoveries to a larger and larger audience; the *wishfuls* are just not with it.

But most of us do not fall under any of the three groups discussed. We are not the producers, but the consumers. And—we make our choices on that level where we believe art to exist: *on the level of skill*—If it looks hard to do, it is art, e.g. the illusion of lace in an old Dutch portrait, flagpole sitting, etc. *On the level of liberal arts*—If it is mentioned in art history books, or in art magazines, if custom and tradition acclaim it, it is art. *On the level of taste*—Where impeccable choices are made concerning the form of the thing itself, by the discerning few. *On the level of beauty*—or vitality. Even the most discerning rise to this level but seldom. They tend to find their joy on the level of taste, which is the highest of the levels that can be aimed at through training. The level of beauty or vitality is not a matter of years of training, but of insight. It frequently by-passes the other three levels: how many times a thing of beauty seems unconcerned with polished skills; how many time a thing of beauty is unheralded or even rejected by art historians and art critics; how many times the prevailing taste excludes a thing of beauty.

The level of beauty may be and probably is more often approached by the seemingly unprepared. In fact the prepared are, more frequently than not, marooned on one of the other levels, due to the lack of real insight or perspective on the part of the prepare-ers. Art is probably the only field of investigation today in which the ones-being-prepared (the students) are still required to waste precious time in *drilling* with already found solutions to far removed problems of other centuries and other cultures, leaving no time to tackle the problems of their own. There is a desperate clinging to "basics" (basic problems that have long since ceased to be problems—when they are basic to anything at all—which is seldom) that smells strongly of insecurity among the prepare-ers.

Consumers are and must be brave, for they risk hundreds of dollars purchasing paintings which may not prove even *less than great.* But the artists risk whole lifetimes. The great difference between consumers and artists is that consumers weigh the risks, and artists neither weigh the risks nor measure gain. They are akin to lovers whose measure is that they do not measure. They are amateurs (amateur—one who loves; professional—one who knows how-to-do-it) always working beyond known frontiers in areas where they do not know how-to-do-it. Nothing great was even invented or discovered by a professional, except at that moment when he recaptured his amateur-status.

[2] Etienne Gilson, *Painting and Reality.* The A. W. Mellon Lectures in the Fine Arts. New York: Meridian Books, 1959.

[3] The Rodgers and Hammerstein Award was presented "for having done the most for theatre in Boston."

[4] The Croix de Chevalier des Arts et des Lettres was presented for "furthering French artistic and cultural endeavors in Boston."

[5] What is being referred to here is that Alfred A. Knopf, Pantheon Books, and Random House are divisions of Random House, Inc., where each division is editorially independent of the other. While a project may not fit within one division, it may fit within the publishing scheme of another.

[6] Ole Risom, associate publisher of children's books for Random House.

[7] D. B. Thomas, *The Origins of Moving Pictures: An Introductory Booklet on the Pre-History of the Cinema.* A Science Museum booklet (London: Her Majesty's Stationery Office, 1964).

[8] The *Peek-a-Boo ABC* is a book of childhood objects in alphabetical order using objects only familiar on a worldwide basis. The appeal had to be universal because so many countries were involved in the international simultaneous printing.

[9] Anna Bier, editor of children's books for Harcourt Brace Jovanovich.

[10] Demi's "Magic, Magicians and Chinese Painters" speech, incorporating *The Mustard Seed Garden Manual of Painting,* follows.

## MAGIC, MAGICIANS AND CHINESE PAINTERS

Life is magic.
Everything alive is magic.
To capture life on paper is magic.
To capture life on paper was the aim of Chinese painters.
That is my aim too.
The dictionary defines a magician as: An artist who can produce
wonderful effects by the mastery of secret forces in nature.

Painting was regarded in early China as an art of magic.
And painters, through their creative powers were magicians.

Something magical indeed happened, when,
skill with brush could transmit the magical spirit of life to paper.
To express life pervading the universe, and
to transmit a spiritual influence with imagination, spontaneity
and humor, the painter had to transcend the limitations of the eye
and delve into the secrets of nature.

With the power of their spirit,
painters were said to, "Comb the wind, and sweep clear the full moon;
reveal the brilliance of the sun and penetrate the limits of
heaven and earth."
("Such height would be hard going for even a yellow crane.")-li Po-
*Hard Roads in Shu*

These Chinese magicians were keen observers of life.
Their spirit came from a deep conviction that every phenomenon of life,
however small, was of compelling concern.
Everything possessed CH'I
or the essence of life.
and there was no place that it was not.
It was in the rock, it was in the houses, the birds, the wind, the ant—
it was in everything.

And that Ch'i, being a part of things so low— it followed that every act
of living, was an act in the celebration
of living, was an act of celebration in the festival of life.
Every moment in time would merit celebration as a part
of the thread of life.

Every painting would become a masterpiece to serve as a distillation
of all paintings,
as if it were the first with no others to follow.

The high standards
of Chinese painters were recorded in
THE MUSTARD SEED GARDEN MANUAL OF PAINTING
by Wang Kai 1679
It is something I like to read a lot for its extraordinary
perceptions and sensitivities, and the way it suggests
you look at life.

It begins:
Take ten days to paint a stream and five to paint a rock.
Above all, learn to hold your thoughts on the five peaks;
the harmony of the universe, the outer and inner harmony of man.

Study all things in all seasons.
See the different shape of the wind blowing through willow
branches in summer and fall.

Study ten thousand volumes. Walk ten thousand miles.

Study the great; With one stroke of the brush, they can
release a kite on a thousand foot string.
When they paint, mountains soar, springs flow,
water runs clear,
and forests spread vast and lonely.
If you aim at facility, work hard.
If you aim at simplicity, master complexity.
If you aim to dispense with method, learn method.
for the end of all method is to seem to have no method.

The TAO TE CHING
also has wonderful verses for spatial imaginings:
We put thirty spokes together and call it a wheel;
But it is in the space where there is nothing, that
the magic of the wheel depends.
We turn clay to make a vessel;
But it is in the space where there is nothing that
the magic of the vessel depends.
We pierce doors and windows to make a house;
And it is in the space where there is nothing
that the magic of the house depends.
Therefore, just as we take advantage of what is,
We should recognize the magic of what is not.

[11] Janet Chenery, former editorial director of children's books for Doubleday & Company.

[12] Ellen Roberts, former editor-in-chief of children's books for Prentice-Hall.

# BIBLIOGRAPHY
## As Demi:

*The ABC Block.* New York: Intervisual Communications/Metropolitan Museum of Art, 1982.

*Adventures of Marco Polo.* New York: Holt, 1982.

*All about Your Name, Anne; Anna, Annie, Annette, Hannah, Anita, Nan.* By Tom Glazer. Garden City, N.Y.: Doubleday, 1978.

*All about Your Name, David; Davies, Dave, Davis, Davidson, Davy.* By Tom Glazer. Garden City, N.Y.: Doubleday, 1978.

*All about Your Name, Elizabeth; Beth, Bette, Eliza, Betsy, Betty, Lizzie, Liz.* By Tom Glazer. Garden City, N.Y.: Doubleday, 1978.

*All about Your Name, James; Jim, Jamie, Jimmy.* By Tom Glazer. Garden City, N.Y.: Doubleday, 1978.

*All about Your Name, John; Johnny, Jack, Jackie.* By Tom Glazer. Garden City, N.Y.: Doubleday, 1978.

*All about Your Name, Joseph; Joe, Joey, Jo-Jo.* By Tom Glazer. Garden City, N.Y.: Doubleday, 1978.

*All about Your Name, Katherine; Catherine, Cathy, Kate, Katie.* By Tom Glazer. Garden City, N.Y.: Doubleday, 1978.

*All about Your Name, Mary; Maria, Molly, Marie, Miriam, Marion, Maureen.* By Tom Glazer. Garden City, N.Y.: Doubleday, 1978.

*All about Your Name, Susan; Susie, Susanna, Suzanne, Sue.* By Tom Glazer. Garden City, N.Y.: Doubleday, 1978.

*All about Your Name, William; Will, Bill, Willie, Billy, Willy.* By Tom Glazer. Garden City, N.Y.: Doubleday, 1978.

*Bong Nam and the Peasants.* By Edward Yushin Yoo. Englewood Cliffs, N.J.: Prentice-Hall, 1979.

*The Book of Moving Pictures.* New York: Pantheon, 1979.

*Book of Opposites.* New York: Intervisual Communications/Metropolitan Museum of Art, 1982.

*Cinderella on Wheels.* New York: Holt, 1983.

*Dragon Night and Other Lullabies.* By Jane Yolen. New York: Methuen, 1980.

*Fat Gopal.* By Jacquelin Singh. New York: Harcourt Brace Jovanovich, 1984.

*Follow the Line.* New York: Holt, 1981.

*Hide and Seek with Wilma Worm.* New York: Random House, 1983.

*The Leaky Umbrella.* Englewood Cliffs, N.J.: Prentice-Hall, 1980.

*Liang and the Magic Paintbrush.* New York: Holt, 1980.

*Light Another Candle: The Story and Meaning of Hanukkah.* By Miriam Chaikin. New York: Clarion, 1981.

*Lu Pan, the Carpenter's Apprentice.* Englewood Cliffs, N.J.: Prentice-Hall, 1978.

*Make Noise, Make Merry: The Story and Meaning of Purim.* By Miriam Chaikin. New York: Clarion, 1983.

*Peek-a-Boo ABC.* New York: Random House, 1982.

*The Shape of Water.* By Augusta Goldin. Garden City, N.Y.: Doubleday, 1979.

*Six Performances.* New York: Intervisual Communications/Metropolitan Museum of Art, 1982.

*Three Little Elephants.* New York: Random House, 1981.

*Tony's Tunnel.* By Ann Sperry McGrath. New York: Holt, 1981.

*Under the Shade of the Mulberry Tree.* Englewood Cliffs, N.J.: Prentice-Hall, 1979.

*Watch Harry Grow.* New York: Random House, 1984.

*Where Is It?* Garden City, N.Y.: Doubleday, 1979.

*Where Is Willie Worm?* New York: Random House, 1981.

### As Demi Hitz:

*Cats:* Based on the television series *Wild World of Animals.* New York: Time-Life Films, 1976.

*The Classic of Tea.* By Lu Yu; tr. Francis Ross Carpenter. Boston: Little, Brown, 1974.

*Feelings.* By Carl B. Smith and Ronald Wardhaugh. New York: Macmillan, 1975.

*The Old China Trade: Americans in Canton, 1784-1843.* By Francis Ross Carpenter. New York: Coward, McCann & Geoghegan, 1976.

*The Surinam Tales.* By Partap Sharma. New York: Harcourt Brace Jovanovich, 1973.

*The Tom Glazer Guitar Book.* New York: Warner, 1976.

## AWARDS AND HONORS

*Liang and the Magic Paintbrush*
    Library of Congress list
    Notable Children's Trade Book
      in the Field of Social Studies

*Lu Pan*
    Library of Congress list

*The Old China Trade*
    Library of Congress list

*Where Is It?*
    Library of Congress list

## ADDITIONAL SOURCES

Commire. *Something about the Author.*
*Contemporary Authors.*

_Jean Fritz_

**Jean Fritz**

## BIOGRAPHICAL NOTE

The award-winning author of *Homesick* was born on November 16, 1915, in Hankow (now Wuhan), China. She graduated from Wheaton College in Norton, Massachusetts, in 1937 and has also studied at Columbia University. She has been a children's librarian, reviewer, and teacher, most recently at Appalachian State University in Boone, North Carolina, from 1979 to 1982. She married Michael Fritz in 1941 and they have two children, David and Andrea. Ms. Fritz has donated some of her manuscripts to the Kerlan Collection and to the library at the University of Oregon.

## PRELUDE TO THE INTERVIEW

Jean Fritz has done one thing few authors can ever hope to accomplish: she has irrefutably changed an entire style of writing for children.

Up until she started writing biographies for children, the genre was, with few exceptions, essentially a dull and lifeless one. Historical scenes were recreated, often without attention to accurate detail. Dialogues were invented, sometimes in contemporary jargon, thus negating the impact of an historical biography. Facts were frequently distorted and distilled to the point of futility.

It was her attention to detail, her refusal to romanticize a person or event, and her impeccable searching out of diaries, journals, and letters to re-create the past that has brought Jean to the forefront of biographical writing for children.

This interview was conducted twice, because of faulty tapes. The first took place just as *Homesick,* the book in which she looks at her own self, was capturing the public's attention and winning the first of many of its awards. The second occurred just as she returned from a long-overdue trip to her birthplace in China—an exciting time for her.

Jean is a personification of her books. She is witty; she is precise. She pays great attention to detail, leaving no room for misinterpretation or misunderstanding. The person one "sees" in Jean Fritz's books is very much the person the real Jean Fritz is.

## THE INTERVIEW

J.R.     You certainly did a turnabout with *Homesick,* your story. Up until the publication of it, you researched only historical figures. Working from your own memories and history must have proven to be a real challenge for you. What was the impetus behind it?

J.F.     I tried so many times to do it and hadn't been able to. I had the feeling that no one was left who had shared my childhood in China at all. My father had just died and I was afraid that now my whole childhood was going to melt away.

No one could ever say, "Do you remember such-and such?" No one knew. That very isolating experience was really the impulse to write the book. That partly, and to write it because I had always wanted to.

When I wrote the first sentence of that book the whole tone came to me. "In my father's house was a globe." When I put that down I knew finally how to go on.

J.R.     After *Homesick* was published, it went on to great success for you. Is there a plan to continue the story in a future volume?

J.F.     Yes. I knew then I had to go back to China and that story would be my next book.

J.R.     In what way?

J.F.     I didn't want to go with a group tour. It took many months of negotiation before I finally received permission for my husband and me to go as individuals and to stay in Wuhan[1] where I had lived. We went under the sponsorship of the Foreign Affairs Bureau, which took wonderful care of us. Not only were we escorted to all kinds of off-the-usual-route places, but we had complete freedom to wander as we pleased. And I had the chance to use my Chinese with people on the street! My greatest pleasure.

J.R.     Have other adults who spent time in China discovered the book?

J.F.     Oh, yes! I get two or three letters a week from adults who were children in China and who have read the book saying "You've said what we would have wanted to be said." Even Katherine Paterson[2] in her *Washington Post* review wrote, "All those writers who wanted to write about their experience in China don't have to anymore because Jean Fritz has done it." She wrote me later saying, "I think *Homesick* is *our* book."

China was a special experience. And I think it is for anyone who lived there.

J.R.     In what way?

J.F.     People who spent their childhoods there feel the experience was special. I cannot put it into words. I'm not sure people born in Russia or El Salvador, or anyplace else, have the same feeling. I don't really know what it is, but there is something about the Chinese people that binds you to the country. I asked a tour guide while I was there, "Are there any differences between tourists of different nationalities?" "Oh, yes," said he. "Americans have a sense of humor." And my mother used to say this. "No one brings this out except Americans. The American and Chinese have the same kind of sense of humor."

J.R.    I assume that you haven't kept up with the number of people you mention in the book by name. Because of the book, have you been able to strike up reacquaintances with people in the book?

J.F.    Actually, yes. I met up with Andrea[3] who's in the book after many years after losing touch with her.

A woman in Texas, whom I don't know, wrote to me after reading the book. She thought the Andrea in the book was the same one as she had known when she was a girl in China. It turned out she went to high school with Andrea's younger brother. She gave me his phone number and his wife gave me Andrea's.

So I called her and said, "This is Jean Guttery.[4] I've just written a book in which you're a character." I worried about it because I hadn't seen her in years. I didn't know if she would like it or not. Her voice sounded so *controlled,* I wasn't sure I could find the old Andrea. So I heard myself say, "But Andrea! You sound so *grown up!*" She answered back, "Well, Jean, I am 69!" My daughter Andrea, who is named after the Andrea in the book, was, I think, both amused and embarrassed.

Well, I sent out a book immediately. The letter I received back was enthusiastic. She sounded *just* like the person I hoped she would be after all this time.

When I went to the ALA[5] in Los Angeles we got together and it was just as if we'd been reading the same books, doing the same things, after all this time.

We had a wonderful visit. Michael[6] asked her, "If you could have seen this in manuscript and Jean had asked you to be frank and if you'd like to have anything changed, what would you have changed?" "Nothing," she said.

J.R.    Did she remember the same incidents you described? And in the same way?

J.F.    Some. Do you remember the orphan girl in the Christmas part of the book? Andrea remembered her as a good-looking, sexy girl her brother took quite a shine to. I remembered her as homely little stub, probably because she was so mean to me.

J.R.    Have you found anyone else?

J.F.    In Wisconsin a man came up after a talk I gave and said, "I think my father delivered you." I mean, at my age, it's an overwhelming thing to have happen!

J.R.      What about Ian Forbes, your great nemesis in the book?

J.F.      I haven't found him yet, but I'm hoping to. I didn't change his name because I'm hoping when I meet him I'll be with Michael. Then Ian can pull up his trousers and I can see if his knees are still square. And Michael can take over from there.

J.R.      Let's change to your historical books. Your younger books, the so-called question books, have a light, witty quality that is difficult to achieve. How do you do this?

J.F.      None of it comes easily. I may do it one way, and when I come back to it in rewriting, I may say, "Hey! That's heavy. That's not right." Suddenly it comes after you think about it. It's always working at you somewhere, but you don't always know it.

My style is the way I talk, I think. I feel humor is a lifeline. Conversation is boring to me if it doesn't have life. It seems to me that human contact is made by light sparks between words not only in conversation but also in books. I want to make contact.

J.R.      How do you handle those critics who think your style is too light and humorous for children?

J.F.      If anybody thinks that something to be true has to be ponderous they're not on my wavelength. So what is there to talk about with them?

Since I work with heroes—I avoid the conventional textbook way, the man who is generally bigger than the normal run-of-the-mill person—but you can't, *I* can't, take away the humanity or the faults.

Traditionally George Washington is often presented as faultless. I would have no reaction to him if he were like that. I admire him for his enormous will at being able to single-handedly hold the country together and for his enormous integrity.

But I warm up to him when I know at the Battle of Monmouth that he is said to have cursed Charles Lee until the "leaves shriveled off the trees." Although he didn't usually let it get out of control, he had a terrible temper. He had good reason to be mad at Charles Lee and I'm with him the whole way.

I like surprises like that. I like that in my books.

J.R.      Expand on that a little bit.

J.F.      I want to come up with surprises in my books. I like to jolt people into the past. I don't think you can walk casually into it. I think you have to be *jolted* into it.

For instance, I had a hard time finding out what Patrick Henry was like as a kid. Finally I came across a source that said that unlike his friends, Patrick Henry liked to wear clean underwear! Now, that's jolting!

J.R.     But by doing that, don't you stick your neck out and risk the wrath of pressure groups? After all you are making a hero an ordinary mortal in a sense.

J.F.     Oh, of course.

I've been censored for not treating Paul Revere with reverence. And it went to court but I don't want to discuss it.

Reverence is a national hero's due to some people. They feel it's unpatriotic to treat anybody as if they were human. Leaders should be on pedestals. But I can't do that.

J.R.     From what I understand you came to writing for children after raising your children. Is that correct?

J.F.     Not quite, because I had worked before I was married. Like so many others I stopped work to raise my family. After they were beyond being little I eased back into things.

My first book was *Bunny Hopwell's First Spring* in 1951. I called it *The First Spring* but the editor changed that. I kept looking for an avenue in writing. I accepted the chance to be editor of my college alumni bulletin for the experience of it. Two weeks after accepting I received a letter from the president of the college saying the present editor had decided to stay on. That was the best thing that could have happened. If I had gone on with that, I would have been up a blind alley.

When I had worked as a research assistant at Silver-Burdett, I took a course in children's literature, which was how I got into children's books. I did a term paper on style in children's literature for the course. The professor thought I could get it published if I tried. *That* just knocked me over! *I* could get *published!* I sent it to a magazine and it was accepted and published. That was about 1939. Recently an anthology of writings was put out and the editor discovered that old manuscript and put it in![7]

Also I read constantly when I was young. In high school, I remember, I went to Valentine Mitchell Bookstore in Hartford, Connecticut, where they had big easy chairs and one room for poetry. You could read the books right there and I was at the poetry age. I would save up my money, go into that bookstore, and read. Then I'd buy a thin book of poetry and get a little pot of narcissus. There was something so great about that. I felt like Omar Khayyám!

Later I volunteered to conduct a story hour for the Dobbs Ferry (New York) Public Library, too. We put up a big umbrella for story times and invited children to come and meet "The Umbrella Lady" under "The Magic Umbrella!" After that I was asked to be the children's librarian and design the children's room at the library. It was a great experience.

J.R.     So what turned you toward historical subjects then? You first did *Bunny Hopwell,* a mass-market book, and then some picture books and novels.

J.F.     *The Cabin Faced West* was my first introduction into research and it was about my family. When I did *Early Thunder* I kept thinking that real life is so much more incredible than fiction. It's all three hundred years old but still news. Still a surprise. "Guess what happened?", I want to say.

J.R.     It was certainly the "young question" books that brought you to prominence in writing for children. Is there a story in that?

J.F.     Well, *Sam Adams* was written first but *Paul Revere* was published first. Sam was the first one I thought of, but I knew enough of Paul that I did him first.

The incident of the horse and Sam Adams was buried in history. I found it in a letter from John Adams to James Warren when I was doing my adult book, *Cast for a Revolution.* I came across that letter saying two of the most unexpected things in the world had just occurred. One was that John Hancock got married. The other was that Sam Adams actually got on a horse. And then John Adams told the whole story about the horse. When I read that, I knew I wanted to turn it into a story.

The idea of the question books series began with *Paul Revere.* I started out with a question and then worked the book around it. I had broken away from the chronological telling of the story and tied it together by theme rather than time. In order to move the story along, I used the phrase "and then what . . . and then what?"

J.R.     Well you certainly have established a recognizable pattern with the question books. What's next in the series?

J.F.     I don't like getting stuck in molds. I don't think I'll ever do another question book.

J.R.     You evidently made a historical discovery with the Sam Adams incident. Have you found this for any of your other books, that is, where some new light is shed on the person in question?

J.F.     Well, in *Pocahontas* her whole psychology has never been exposed. (There is a short pause.) Not in my way, at least!

And I don't think Stonewall Jackson's terrible conflict between his religion and ambition has ever been emphasized in a biography as a central thing. Which I do.

I read a quotation once that biography is a series of coups d'état. You're inside the person and you have lived and lived with him or her, trying to get the story down on paper. But suddenly, when you're doing something entirely different, you have a—(she snaps her fingers sharply here)—strike! All at once you understand something you didn't quite understand before. And there is a feeling of truth about it.

J.R.     Besides books, what else do you rely on for source material?

J.F.     Newspapers definitely, but the newspapers of the eighteenth century aren't too helpful. Most of the news they told about was what was going on in Europe. They figured you knew what was going on in your city.

With *Paul Revere* I read his letters in his handwriting. I find sources in bibliographies of some of the most scholarly books. And I follow through to their primary sources.

J.R.    You must have some extraordinary form of note- and record-keeping. Do you?

J.F.    Of course not.

I used to keep things on cards, but cards are difficult. Now I do it in a binder notebook, an eighty-nine-cents thing. I put at the top what book it is I'm making notes from, and for every quote, I put the page number. I mark the books "1," "2," "3," and so on. At the end I go through and make my index topics and mark which pages of which notebook I'll find what I need. At that point I have a reference for everything.

I do keep long hours. I usually work from after breakfast until dinner. But I *never* write after dinner!

J.R.    Of the historical books, which gave the most problems and why?

J.F.    *Pocahontas.* I would never try again anything that requires so many "perhaps, must have beens, possibles, would haves, or could haves."

The problems were terrific because she wrote nothing. I had only the Jamestown settlers talking from their view. To do Pocahontas you have to begin with John Smith. Then you have to study what you can about the Algonquin Indians of that period to reconstruct the psychology and what they must have felt. I reconstructed that book from books by and about Indians.

With *Stonewall* and *Traitor* I had quotations from them or from the time that I could put in that served my purpose. With Pocahontas I didn't know what she thought about anything. I had to follow her imaginatively to re-create her feelings.

J.R.    Do you travel to the locations of the characters and books, too?

J.F.    Yes. I always travel. I have for everyone but St. Columba of *The Man Who Loved Books.* And *Brendan* was an excuse for an adventure.

While I was working on *Brendan, The Man Who Loved Books* began. I had this very old book of saints with all the saints in alphabetical order. When I was looking up Brendan, I thumbed through and came across Columba and thought, "What a neat guy!"

J.R.    If you had the chance to teach American history in the classroom, and knowing how you do disagree with the current approaches, what would you do differently?

J.F.    Well . . . I talk a lot about teaching history. And, you know, I have some very strong feelings on how history should be taught. It isn't always a laugh a minute nor is it something that is remote from you. The  past has to be brought close enough so you will feel, "I can understand that." It has to be made believable enough. And I try to do that.

You *cannot* do the bit of "way back there long ago, in the dear dead days." All of that removes history from reality. That makes it a story and you don't really believe that. It has to be believable, it has to come out from behind that curtain, the textbook.

J.R.      How do you do that, especially considering most teachers follow the textbook closely?

J.F.      With trade books. And you start right off with the kid himself. I'd start off with Robert Lawson's *They Were Strong and Good*[8] for the younger ones. And move from there. Start off with family histories and go back. Go to towns, use oral histories, all that.

You do that in a classroom and you'd be amazed at how many different strands of American history you're pulling out that you can follow through. Maybe always not in a linear way, but a time chart going around the room helps keep things straight.

J.R.      Because you do set the historical record straight, you must get some interesting mail. Especially from people who might disagree with you.

J.F.      I had a letter from an adult recently who had always felt sorry for Benedict Arnold. She thought he had gotten a bum rap in history, that he had been so misunderstood and treated so badly. After reading my book, she wrote, "I have taken all my sympathy away from him."

Then I got a letter from a little boy who wouldn't sign his name. "Dear Mrs. Fritz. I have enjoyed your book on Benedict Arnold. But after all he did in Canada and after being such a hero at Saratoga, I want you to know there is still one person in this United States of ours who sheds *tears* for Benedict Arnold."

I couldn't write back because he didn't give his address. If I could have answered, I would have said, "Good for you! I'm glad you cared." That's all anybody wants from a book. You don't have to agree with it.

J.R.      One of the criticisms I've heard about you is that you write only about men. Why don't you write about women?

J.F.      Well, I've done Pocahontas. She was certainly a victim of white and male arrogance.

But I can't be bothered with that criticism. I don't write on a soapbox. I'm not out there. I'm a woman doing my thing. I don't have to tell other women to do their thing. I don't have to run around creating role models.

J.R.      I note that your publisher has billed you as the premiere biographer for young people. Is that a fair assessment?

J.F.      I have no idea. But it sounds good, doesn't it?

# Notes

[1] Wuhan is the contemporary name for the city of Hankow, China.

[2] Katherine Paterson, the Newbery Medalist, who often reviews books for the *Washington Post,* in *Washington Post Book World* 12, No. 45 (July 7, 1982): 13.

[3] Andrea, Jean's best friend in *Homesick.*

[4] Jean's name before marriage.

[5] American Library Association annual conference.

[6] Jean's husband.

[7] Jean Fritz, "Style in Children's Literature," *Elementary English* (October 1941): 208-212. Reprinted in *Children's Literature Criticism and Response* by Mary Lou White (Columbus, Ohio: Merrill, 1976).

[8] Robert Lawson, *They Were Strong and Good* (New York: Viking Press, 1940).

# BIBLIOGRAPHY

## As Jean Fritz:

*And Then What Happened, Paul Revere?* il. Margot Tomes. New York: Coward, McCann & Geoghegan, 1973.

*The Animals of Dr. Schweitzer.* il. Douglas Howland. New York: Coward, McCann & Geoghegan, 1958.

*Brady.* il. Lynd Ward. New York: Coward, McCann & Geoghegan, 1960.

*Brendan the Navigator: A History Mystery about the Discovery of America.* il. Enrico Arno. New York: Coward, McCann & Geoghegan, 1979.

*Bunny Hopwell's First Spring.* il. Rachel Dixon. New York: Wonder Books, 1954.

*The Cabin Faced West.* il. Feodor Rojankovsky. New York: Coward, McCann & Geoghegan, 1958.

*Can't You Make Them Behave, King George?* il. Tomie dePaola. New York: Coward, McCann & Geoghegan, 1977.

*Cast for a Revolution: Some American Friends and Enemies, 1728-1814.* Boston: Houghton Mifflin, 1972.

*Champion Dog, Prince Tom.* With Tom Clute. il. Ernest Hart. New York: Coward, McCann & Geoghegan, 1958.

*The Double Life of Pocahontas.* il. Ed Young. New York: Putnam, 1983.

*Early Thunder.* il. Lynd Ward. New York: Coward, McCann & Geoghegan, 1967.

*Fish Head.* il. Marc Simont. New York: Coward, McCann & Geoghegan, 1954; new ed., 1972.

*George Washington's Breakfast.* il. Paul Galdone. New York: Coward, McCann & Geoghegan, 1969.

*The Good Giants and the Bad Pukwidgies.* il. Tomie dePaola. New York: Putnam, 1982.

*Growing Up.* il. Elizabeth Webbe. Chicago: Rand McNally, 1956; 1958. (This book was issued in two different formats.)

*Help Mr. Willy Nilly.* il. Jean Tamburine. New York: Treasure Books, 1954.

*Homesick: My Own Story.* il. Margot Tomes. New York: Putnam, 1982.

*How to Read a Rabbit.* il. Leonard Shortall. New York: Coward, McCann & Geoghegan, 1959.

*Hurrah for Jonathan!* il. Violet LaMont. Racine, Wis.: Whitman, 1955.

*I, Adam.* il. Peter Burchard. New York: Coward, McCann & Geoghegan, 1963.

*The Late Spring.* il. Erik Blegvad. New York: Coward, McCann & Geoghegan, 1957.

*Magic to Burn.* il. Beth and Joe Krush. New York: Coward, McCann & Geoghegan, 1964.

*The Man Who Loved Books.* il. Trina Schart Hyman. New York: Putnam, 1981.

*121 Pudding Street.* il. Sofia. New York: Coward, McCann & Geoghegan, 1955.

*San Francisco.* il. Emil Weiss. Chicago: Rand McNally, 1962.

*The Secret Diary of Jeb and Abigail: Growing Up in America, 1776-1783.* il. Kenneth Bald and Neil Boyle. Pleasantville, N.Y.: Reader's Digest, 1976.

*Stonewall.* il. Stephen Gammell. New York: Putnam, 1979.

*Surprise Party.* il. George Wiggins. New York: Initial Teaching Alphabet Publications, 1965.

*Tap, Tap, Lion—1, 2, 3.* il. Leonard Shortall. New York: Coward, McCann & Geoghegan, 1962.

*The Train.* il. Jean Simpson. New York: Grosset & Dunlap, 1965; also issued as *The Traen.* New York: Initial Teaching Alphabet Publications, 1965.

*Traitor: The Case of Benedict Arnold.* New York: Putnam, 1981.

*What's the Big Idea, Ben Franklin?* il. Margot Tomes. New York: Coward, McCann & Geoghegan, 1976.

*Where Do You Think You're Going, Christopher Columbus?* il. Margot Tomes. New York: Putnam, 1980.

*Where Was Patrick Henry on the 29th of May?* il. Margot Tomes. New York: Coward, McCann & Geoghegan, 1975.

*Who's That Stepping on Plymouth Rock?* il. J. B. Handelsman. New York: Coward, McCann & Geoghegan, 1975.

*Why Don't You Get a Horse, Sam Adams?* il. Trina Schart Hyman. New York: Coward, McCann & Geoghegan, 1974.

*Will You Sign Here, John Hancock?* il. Trina Schart Hyman. New York: Coward, McCann & Geoghegan, 1976.

### As Ann Scott:

*December Is for Christmas.* il. Alcy Kendrick. New York: Wonder Books, 1961.

# AWARDS AND HONORS

*And Then What Happened, Paul Revere?*
  Best Book of the Year
  Best of the Best Book
  *Boston Globe-Horn Book* Award
    honor book
  Fanfare Book
  Library of Congress list
  Notable Children's Book
  Notable Children's Book, 1971-
    1975
  Notable Children's Trade Book
    in the Field of Social Studies

*Brady*
  Notable Children's Book
  Notable Children's Book, 1940-
    1970

*Brendan the Navigator*
  Library of Congress list
  Notable Children's Trade Book
    in the Field of Social Studies

*Can't You Make Them Behave, King
  George?*
  Best Book of the Year
  Children's Choice Book
  Library of Congress list
  Notable Children's Trade Book
    in the Field of Social Studies

*The Double Life of Pocahontas*
  Best Book of the Year
  *Boston Globe-Horn Book* Award
  Notable Children's Book
  Notable Children's Trade Book
    in the Field of Social Studies

*Early Thunder*
  Fanfare Book
  Library of Congress list

*The Good Giants and the Bad
  Pukwudgies*
  Notable Children's Book

*Homesick*
  American Book Award
  Best Book of the Year
  *Boston Globe-Horn Book* Award
    honor book
  Child Study Children's Book
    Committee Award

*Homesick*—continued
  Christopher Award
  Fanfare Book
  Library of Congress List
  John Newbery Medal honor
    book
  Notable Children's Book
  *Parents' Choice* Award
  Reviewers' Choice Book
  Teachers' Choice Book

*I, Adam*
  Fanfare Book
  Notable Children's Book
  Notable Children's Book, 1940-
    1970

*Stonewall*
  Best Book of the Year
  *Boston Globe-Horn Book*
    Award, honor book
  Fanfare Book
  Library of Congress list
  Notable Children's Book

*Traitor*
  American Book Award finalist
  Best Book of the Year
  *Boston Globe-Horn Book* Award
    honor book
  Library of Congress list
  Notable Children's Book
  Notable Children's Trade Book
    in the Field of Social Studies

*What's the Big Idea, Ben Franklin?*
  Children's Choice Book
  Library of Congress list
  Notable Children's Trade Book
    in the Field of Social Studies

*Where Do You Think You're Going,
  Christopher Columbus?*
  American Book Award finalist
  Best Book of the Year
  Library of Congress list
  Notable Children's Book

*Where Was Patrick Henry on the 29th of May?*
  Library of Congress list
  Notable Children's Book
  Notable Children's Book, 1971-
    1975

*Who's That Stepping on Plymouth Rock?*
  Library of Congress list

*Why Don't You Get a Horse, Sam Adams?*
  Fanfare Book
  Library of Congress list
  Notable Children's Book
  Notable Children's Book, 1971-
    1975

*Will You Sign Here, John Hancock?*
  *Boston Globe-Horn Book* Award
    honor book
  Children's Choice Book
  Library of Congress list
  Notable Children's Trade Book
    in the Field of Social Studies

Children's Book Guild Nonfiction Award for the total body of her work.

Honorary Doctor of Literature, Washington & Jefferson College (Washington, Pennsylvania)

May Hill Arbuthnot Lecturer

Pennsylvania Author of the Year, Pennsylvania School Library Association

Regina Medal

## ADDITIONAL SOURCES

Commire. *Something about the Author.*
*Contemporary Authors.*
de Montreville and Hill. *Third Book of Junior Authors.*
Hopkins. *More Books by More People.*
Kirkpatrick. *Twentieth-Century Children's Writers,* 1978 and 1983.
Ward. *Authors of Books for Young People.*

_Patricia Lee Gauch_

Patricia Lee Gauch

## BIOGRAPHICAL NOTE

Patricia Lee Gauch, born in Detroit, Michigan, on January 3, 1934, graduated from Miami University in Oxford, Ohio, in 1956. She has received master's degrees from Manhattanville College in Purchase, New York, and from Drew University in Madison, New Jersey. She began her writing career as a reporter for the _Louisville_ (Kentucky) _Courier-Journal_. With her husband, Ronald, whom she married in 1955, she has had three children, Sarah, Christine, and John. Ms. Gauch's original works can be seen in the Kerlan Collection and at Rutgers University.

## PRELUDE TO THE INTERVIEW

Patricia Lee Gauch, more informally known as Patti, is an unabashed children's literature advocate. A passionate and articulate speaker on the subject, she enjoys healthy dialogs about books, authors, artists, styles, themes, sales, promotion—the range of the book world. She is as eager a listener as she is a speaker. And when she finds another advocate, the time passes quickly.

As a writer, she sits and immediately writes the book through. After the first draft she goes back and begins to work each section until it is just right—character motivation, scenes, moods, tempers. She approaches the book-in-progress as a movie scriptwriter does, carefully blocking out each scene, developing the characters, developing the relationships, developing the book.

Shortly after this interview she stopped teaching in public schools, deciding to focus her full energies on writing and lecturing about writing. These days when she is not behind a typewriter, she is behind a podium talking about her favorite subject.

Patti is an intense speaker and listener. While she talks, she looks directly at you, seemingly inside of you. She doesn't move. She is listening carefully. You can almost see her assimilating what you are saying and at the same time forming her response. But there is a dichotomy: underneath the penetrating watching, she is playing with napkins, coffee cups, silverware: an indication of the eagerness inside.

## THE INTERVIEW

J.R.   As a teacher of writing, how did you approach the subject with your students?

P.L.G.   Through the senses and the subconscious. I asked, What did you see? What did you feel?

In a writing class you have to give students pieces of information. To that degree they can't be free. To another degree they must be free. So you work the two off against each other.

I tell new writers, if you're very lucky you'll be able to see the practical, the plotting, the stylization, all those rigid words. You can see them someplace in your head.

Then you go to your subconscious and have to trust it. Eventually the subconscious will integrate the other more practical information into it.

What I am saying is a writing class has a double thrust. I always have the left side of their brains looking for structure. What is plot? What is character? What is tension? All those things. But they must always work this against simple experience and the spontaneous, intuitive responses to that experience.

In order to create, in the writer's sense, in new forms you have to let go of old forms.

J.R.   Please elaborate.

P.L.G.   You can't lean on formulas. When you let go, you are exploring a consciousness beyond the rigidly conscious.

There are certain writing forms that have been developed by a lot of people. As long as writers stay in those forms they may be competent, but in order to create something beyond just competency, a new form, they have to let go. Then they get into their creative selves.

J.R.   Can you give an example here?

P.L.G.   Virginia Hamilton. She is good because she knows the basics. And then she departs.

For example, she suddenly has a character climb a flagpole and sit on it to figure his world in *M. C. Higgins, the Great.*[1] Who ever heard of such a thing? That doesn't come from her form side. The *idea* that she needs a focus for her story comes from her form self, the flagpole comes from the creative self.

It's a nice little tuning, isn't it? The one side of her head thinks of the need. The other side says, "Ah, now how can I fill that need?" Sometimes the sequence is reversed, but it is an input from two different sides of the writer. You see?

J.R.   I think so. But keep on.

P.L.G.    Jean Fritz once said it's very difficult to transcend the limitations of your own spirit. And she's right. You do run up against the limitations of your personality, how far you can plumb the depths, and what you see there. And how much of a risk you're willing to take in putting out what you do see there.

Most people aren't risk-takers. They've been covered up for so long. They've played it emotionally safe for so long, they can't tap their own resources.

Jean is right. She really trained me. I was fascinated with her critiquing as well as the process she was giving me as a writer.

J.R.    I think I missed something here. What do you mean by "Jean trained me"?

P.L.G.    I was in one of her writing workshops.[2]
Let me back up.

I had a huge ego when I was twenty-one. I lost a lot of it when I was a young mother. When you have someone at the table going, "Yuck" when you put food on, or "Where is my laundry?", or "Don't you have it done yet?", that's a lot of negative input. I learned to mistrust myself and it was a little scary.

When Ron came home one night I said I must do something besides raise children. I said I think I have to go back to school or write again. That was when I started Jean's workshop.

She taught me the inner working of a story. She could put her finger on an idea and bring it up. Just like *that!* (Patti snaps her fingers.) It was the most miraculous thing. When anyone ever asks me about her I say Jean Fritz is a genius. She is.

She trained me as a writer, and because of what I learned from her, I can read someone else's manuscript as an editor. But I can't always edit my own manuscript! That's where I need Margaret.[3]

J.R.    Following that, what do you view as the editor's role?

P.L.G.    Margaret is very receptive to my ideas. So she's good for me. She senses I need certain freedoms and gives them to me. She could force my style into molds, but she doesn't. I think that's the sign of a good editor.

And she supports me, with notes, telephone calls! If I send in a chapter or two she'll react, which is terrific. She is one of the finest editors around. She is very respectful of marketing needs and at the same time is respectful of art. She's willing to look at something two ways.

There are a great many writers who are thirsty for support. Their editor becomes part of their daily framework. Some of the new writers never hear from their editors. And they are thirsty for attention, for feedback. Writers spend so much time alone, they need that attention.

J.R.    Anything else?

P.L.G.    Well, I think a writer appreciates an editor for two reasons.

It's nice to have line-by-line editing, which is useful to catch little inaccuracies or something that sounds overwritten or underwritten. It's very useful left-brain stuff.

But, a joy, a *gift,* is the editor who can see inside the writing and say, "I know what you want. I know what you're trying to do. Perhaps you will get there if you. . . ." It takes a special editor to understand a manuscript in that way. You can only hope you get that kind of editing.

Authors love certain publishers out-of-hand. It's because of the way they're treated. And it has as much to do with the marketing director as with the editors these days.

J.R.     And of marketing? It has become increasingly important in the last few years. Certainly among the years you've been writing, there have been dramatic changes. Any views on that?

P.L.G.     I think children's books is one field where you don't need a big splash of advertising. It helps, for sure, but if you write a good book the reviewers are fair. And if the reviews are good, your book will be bought. Those reviews really do help.

J.R.     Certainly though, you can argue with the way some children's book reviewing is done.

P.L.G.     Yes. A reviewer once told me he didn't like the *kind* of story I told in one of my books. And I don't think that should be a consideration for a reviewer. The consideration is, did you believe this story for the length of the book? Did it compel you? Did you like the characters? Did you see what was happening? That's what I want to hear. Not if some adult liked the *kind* of story it is. That's very disturbing to an author. *So what* if some reviewer doesn't like some kind of story or some kind of character? Who cares? They're reviewing books for children's use, not their own, and for the quality of the book, not for personal use.

J.R.     Describe your writing style in one sentence.

P.L.G.     It's more like drama than it is narrative.

J.R.     All right, explain.

P.L.G.     I am very visual. I see scenes. I've seen every scene I've ever written.

When I wrote *Kate Alone* I could see J. running up the hill after his sister. I could see him tumbling in the brush. I could see him looking for Kate by the water tower on the hill.

I could see all of it. My task was to find the words. I write as I see. Almost simultaneously. I don't sit down and see, then write.

J.R.     You had better explain this, too.

P.L.G.     I usually work from blocks. Before I started writing *Night Talks* I had paper taped up all around the four sides of my upstairs hall. Chapter one, chapter two, chapter three, just globs of paper. On the paper, I would see the scenes—jot notes about them. The paper helps me to see things spatially. Then I sat in the middle of the room and looked at my chapters.

I can't work from outlines because they're words. What I usually do before I sit down to write is consciously structure a book, at least in my mind. Then I write. That's when the two selves come together.

J.R.    For instance?

P.L.G.    Take *Kate Alone* again.

My form self, the side of me that knows form, knows that Kate who is faced with losing her dog, Duffy, has to confront herself at a certain point. She has to confront all the things she's running away from. A book isn't a good book if there's no growth or at least a change in the character.

In *Kate,* which of all the books I have written is the one written the most out of my subconscious, I have Kate running out of the house after just finding out her dog has bitten somebody. I didn't really know where she was going. So I just let her go and started writing.

The sequence would be something like this:

I'm Kate as I'm writing. The house is half-dark. Kate hears voices downstairs. Where does she go? I just started typing. What is happening is that the ideas are going directly from my head to my fingers. She comes downstairs and finds out Duff has hurt someone. She starts to hide. I know the house perfectly. I know right where she would go. First she goes into the kitchen and then she goes to the laundry rooms and hides under the tubs. She does all this and I'm typing. And then where does she go? Somehow it's still not concluded. It's still unfinished. She goes outside. She's trying to get away from all of the things happening in the house. Where does she go? She goes down the street. And then what? What's down the street? Suddenly there is a water tower. I had no idea there would be a water tower, but there it is.

See?

J.R.    Right. There is a tone about *Kate* that strikes me as autobiographical, or at least partially autobiographical. Is that correct?

P.L.G.    *Kate,* you're right, was autobiographical. It really happened to my family. The main character was my daughter, Chris, the same Chris as in *Christina Katerina.* But the father was *not* my husband and the woman was not me! To have put myself and my husband in the book would have been getting too close and I back off from that sort of thing. I don't want to be in my own books.

I wrote *The Green of Me* out of my insides. Sometimes I'd be crying when I finished certain parts of it because it was so personal.

And *Fridays!* I was one of the kids who did nothing when the girl was destroyed in *Fridays.* That story happened to me when I was an eighth-grader, but with slight distortion. The story is basically about the reduction of one girl by other girls because no one speaks up, no one has the courage to stop what is going on. And I purposely set the book on Friday nights because that's when the kids in our town went to the movies to meet the other sex. We knew we'd all be there in the second row raising the devil and driving the ushers crazy.

J.R.     Oh, yes. I remember those sessions, too. Now what about your other books? Can you follow your development as a writer through them?

P.L.G.     My first book was *Grandpa and Me.* That came out of Jean's class. *Christina Katerina & the Box* followed. That came from Jean's workshop, too. I wrote it in about two hours and it was printed almost exactly the way I wrote it. It's a from-the-subconsious book, almost right when I first did it. There's a lot of form in that story. The first consciously plotted book was *Aaron and the Green Mountain Boys,* an easy reader. That was Ferd's[4] idea. Then I did *Tempe Wick* and *Thunder at Gettysburg.*

Those first books of mine are fairly amorphous. I hadn't learned the craft of writing a book yet, although *Christina* has form to it. If you look at it you see it breaks down into four parts, almost like four squares and a twist.

If you take a close look at all my books you will see they've become increasingly complicated, but even now plotting is hard for me. It's far easier to write a *Tempe Wick* where the plot is all there in the original legend for me.

Plotting is a complicated process, and frankly, I'm more interested in character. It's hard to give characters and thoughts all the time they need when at the same time you're pulling through different threads of a plot.

J.R.     You mentioned the creative side of writing earlier. What do you consider one of your most creative books?

P.L.G.     *Morelli's Game.* That was a hard book to write because it was all fiction. I modeled the characters after six boys I knew well, but I put them in a new situation. None of them had ever taken a bike trip together. I drew a big chart for each boy, what he would do, what he would wear, what he'd do on a Sunday morning, what his response would be to an abstract question. Before I ever began writing, I *knew* those boys!

Everything about that bike ride, the boys' adventure was totally creative. Totally creative.

J.R.     Writers and illustrators generally lead, if you will, lonely work lives. What do you do to keep yourself in touch with other people?

P.L.G.     Oh boy. One thing I see in authors over and over again is self-deprecation. Part of the reason that happens is because you don't have an everyday support system. You have only yourself and your typewriter.

I'm a people person and I play off of that reality. I like relationships. I get joy from them. I grow from the banter. This is one of the reasons I like to teach.

When you're alone in a room with a typewriter, or a word processor, you have to adjust to that. You're not getting the hello of the switchboard operator or the stimulation of the kids. You work that out for yourself. And then you have to get a boost.

Let's say you give a speech once a month, maybe twice a month. That's a boost. You meet new people, see new cities, and hear about new ways of doing things. Your ego blooms. And then you go home. There's almost a withdrawal after the effusive praise you get. It's not there. I'm very careful with myself the day after a very "high" speech. I can't quite believe the checkout clerk at the supermarket is yelling at me to hurry along.

J.R.     But what do you do to keep in touch with people, other than speeches or listening to a telephone buzz?

P.L.G.     Well I've recently joined a group with four other authors. We meet once a month. We all write for young adults, but differently. So we talk craft. We talk transition. We talk ideas. We talk of what's going on in our minds. It's a way of keeping ourselves sane. You can't always talk to your spouse. The neighbors all work. And your friends don't read your books.

I was at a party once in New Jersey when this friend of mine was receiving an award. I was talking to a man when she came up. I had told him I was a writer but had not identified myself further. Then he said to my friend, "What does she write?" "Oh," my friend said, "she writes children's books." As if to say *that's all,* just children's books.

J.R.     That shouldn't really be that big of a surprise to you. Or is it?

P.L.G.     Well, you know, that's quite common. Most people don't know that children's books have some interesting expectations.

If you wish to write literature, something that affects the human spirit, something that when you read it changes you or makes a connection for you with another time or a new time, then you're talking about writing a special kind of language. You're talking about emphasis and rhythm and all sorts of things literature can mean as opposed to a straight narrative that just tells a story.

At the same time, when you're writing children's literature you can't get away with the *Garp*[5] approach. John Irving can give you a collage. He can lay in a dog story here. He can tell you a whole short story in the middle of a novel. He can play with internal ideas.

Whereas, if you wish to write children's or young adult literature, you have some freedom to try forms but you must tell a good story as well.

In a funny way, writing for children asks for more than writing for adults. You can't forget the story line. You can't forget connection. You can't leave the reader confused.

There are those who will disagree, I know. All I'm really saying is, there is an added amount of pressure on us, not a lack of pressure as so many people seem to think.

J.R.     I don't think many people who are actively involved with children's or young adult books will readily disagree with that.

P.L.G.   What I'm really impassioned about is writing a book not just as three hundred or two hundred or one hundred pages, something a person looks at, reads, and closes, but as an experience. Something that can endure as idea or feeling or story. I have to say what I believe in my books.

   I don't quote other craftsmen about writing endlessly as I once did. I used to quote Forester, Jean Fritz, and all the other people I believe in. I realize I've reached a point when my own voice is the most valid voice I can use. Both in my writing and teaching. My ideas, my views, are valid and have validity because I've lived through them and I've used them. I've worked with them. They're mine. I have earned the right to say them.

## Notes

[1] Virginia Hamilton, *M. C. Higgins, the Great* (New York: Macmillan, 1974).

[2] For a time, Jean Fritz taught writing classes to aspiring writers.

[3] Margaret Frith, publisher of children's books for the Putnam Publishing Group.

[4] Ferdinand N. Monjo, former editor-in-chief of children's books for Coward, McCann & Geoghegan, who was also an author of children's books.

[5] John Irving, *The World According to Garp* (New York: E. P. Dutton, 1978).

## BIBLIOGRAPHY

*Aaron and the Green Mountain Boys.* il. Margot Tomes. New York: Coward, McCann & Geoghegan, 1972.

*Christina Katerina & the Box.* il. Doris Burn. New York: Coward, McCann & Geoghegan, 1971.

*Christina Katerina and the First Annual Grand Ballet.* il. Doris Burn. New York: Coward, McCann & Geoghegan, 1973.

*Fridays.* New York: Putnam, 1979.

*Grandpa and Me.* il. Symeon Shimin. New York: Coward, McCann & Geoghegan, 1972.

*The Green of Me.* New York: Putnam, 1978.

*The Impossible Major Rogers.* il. Robert Andrew Parker. New York: Putnam, 1977.

*Kate Alone.* New York: Putnam, 1980.

*The Little Friar Who Flew.* il. Tomie dePaola. New York: Putnam, 1980.

*Morelli's Game.* New York: Putnam, 1981.

*My Old Tree.* il. Doris Burn. New York: Coward, McCann & Geoghegan, 1970.

*Night Talks.* New York: Putnam, 1983.

*On to Widecombe Fair.* il. Trina Schart Hyman. New York: Putnam, 1978.

*Once Upon a Dinkelsbühl.* il. Tomie dePaola. New York: Putnam, 1977.

*A Secret House.* il. Margot Tomes. New York: Coward, McCann & Geoghegan, 1970.

*This Time, Tempe Wicke?* il. Margot Tomes. New York: Coward, McCann & Geoghegan, 1974.

*Thunder at Gettysburg.* il. Stephen Gammell. New York: Coward, McCann & Geoghegan, 1975.

## AWARDS AND HONORS

*Fridays*
　　Children's Choice Book

*Kate Alone*
　　Children's Choice Book

*On to Widecombe Fair*
　　*Boston Globe-Horn Book* Award
　　　honor book
　　Fanfare Book

*This Time, Tempe Wick?*
　　Library of Congress list
　　Notable Children's Trade
　　　Book in the Field of
　　　Social Studies

## ADDITIONAL SOURCES

Commire. *Something about the Author.*
*Contemporary Authors.*

Bette Greene

# BIOGRAPHICAL NOTE

The celebrated author of *Summer of My German Soldier* was born in Memphis, Tennessee, on June 28, 1934. She attended the University of Alabama, Memphis State University, and Columbia University. Besides writing fiction for many years, Ms. Greene has worked at every job from secretary, reporter, and waitress to copywriter and recreational director for a retirement home in Brooklyn, New York. She married Donald Greene in 1959 and has two children, Carla and Jordan. She is represented in the Kerlan Collection.

# PRELUDE TO THE INTERVIEW

Bette Greene and I were determined to get together for this interview session. Our difficulties developed because we live so far apart, over six hours by car. After months of planning we arranged to meet each other at a hotel while she was in New York City on a publicity tour.

There is a quality about Bette that is not immediately seen. It is only after you have separated that you realize she has made an indelible impression. Bits of conversation come back, visual images of postures along with them. This is the same quality that is in her books. Perhaps this is, as she says, because she is "connected."

She has learned to trust her judgements from an early age. She discovered early on that she is one of those people who cause other people to react, whether she wishes it or not. It is a fact of her existence and one she has adapted comfortably to. And she has emerged a winner, or in her words, 'vindicated.'

Bette is a forceful and quiet speaker. While speaking she does not deal with the superficial. If it does come up, as it often does, she brushes it away with her hand. It is a motion that one can interpret as being abrupt; it is not. It's a motion to do away with the nonessential, nothing more; a motion that can also be interpreted to allow room for more expression and discussion of a question or development of a thought.

# THE INTERVIEW

J.R.　　Let me start off with a question you have probably heard one thousand times.

B.G.　　　No, two thousand.

J.R.　　What's the question?

B.G.　　　Is *Summer of My German Soldier* autobiographical?

J.R.　　Yes.

B.G.　　　Oh, I was hoping you'd surprise me. The best I can say is that it was an incident that is the basis of the novel.
There.

J.R.　　But did it actually happen to you?

B.G.　　　Well, yes.
There are a lot of fictional elements in it. It was only an incident worked up to a higher key.
That book has gone through a lot.

J.R.　　What do you mean?

B.G.　　　It goes way back.
I was taking a writing class at Harvard from a well-known professor of writing. He wouldn't read *German Soldier* to his students. It was the only book he refused to read aloud. Apparently the book, because of its emotional exposure, made him uncomfortable.
This was a very expensive at-night class and the professor read everybody's stuff two or three times, stuff about sex, brutality, incest. But still he became obviously disturbed by *German Soldier*. He wasn't German or Jewish. He was very WASP-y. Even his ties were WASP-y.
Instead his assistant read it and she hated it. She told me she thought the plot was good but I didn't write well, that what I needed was a ghost writer. On one level, I was devastated and yet on another level, I thought that her statements were absolutely crazy because I had been published in literary journals and knew I wrote well. I couldn't believe it! I think she was doing a number on me.
When I left I said, "I appreciate your comments and I will take care of all the things before I get the book published." I knew that would set her off. She told me, with a flash of intensity, "I'm a summa cum laude graduate of Hunter College." The assistant professor reeled off her scholastic accomplishments and even the scholastic accomplishments of her parents. "And I'm not sure I'm going to be published." So I said, "You know, you should be more confident of your work." And I closed the door.

She did her job on me but I felt good that she didn't come out unscathed, too. The tables turned and I became the teacher. She obviously didn't like my confidence. A lot of people don't. But it was the only thing that kept me alive for a long time. I had been told I couldn't write, that I was a bad student, these things. So the only thing I had left was either I was good as I thought I was or I was crazy.

Getting my first book published was a tremendous vindication.

J.R.     But the problems with the book only began there?

B.G.     Yes.

The Jewish Defense League asked that the book be taken out of bookstores.

I got a call one night from a very well-known woman critic and one I think who has tremendous integrity. She had tears in her voice.

She called me saying, "We've never met. It's eleven o'clock at night." I was working on something and you know a woman of great following doesn't call somebody at that hour whom she hardly knows. She said, "I'm sorry to disturb you." She told me who she was. She said, "I've just finished reading your book and I'm very disturbed by it. You're a woman of obvious talent but I think your book does a disservice to Jews." I said I felt terrible that she would think so.

Then she went on to say she'd just come back from a visit to former concentration camps in Poland. And said what I'm doing is "stimulating anti-Semitism all over again." And I said I hoped that wasn't true. "I would feel terrible if that was true."

She was accepting Harry Bergen as a symbol of Jews everywhere. I didn't write Harry Bergen to be a symbol of Jewish men or Jews. And I said, "I don't think you should view him like that. What I wrote is of one man who's highly disturbed and highly upset."

And, a Jewish novelist got involved in *The Alan Review* of the whole controversy of that book.[1]

J.R.     I don't know what that controversy is.

B.G.     This novelist said the book was pro-Hitler. Some librarians wrote in defense of me. It was the first time I ever answered a reviewer. When I wrote to the editor I said I was breaking my own policy of never responding to reviews because I believe they have a right to their opinion. But however I am very saddened to think you would publish this because you really don't know what would be pro-Hitler and wouldn't be pro-Hitler. And that as a practicing Jew, this was not my intention and would hope that readers everywhere would read it as Harry Bergen, one man, who happens to be Jewish, responding to a misguided psyche, and that he's a disturbed man. And that Jews everywhere, as well as non-Jews, can accept the fact that there might be a Jewish man who can be upset and disturbed and cruel. And if he is the archenemy why can't Patti Bergen be viewed as the Jewish archheroine? But they don't think Patti Bergen is all Jewish women the way they think Harry Bergen is all Jewish men.

But that was vindicated, too. The book is now used in a lot of Jewish schools and used as part of Holocaust literature. It seems to be at least accepted now. And since it's considered important Holocaust literature, I take it as a vindication.

J.R.     But it didn't stop there, either.

B.G.     No.

I was at a conference at the Harriet Tubman House in Boston attending a session on racism in literature. A publisher had come up for it and invited me to go with her.

We no sooner sat down, now nobody knew who I was, and the first person started talking on the panel about racism in children's literature. She had one book in her hand and said, "Now this is a book we can't tolerate. And the only book worse than this is *Summer of My German Soldier.*"

I couldn't believe it! I waited until she got through and at the time of questions and answers I raised my hand and said I was saddened for her that she felt that way about my book.

At that point she pointed her finger directly at me, "*You're* Bette Greene?" She knew my book so well she knew the pages she was referring to, where the "racism" was.

One part that particularly offended her was when Ruth, the black housekeeper, says, "I've loved children white and I've loved children black. But I love you most of all." She said, "that's exactly what the white person believes. No matter how many children you have of your own, they always love the children they care for more," meaning Patti Bergen in the book.

Julius Lester, who moderated the panel, wrote an article about that encounter in *Parents' Choice.*[2]

J.R.     Well, certainly getting a Newbery honor medal for the book proved to be yet another vindication.

B.G.     But it didn't! Everybody thinks *Summer* was an honor book, but it's not. That was for *Philip Hall Likes Me. I Reckon Maybe.*

It happens all the time in introductions. I don't even correct people anymore. I just let it go by. I've received a lot of things, but never the Newbery. And I never expect to. I'm pretty accurate about things like that.

J.R.     Speaking of *Philip Hall Likes Me,* that received its share of critical press, too, didn't it?

B.G.     Oh, yeah. It came from a white critic who said the book was racist because 'Philip Hall' ate watermelon in one of the scenes. I knew when I wrote it that I should make the watermelons cantaloupes because some person invariably was going to call it racist. But I didn't change it because it was watermelons, not cantaloupes, that was most Southerners' pause that refreshes.

A magazine critic from New Jersey said they weren't sure about my Arkansas accent in the book. Well, I've lived in Arkansas and I wondered how a New Jersey critic could ever legitimately question my Arkansas accent.

I'm amused more than offended by things like that. I don't expect the world to make sense so I'm ahead of the game. The world is not a rational place. I learned that a long time ago.

It's like children in school. I heard a fight in the hall when someone said, "It's not fair." Well, the older you get, you think, "Fair? What is that?" Of course it's not fair. But everything works out.

J.R.     You're right that nothing is fair and you shouldn't expect it to be. But following up on vindication for a moment, after all the noise and banter, *Summer of My German Soldier* went on to enjoy television success when it was made into a TV movie. Were you involved in that?

B.G.     Yes, I worked with the screenwriter. One reason I think the movie was so good was the producers asked me how the novel should be handled.

They were very kind about it. I thought they were either doing a number on me or they were being honest. I hoped, though, they were really being honest when they told me that they wanted me to work with the screenwriter.

I told them the screenplay had to be done by a Southern woman who felt outside the Southern structure. They found a woman who felt just that. Jane Howard Hammerstein wrote a wonderful script. She had a real knack for characters.

She was terrific. She wanted a good script and would do anything to get one. And she did.

I didn't expect the book on TV word for word. It was emotionally true, which was all I really expected and was concerned about.

J.R.     You mentioned something about the people at Harvard "not liking my confidence." What do you mean by that?

B.G.     I have a strong sense of self and I think you need that if you're going to be a writer.

I've never felt like a newcomer to publishing. I had written for newspapers and magazines before books.

And I didn't come to publishing saying, "I'm so *glad* to be here. Thank you." I came in with, "You've found me. Let's help each other." I was thrilled my book was finally accepted but my attitude was one of "Boy, it took you long enough!" I wasn't one to be abjectly thankful!

J.R.     Can you trace back when you received that strong sense of self?

B.G.     Absolutely. I was fourteen.

There was a patriotic contest in Memphis. The person who won the contest won a thousand dollars, a plaque or something. I forget what it was, but it was heavy stuff in those times. Your picture in the paper, and a prize.

As I remember it you gave your essay to the English teacher and then forgot all about it. Six months later the prize was announced.

One day, I was called into the principal's office. They wanted to know where I plagiarized my story from. I told them I did it myself and they asked for my library card.

So they tried to find all the books I had been accused of plagiarizing from. Of course they couldn't. I was accused because I was making D's in English, C's at the most. So naturally they thought I plagiarized my essay.

It was decided in all fairness I should get honorable mention. Honorable mention got a notice in the newspaper along with the winner. But no picture and no prize.

I said, "No. I didn't really want to be honorable mention. What I really wanted to be was the winner." They said I couldn't be. I could be honorable mentioned or nothing.

I suddenly got very angry and told them what I thought of their honorable mention.

I was very angry, very bitter, and very tearful. I felt wiped out and felt life wasn't fair and all of that. I was upset about it for a long time.

But at some point afterwards it struck me that I had won. I had won! I didn't care what the others thought, *I had won!*

So I went out and bought myself a prize, a Parker pen set. It cost about five dollars and came in a box with a little satin background. I knew I had won.

That experience gave me a sense of self.

And when I was first told by publishers I wasn't going to be published in book form, I kept thinking they were making a big mistake. That feeling got me through the hard times when publishers were sending me second-rate books to read, saying, "This is what we want to publish."

J.R.     So when you sat down to write books did you intentionally write for a young adult audience?

B.G.     No, no. I wasn't that sophisticated. I didn't know that much about the marketplace.

I didn't know *Summer of My German Soldier* was a juvenile. Nobody would publish it because it didn't fit into their marketing plans.

The problem, according to the editors, was it was a book narrated by a twelve-year-old. "And we all know that twelve-year-old books are read by kids twelve and under," they said. It was also too heavy, too psychological, too strong for them.

So I said, "Market it to older kids." And they said, "Oh, but you don't understand. It can't be marketed for older kids or adults because no adult in their right minds would read a book narrated by a twelve-year-old." So I said, "What about *Catcher in the Rye?*"[3] Their response was, "That's a classic."

J.R.      So what do you expect from your editors?

B.G.      I think I expect them to read my manuscripts and make overall comments on them. Generally I'm very receptive because most of the time I agree with them. Most of the time their comments are well thought out. But there have been times we've disagreed.

J.R.      Such as?

B.G.      Well, originally they wanted Philip Hall to be white, not black. It would have been very easy to do, because all that was necessary was to remove two references to race. Then it would have been a white book. It was an anguishing decision. But *Philip Hall* really is a black book. It's black in spirit.

Anyway. I really like editorial comments and criticism. Especially if it's flattering!

J.R.      Do you work with newer writers the way some writers do, passing along your comments and criticism, much in the way an editor does?

B.G.      Sometimes. I do comment the best I can. I do feel there need to be young authors coming up. I am interested in making authors better.

But I also teach them to be confident. You never know.

J.R.      What do you mean?

B.G.      A literary agent once told me his client was the publisher. And I asked, "What do you mean your client is the publisher?" His answer was, "That's where the money is."

I said, "That's where the money is all right, but the source is the author. And if you forget that. . . ." Of course he backtracked, "Well, I didn't mean." I said, "Oh, I understand what you mean."

J.R.      You have the knack of writing very real, very memorable characters. They stay with you long after reading. How?

B.G.      Thank you.

I think it's all because I'm very connected to myself. And it comes out in my work.

Why was Judy Garland so great? She didn't have a great voice. She wasn't all that gorgeous. She was short and overweight and her voice as an instrument wasn't great. But when she sang we were *connected*. Somehow Garland let us know those songs came from her personal experience. She took "Somewhere over the Rainbow" and you knew that each line had a meaning for her and it came through.

I've learned from Judy Garland, and I've learned from people who take their own lives—the dark angels, as I call them—they supercede their art. Their art goes beyond. It's their own connection. I'm sure when Michaelangelo did the Pieta he was in some very strong way connected to a mother-son relationship. I'm sure he had a very emotional connection to his own mother . . . or to a mother of his fantasy in ways that I won't begin to understand.

I want to do in words what Judy Garland does in song, which is to be constantly connected. I don't want to just parrot them. Getting the connection is the most important thing to me. I can never do a book superimposed on me because of that. If the connection is missing, I can't do it.

J.R.    How do your readers react to your work?

B.G.    They all say the same thing. "I am more alive because. . . ." Over and over they use the same words. I think my readers are connected to all my books. There's an involvement there.

I'm told by my publishers that both the volume and the intensity of my fan mail is extraordinary.

It's my readers' internal reaction that interests me, not the external. I mean I'm not all that fascinated about when you were born, how old you are, what your social security number is. I am interested if you've gone through hardships and how you kept your sunny side up most of the time, how you go on. How you get through the whirlwind. How you fall back on yourself. That sort of thing. We pick up, my readers and I, on each other in so many ways.

J.R.    You're very fortunate to have that response. Have you been that fortunate in other aspects of your life?

B.G.    Life has been as good to me as anybody else. I've certainly been through bad times but I've always come through. I've enjoyed the ride. I've been lucky. I guess what I'm really trying to say is that I've been ahead of the game. And any day or anything I get after that is a plus. I've reached the point where I'm adding up all the pluses and minuses. There are a lot of minuses. But there are a lot of pluses, too. And there is one thing I do that nobody does better.

J.R.    Which is?

B.G.    When I dig deep and hard enough, I can sometimes strike connections with my emotional source. And when I'm writing from those depths, readers respond. They say, "Hey! I know exactly how that feels. I think you must be writing about me."

## Notes

[1] Bette refers here to a controversy about *Summer of My German Soldier* that appeared in *The Alan Review.* The President's Podium (6, No. 1 [Fall 1978] : 11) is the column that began the discussion, referring to *Gentlehands* by M. E. Kerr (Harper, 1978). "Critical Criteria Challenged" (6, No. 2 [Winter 1979] :14), a reader's response to The President's Podium had implications for *Summer of My German*

*Soldier.* Two subsequent letters to the editor (7, No. 1 [Fall 1979] :13) also figure: one contains a reference to *Gentlehands* and brings in *Summer of My German Soldier.* The second refers to the first printed letter regarding *Gentlehands,* Bette's letter appears in winter 1980 (7, No. 2:30).

[2] Jules Lester, "To Be a Writer and Be Black," *Parents' Choice* 4, No. 1 (Spring 1981): 8.

[3] J. D. Salinger, *Catcher in the Rye* (Boston: Little, Brown, 1951).

## BIBLIOGRAPHY

*Get on out of Here, Philip Hall.* New York: Dial, 1981.

*Morning Is a Long Time Coming.* New York: Dial, 1978.

*Philip Hall Likes Me. I Reckon Maybe.* il. Charles Lilly. New York: Dial, 1974.

*Summer of My German Soldier.* New York: Dial, 1973.

*Them That Glitter and Them That Don't.* New York: Dial, 1983.

## AWARDS AND HONORS

*Philip Hall Likes Me. I Reckon Maybe.*
    Children's Choice Book
    Library of Congress list
    John Newbery Medal honor
        award
    Notable Children's Book

*Summer of My German Soldier*
    Best of the Best/YA
    Emmy Award for television
        movie

*Summer of My German Soldier—*
    continued
        Golden Kite Award
        Library of Congress list
        Massachusetts Children's Book
            Award
        National Book Award finalist
        Notable Children's Book

*Them That Glitter and Them That Don't*
        *Parents' Choice* Award

## ADDITIONAL SOURCES

Commire. *Something about the Author.*
*Contemporary Authors.*
Kirkpatrick. *Twentieth-Century Children's Writers,* 1978 and 1983.
Ward. *Authors of Books for Young People.* Supplement.

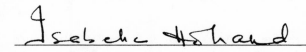

Isabelle Holland

## BIOGRAPHICAL NOTE

Born in Basel, Switzerland, on June 16, 1920, this well-known young adult author was educated at the University of Liverpool in England and graduated from Tulane University in New Orleans in 1942. She began a varied career in publishing in 1944, and worked in publicity and public relations positions with various publishers. Since then she as been a free-lance writer. She is also known as Francesca Hunt. Ms. Holland's works are part of the de Grummond and Kerlan collections.

## PRELUDE TO THE INTERVIEW

Isabelle Holland was born in a family with nineteenth-century values while living in the twentieth. Because of this, she has had exposure to a life spanning two centuries of ideas and cultures. These experiences caused her to be a late rebeller to allow development of her own style, which is discussed here.

Her involvement with children's books has been increasing over the past twenty-five years. An "insider" of magazine and book publishing, she decided to opt for a free-lancer's life, a life that can be as precarious as it is fulfilling.

It was *Man without a Face* that catapulted her to national attention. For a woman with nineteenth-century values, it was somewhat of a shock for her to realize she had unwittingly touched a nerve that set off a controversy that didn't settle for years. Her book, along with others', paved the way for what has been labelled "the new realism" in children's books. The criticism that erupted and the effect it had upon her as discussed here presents new insights to Isabelle the author when her background and intentions are considered.

As befits a writer, she has her pets. We are accompanied in the interview by Susan, Peter, Paul, Amanda, and Widget, her cats of various breeds and nationalities. It is Susan, however, who is described as "the only one  of  good family in this household."

## THE INTERVIEW

J.R.     You have what can be called an exotic background. Can you give a quick summary?

I.H.     I was born in Switzerland. And I visited the U.S. at the ages of three, five, seven, and eighteen.

J.R.     Now, can you fill in some gaps?

I.H.     My parents were born in 1878. They were forty-three when I was born. My grandfather, mother's father, was a Confederate soldier. Admittedly, he was only sixteen and fought the last year of the Civil War, but it still counts.

My mother grew up in the nineteenth-century South in Tennessee. When she sang songs to me that were fashionable in her girlhood, they were things like "After the Ball Is Over" and "Daisy, Daisy." You know, songs we associate with the gay nineties. Well, it *was* the nineties!

She and my father were married in something like 1903, and my father got his first diplomatic post abroad in 1910. He never lived in the U.S. after that until he retired in 1942, after thirty-two years of foreign service. They left the United States as residents before World War I.

My knowledge of "home," was what my mother told me of Jackson, Tennessee, circa 1890. When I came to live here in the States at the age of twenty in 1940, it was an enormous culture shock. And if some of my books seem slightly nineteenth-century to you, that's why.

J.R.     Were you raised, then, with the nineteenth-century mode of upper-class families, reading in the home and all that?

I.H.     Yes. I grew up in pre-World War II Europe. America was still a powerful nation, but not the giant we're perceived to be now.

My mother, to whom I owe all my storytelling ability, was a wonderful storyteller. Afterwards, I came to read many of those same stories she told me in mythology, history, novels, and the Bible. But she would tell me these stories as a form of entertainment. I think this is where the story as a mode of expressing everything was planted in me early. It's a very Southern way of doing things, I came to realize later. It's very biblical.

In the New Testament Christ rarely talks about abstracts such as poverty or social responsibility. Somebody says to him, "Who is my neighbor?" And He says, "A certain rich man went down from Jerusalem to Jericho and fell among thieves." That's what my mother would do. She would never give me a dissertation in the abstract. She would tell me a story. It came out of her Southern heritage and she came from a Bible-oriented society.

But her sense of reality was not strong. In her long absence abroad, she had idealized the United States. In her own mind, when she returned, she was going back to what she had left. Going back to the South in 1940 and expecting it to be like Jackson, Tennessee, in 1910 was one terrible shock.

I never saw my family reading the post-World War I generation authors such as Fitzgerald or Hemingway. What I was brought up with and what they read to each other at night was George Eliot, Scott, Austen, and Thackeray.

J.R.     So you came back to the U.S., the deep South. How did you find your way to New York? I would imagine that as a young woman with your background, that was a particularly daring thing to do.

I.H.     We had moved to New Orleans and I wanted to get out. First of all I had this idea I was going to return to Europe. New York is much nearer to Europe than New Orleans. Second, I planned to work in publishing. The third thing I wanted was to be on my own. I was twenty-four.

I tell kids today that I ran from home at twenty-four and they "die laughing." It took me more anguish and guile to do it at twenty-four than they would need now at fourteen.

My parents handled it very poorly. I didn't tell them the entire truth. I told them I was going to visit friends from New Orleans who had taken a cabin in Canada. That was all right. Mother, you see, didn't want me to leave home until I married because girls didn't leave home until they married. And I would say to her, "But mother, if I married a man and he went to live in China or Hawaii you wouldn't question it." Her answer was, "No, dear, but that's different." I make her sound like an idiot, but she wasn't. She was a highly intellectual woman but she was also a complete product of her time.

My father just didn't want anybody to get out of his control. He was a man of many admirable qualities but he and I did not have what is now called "a good relationship."

Anyway. I went to Canada, telling my parents that on my way home I was going to stop in New York and visit an old friend from Europe who lived there. Which I did.

My first act on arriving in New York was to go out and look for a job. That was 1944. The war was still on, I had an unusual background, which I glamorized of course, and landed a job almost immediately.

J.R.     Something in publishing, I presume?

I.H.     Well, I came to New York to be a writer. I put on my passport that I was a writer, more as an act of faith than anything else.

I landed a job at *Life Magazine* in the Letters section. I would write, "Dear Mr. Smithers, We are sorry we cannot send you the address of the girl on page twenty-eight. But if you would like to write a letter to her, we will be glad to forward it for you." Or, "We are sorry you do not like our editorial on Palestine." Since I was not trusted, and quite rightly, to discuss Time, Inc.'s policy on the Palestine question, they had three or four paragraphs I would copy to express their view. Then, again, I would say thank you, "Yours, For the Editors," and sign my name.

So I phoned my parents that I had found a job. I thought my father would have a heart attack right there on the phone. He was livid! But my mother, I think, had from the beginning realized on some level that I would do that.

For years I carried around a huge load of guilt. Today, most people would say, why?

J.R.     Any regrets?

I.H.     Going back, I wouldn't do anything different. My mother did what is a mistake for any human being to do. She put all of her emotional eggs in one basket, me. You shouldn't do that to a child.

J.R.     What about your brothers or sisters?

I.H.     My brother was nine years older. Mother never expected him to be always on hand. The way his age and their traveling fell out, we were in Guatemala when he was fourteen, and at fourteen all foreign children went home to school. My brother came back here to the States. Mother would not have allowed me to do that, or she would have returned with me. But my brother was a boy. That was the difference.

J.R.     Once in New York, you began to write happily away?

I.H.     Not exactly. I spent the first several years working at various jobs. I've led a very undisciplined life. I had something like twelve jobs in the first five years.

I never really started writing until I was here about four or five years and then I began with short stories. There were a lot of magazines in the late forties and early fifties, many more slots for fiction then than there are now. Today a magazine will have two or three stories and six or eight articles. Then, you had six or eight stories for two or three articles. Fiction was far more popular.

I must have written forty stories and I sold two, which is not a high average. I got *so* discouraged. I would write on Saturdays. I'd sit on the bed, put my portable on my lap and start typing. As I went on and my lack of success grew, I became convinced that I had to envision a story right through to the end before I wrote it. I couldn't do it then and I still can't do it.

J.R.     What do you mean?

I.H.     I have the original sequential mind. Something coming out of something, coming out of something. But game puzzles where you have to see several things at the same time—they do something to me. Just stop my mind cold.

J.R.     So you got blocked? Then what happened?

I.H.     I gave up. I remember sitting there Saturday morning after Saturday morning with the portable on my lap. I'd start all the stories off, but I couldn't see the end of them. So I quit trying. And I did not do any writing for several years. But after four or five years I learned the single most important thing of my writing career: that writing itself was something I liked to do. Not just having written or having something published. I missed writing. It was the physical act I missed.

So I pulled out that same old typewriter from its case and put it on my lap. And I started a line of dialog. I didn't have an idea in my head.

That line of dialog turned out to be from a fat, miserable thirteen-year-old girl in a boarding school. One of the great things about dialog, which is still my device for getting out of a block, is that it requires somebody to answer.

So the second line turned out to be from a teacher, "Miss Marks." Six years and four hundred discarded pages later, that endeavor became my first novel, *Cecily.*

But I had learned the most supreme lesson from that experience: you don't have to know where the story is going to go. All you have to do is start it and keep going.

J.R.     And because of that you don't get bogged down anymore?

I.H.     Well . . . I'll tell you about it.

One day I got bogged down. I'd been there all day, facing the typewriter. And there was nothing. I was very depressed and called six people for advice because I was going crazy. Five of the six people said, "Why don't you declare yourself a holiday? Go to a movie. Forget about it until tomorrow."

The sixth person was a writer. He said, "Isabelle, don't you dare get out of that seat until you've written a page. And if you write nothing but your name over and over again, that's OK." Something told me he was absolutely right. So I sat down and wrote, "My name is Isabelle Holland. My name is Isabelle Holland.", "Now is the time for all good men," et cetera, et cetera. And I did this gibberish for about two-thirds of a page and suddenly the block was gone and I was able to pick up where I left off.

J.R.     Your first novel, *Cecily.* How autobiographical is it? I ask because so many first novels tend to be autobiographical, or at least somewhat so.

I.H.     It was autobiographical in that I was an unhappy fourteen-year-old in an English boarding school. But the story itself is fiction.

Miss Marks, the teacher, was straight out of my head. She was an odd combination of what I most admired and most hated about the almost-idealized English schoolmistress.

After I finished it—quite some time after I finished it—I realized Miss Marks and Cecily were two sides of the same person: me. Without meaning to, I had divided myself to create them.

I was working at *Harper's Magazine* at about that time and bumped into Jeanne Vestal,[1] who was then an editor at Lippincott. This took place in the lobby at Lord and Taylor's, that well-known editorial place. She said, "Isabelle, I think you could write a children's book because of the child, Cecily." About a year later I decided to try.

*Cecily* came out as an adult book as did *To Kill a Mockingbird*[2] and *Catcher in the Rye.*[3] That was the period before young adult books became part of children's book publishing.

J.R.  What was your first children's book then?

I.H.  *Amanda's Choice.* About a year after meeting with Jeanne, I had written an adult book that was never published. I had also quit my job in publishing and had no money. I then remembered Jeanne's offer. So I called her up and she invited me to lunch. Knowing little about children's books, I had compiled a list of possible books I was sure she would like— biographies of queens of England and that sort of thing. So I took this to her. She very nicely listened to my exposition, then said, "That sounds fine to me, but I don't think that's the kind of book you want to write. What are you working on now?"

I told her that I had started one with a perfectly horrible child named Amanda who was having run-ins with her father. She said, "That sounds like the kind of book I'd be interested in." I told her it was an adult book and she said, "Never mind. Finish it and bring it to me." So I finished it and brought it to her.

Then she said, "I will now tell you what a children's book is. We will cut out everything that does not refer to the child." A romance between the governess and the local doctor went out ruthlessly. All conversations that were not either with Amanda or about Amanda went out. It was published in '70. That was my first children's book, *Amanda's Choice.*

J.R.  What followed?

I.H.  *The Mystery of the Castle Rinaldi.* I did it mostly because I had gone to Italy to visit a friend who rented a castle. And I could therefore deduct the airfare from my income tax as a business expense.

J.R.  At some point you wrote a book called *The Man without a Face* which, at the time, seemed to set the children's book world on fire.

I.H.  It's hard to think back that many years. So much as happened since then.

J.R.  Were you aware of what you were writing at the time?

I.H.  Totally *un*aware. But the flap! There was only one other book at the time that touched on the subject and that was John Donovan's.[4] I was soon being asked to talk on controversial books and it was so funny because I'm such a conservative by nature.

I sailed into this in total innocence, in a sense.

I grew up in England. I lived there from when I was seven until I was twenty. What did I read then in the 1920s and 1930s? I was not your literary reader. I read vast volumes of *The Boys' Own Annual,* an annual collection of boys' school and sports stories, because my brother had it, and endless books by Angela Brazil,[5] a popular English writer of school-girl fiction.

Of all the boys' books then, the most famous were two by E. F. Benson,[6] *David Blaize* and *David of Kings.* They went through my boarding school like wildfire.

In them, David is thirteen going on fourteen. He goes to an English public school[7] and becomes great friends with Frank, who is then seventeen. The books deal heavily with the relations between the two boys.

The whole setup of the English public school then was patterned on the Greek model of classical learning, which often included a romantic relationship between the boy and teacher or the boy with an older boy. Or, to bring it up to date in the nineteenth and early twentieth centuries in England, between the boy and the prefect.

In the *David Blaize* books, the physical homosexuality between David and Frank never took place. The relationship remained on a romantic level.

I look back on it now and realize much of what I put in *Man without a Face* was in that same spirit. I imply that Justin, the teacher, had been a practicing homosexual but I didn't go into it. I didn't think it was important. To me, what the book was about was how two people, each isolated behind his own barriers, found the courage to reach out to one another.

J.R.     Did the vocal criticism of the book take you back?

I.H.     I was *stunned!* I got a terrible review in *School Library Journal*[8] on the grounds I had been mealy-mouthed. The criticism was not that I had been daring and adventuresome, but that I had been timorous and given homosexuality a bad name by killing off Justin.

It shocked me that anybody—either of the Right or the Left—would object to *Man without a Face.*

I am frequently taken aback by books for children that are sexually graphic and use a lot of four-letter words. I'm not going to pull them off the shelves or militate against them, because people have a right to write what they want. And teachers have a right to teach what they want. And librarians have a right to choose what they want. And parents have a right to express their own opinions. But, fundamentally, I'm a nineteenth-century writer.

J.R.     By the time you wrote that book you had been writing for a number of years for books and magazines. Do you recall the very first sale?

I.H.     Oh, yes. I had my first sale at age thirteen in *Tiger Tim,* which was part comic book and part story magazine. My father deeply disapproved of it. He thought I should be reading *The Vicar of Wakefield*[9]—in his opinion it was the perfect children's book. In one of its issues *Tiger Tim* offered a prize for a three-hundred word story that the magazine considered good enough to publish. So I wrote a story and they published it. My prize was a book.

J.R.    So how long have you been making your living as a free-lance writer?

I.H.    After the *Tiger Tim* triumph, I spent my adolescent years trying to write another *Gone with the Wind*.[10] Then there was a long gap until my late twenties when I tried to write short stories for the magazines. I've been writing for a living since 1969. My first adult novel sold to paperback in 1972 and that enabled me to do nothing but write.

J.R.    Have any of your book ideas come from your readers?

I.H.    Yes, *Hitchhike*. The idea of a girl hitchhiking was suggested to me over the phone by a librarian in Tucson, Arizona, who said, "I wish you'd write something about how dangerous hitchhiking is. I keep telling my daughter not to do it."

I don't take a suggestion seriously unless I feel like writing it. People have asked me because of *Man without a Face* if I would do a comparable book between a girl and a woman. The answer is no.

J.R.    Because you do write for adults and for children, do you find you have a preference of writing for one group over the other?

I.H.    I like them both, I really do. I enjoy the change of pace.

On a basic level the adult and children's aren't very different. I don't go from being sophisticated to being unsophisticated. I'm equally at ease with both. My degree of sophistication, whatever it is, is about the same. I don't alter my language. My humor is the same. And I write most of my books in first person.

Strange as it may seem, viewing the word from the point of view of an eleven-year-old girl who's run away from her father because he's sold her horse,[11] is not that different from a heroine who is an ordained Episcopal priest and therapist at a church where a murder has been committed.[12] The perceptions are still very much the same.

J.R.    Your perceptions, perhaps memories, of childhood are very acute. How do you manage to get into the mind of a child?

I.H.    I don't.

Malcolm Muggeridge in his autobiography[13] says that people think that those who write children's books do so because they like children. This is not true. They write children's books because on some level they've never stopped being children. I believe that to be true.

J.R.    Then what about your adult books? What is your theory there?

I.H.    The reason I write the kind of adult books I write is that they are only marketable in the format of a mystery.

The love story, the family story, novels that were published as adult fiction when I was growing up are no longer published as adult fiction. Novels are much more sexual than they used to be. And as a whole they reflect a different attitude from those in the '30s, '40s, and '50s.

The chasm between serious fiction and entertainment fiction is much broader than it was, I think, thirty years ago. When you think back, some of the serious writers then like John Marquand,[14] John O'Hara,[15] and Somerset Maugham,[16] were writing books that were much more accessible to the average reader than is much serious fiction today.

For example, romance and courtship have been the staples of English language novels for more than a hundred years dating from Jane Austen and Walter Scott—there's more going on in them than just the romance, but the romance is always there. In the sixties courtship was abandoned as a framework on which you could hang a novel. Thus, it became almost impossible for me to write an adult novel except in a format where that sort of thing is still acceptable, which is why I write young adult novels where romance and courtship are still important and mysteries where the storybook approach is paramount.

The English still cling more to the concept of the novel as entertainment. They've never gotten away from that. But when you read the writings of most American novelists, they have a message they want to get across. I'm not criticizing this. It's just the way it is. If I particularly don't like the message or if it doesn't coincide with my values, they lose me.

As far as my own reading is concerned, I love a good story about interesting people. If it's well-written that makes it even better.

For example, I love Herman Wouk,[17] who is not a favorite among the literary set. I love his stories, his people and share his values.

J.R.    Do you plan your books much in advance? You know, detailed outlines, character analysis, and that sort of thing?

I.H.    Not really.

In the adult books I have a hero and a heroine. They're going to go through a period of conflict and achieve understanding at the end. Not as soon as I would sometimes like, I find out who the villain is. I know where the locale is. I've discovered that the nearer the front of the book that a body is discovered, the more popular the book is. My editor actually discovered that. She said put the body somewhere in the first three pages!

When I go and talk to kids in school I say there are two ways of writing a book and they're both perfectly good ways.

One is the way you make a quilt: you do all the pieces in any order and then put them together. Margaret Mitchell in *Gone with the Wind* wrote the last chapter first. A good friend of mine, Ursula Zelinsky,[18] sometimes also writes the last chapter first. A tremendous scene will occur to her and she'll sit down and write it. And then at the end everything fits together. I would go mad if I had to write a book like that.

The other way to write is the way I write. I try to write a book the way you crochet. You do one stitch, out of another stitch, out of another stitch. I start at page one and go right through. I've tried to write a scene ahead of time when I envision it. The trouble is when I get there, and with my method of writing, it's often no longer applicable.

J.R.    Are some of your books autobiographical?

I.H.    There are large pieces of me in the books. It's impossible not to be there. The central character, Meg, in *Of Love and Death and Other Journeys,* was brought up to be an expatriate. I was brought up as an expatriate.

There is a saying, and I can't remember where I read it, but it's that "writers tell the stories of their lives over and over again," and I believe this to be true. You become preoccupied with certain aspects. It's almost like the neurotic who's stuck in certain behavior patterns and keeps replaying the drama over and over in hope that this time it will come out right. That's what you do in books.

J.R.    In what way were you brought up to be an expatriate?

I.H.    In the sense that I was the *only* American in every school I went to. I was in a bunch of English schools and in many respects there were many advantages. But I grew up with a chip on my shoulder that I've never entirely gotten rid of. So that the feeling about one's country that you take for granted if you grow up in it I've never been able to take for granted. I bridle when it's criticized.

Children of foreign service officers who are fifteen to twenty years younger than I had a much better time of it. The foreign service suddenly woke up to the fact that they were bringing up a whole generation of children abroad with no knowledge whatsoever of their own country. Now what they do is bring the families and the foreign service officer back to Washington for a couple of years so the children can touch base, so they can know what it's like to grow up in their own country.

J.R.    Have you ever tried to write about the experience such as Jean Fritz did in *Homesick?*[19]

I.H.    I have thought about it a great deal. I have never been able to project it out. I have twice had an offer to write my autobiography and I have thought about that, too.

Once I wrote it up till the age of seven. But I stopped there.

J.R.    Perhaps you will someday. From the sound of it, you have had what can be easily called a fascinating life.

I.H.    My life has been very unplanned, very disorderly. I didn't do it in an orderly way.

J.R.    But as a professional writer you must have some sort of order, if for nothing else than just to get through a day's work.

I.H.    I like to get to work as soon after I get up as possible. In actual fact, I get to it two to three hours after I get up. I like to read the paper, feed the cats, make the bed. And then to work.

I can't write in the afternoons very well, just in the mornings. And not very much in the evening because I go out a lot.

It's a *wonderful* life!

## Notes

[1] Jeanne Vestal, then editor for J. B. Lippincott, now editorial director for Franklin Watts.

[2] Harper Lee, *To Kill a Mockingbird* (Philadelphia: J. B. Lippincott, 1960).

[3] J. D. Salinger, *Catcher in the Rye* (Boston: Little, Brown, 1951).

[4] John Donovan, *I'll Get There. It Better Be Worth the Trip* (New York: Harper & Row, 1969).

[5] Angela Brazil, an English writer of popular school stories, including *The Jolliest Term on Record* (1915), *The School in the South* (1922), *Captain Peggie* (1924), and *Joan's Best Chum* (1926).

[6] At the time of the interview, Isabelle was unaware that the *David Blaize* books were actually a set of three, not two, as she states here. The books by British writer E. F. Benson are *David Blaize* (1916), *David Blaize and the Blue Door* (1918), and *David of Kings* (1924, published in the U.S. as *David Blaize of Kings*).

[7] A public school in England is comparable in setup and definition to a private school in the U.S.

[8] *Library Journal* 97 (July 1972): 2489.

[9] Oliver Goldsmith, *The Vicar of Wakefield, a Tale Supposed to Be Written by Himself.* It was first published in London in 1766.

[10] Margaret Mitchell, *Gone with the Wind* (New York: Macmillan, 1936).

[11] *A Horse Named Peaceable.*

[12] *Death at St. Anselm's.*

[13] Malcolm Muggeridge, *The Green Stick* (New York: Morrow, 1973) and *The Infernal Grove* (New York: Morrow, 1974). Collectively the autobiography is known as *Chronicles of Wasted Time.*

[14] J(ohn) P(hillips) Marquand, a popular novelist, wrote *Point of No Return* (Boston: Little, Brown, 1949); *The Late George Apley* (Boston: Little, Brown, 1938); and *So Little Time* (Boston: Little, Brown, 1943), among many others.

[15] John O'Hara is known for *Butterfield 8* (New York: Random House, 1935); *Appointment in Samarra* (New York: Harcourt Brace & Co., 1935); *A Rage to Live* (New York: Random House, 1949); and many other novels.

[16] Somerset Maugham has written *Of Human Bondage* (Garden City, N.Y.: Doubleday, Doran, 1915); *The Moon and Sixpence* (Garden City, N.Y.: Doubleday, Doran, 1919); *The Razor's Edge* (New York: Doubleday, Doran, 1944); and many other novels.

[17] Herman Wouk has written *The Caine Mutiny: A Novel of World War II* (Garden City, N.Y.: Doubleday, 1951); and *Marjorie Morningstar* (Garden City, N.Y.: Doubleday, 1955); among many other bestselling novels.

[18] Ursula Zelinsky, author of *Before the Glory Ended* (Lippincott, 1967), *Middle Ground* (Lippincott, 1968) and *The Long Afternoon* (Doubleday, 1984).

[19] Fritz, Jean. *Homesick: My Own Story.* (New York: G. P. Putnam's Sons, 1982).

# BIBLIOGRAPHY
## As Isabelle Holland:

*Abbie's God Book.* il. James McLaughlin. Philadelphia: Westminster, 1982.

*After the First Love.* New York: Fawcett, 1983.

*Alan and the Animal Kingdom.* Philadelphia: Lippincott, 1977.

*Amanda's Choice.* Philadelphia: Lippincott, 1970.

*Cecily: A Novel.* Philadelphia: Lippincott, 1967.

*Counterpoint.* New York: Rawson, Wade, 1980.

*Darcourt: A Novel.* New York: Weybright and Talley, 1976.

*A Death at St. Anselm's.* Garden City, N.Y.: Doubleday, 1984.

*The deMaury Papers.* New York: Rawson, Wade, 1977.

*Dinah and the Green Fat Kingdom.* Philadelphia: Lippincott, 1978.

*The Empty House.* Philadelphia: Lippincott, 1983.

*God, Mrs. Muskrat and Aunt Dot.* Philadelphia, 1983.

*Grenelle: A Novel of Suspense.* New York: Rawson, Wade, 1976.

*Heads You Win, Tails I Lose: A Novel.* Philadelphia: Lippincott, 1973.

*Hitchhike.* Philadelphia: Lippincott, 1977.

*A Horse Named Peaceable.* New York: Lothrop, Lee & Shepard, 1982.

*The Island.* Boston: Little, Brown, 1984.

*Journey for Three.* il. Charles Robinson. Middletown, Conn.: Xerox Family Education Services, 1974; new ed., Houghton Mifflin, 1975.

*Kevin's Hat.* il. Leonard Lubin. New York: Lothrop, Lee & Shepard, 1984.

*Kilgaren: A Novel.* New York: Weybright and Talley, 1984.

*The Lost Madonna.* New York: Rawson, Wade, 1981.

*The Man without a Face.* Philadelphia: Lippincott, 1972.

*The Marchington Inheritance: A Novel of Suspense.* New York: Rawson, Wade, 1979.

*Moncreiff: A Novel.* New York: Weybright and Talley, 1975.

*Now Is Not Too Late.* New York: Lothrop, Lee & Shepard, 1980.

*Of Love and Death and Other Journeys.* Philadelphia: Lippincott, 1975.

*Perdita.* Boston: Little, Brown, 1983.

*Summer of My First Love.* New York: Fawcett, 1981.

*Tower Abbey: A Novel of Suspense.* New York: Rawson, Wade, 1978.

*Trelawny: A Novel.* New York: Weybright and Talley, 1974.

### As Francesca Hunt:

*The Mystery of Castle Rinaldi.* Middletown, Conn.: American Education, 1972.


## AWARDS AND HONORS

*Abbie's God Book*
> Helen Keating Ott Award

*Alan and the Animal Kingdom*
> Library of Congress list

*Kilgaren*
> Best Young Adult Book of the Year

*Man without a Face*
> Best Book for Young Adults
> Best of the Best/YA
> Fanfare Book

*Now Is Not Too Late*
> Library of Congress list

*Of Love and Death and Other Journeys*
> Best Book for Young Adults
> Fanfare Book
> Library of Congress list
> National Book Award finalist

*Tower Abbey*
> Best Young Adult Book of the Year


## ADDITIONAL SOURCES

Commire. *Something about the Author.*
*Contemporary Authors.*
Kirkpatrick. *Twentieth-Century Children's Writers,* 1978 and 1983.
Ward. *Authors of Books for Young People.* Supplement.

_Lee Bennett Hopkins_ (signature)

Lee Bennett Hopkins

## BIOGRAPHICAL NOTE

Lee Bennett Hopkins was born on April 13, 1938, in Scranton, Pennsylvania. He graduated with a B.A. from Newark State College in Union, New Jersey, in 1960, and received an M.Sc. from Bank Street College of Education in New York in 1964, as well as a professional diploma from Hunter College in 1967. Besides his literary career as a collector and writer of poetry, Mr. Hopkins, a much-honored educator, is represented in the de Grummond and Kerlan collections.

## PRELUDE TO THE INTERVIEW

Lee Bennett Hopkins came to children's books by accident, as so many others have. It was as a young classroom teacher that he discovered his penchant for poetry. Since _Don't You Turn Back,_ seldom does a year go by in which he doesn't publish at least two new books.

His anthologies, in particular, have been thematically arranged which has proved particularly useful in the classroom, fitting in easily with a teacher's lesson plan. A self-proclaimed "children's literature groupie," Lee is among the earliest anthologists to have effectively designed a vehicle to bring poetry to children on a widespread basis.

He is a frequent speaker at education and library conventions across the country. He also conducts workshops for various groups. It is not unusual to hear, when you telephone Lee, "I can't do it then. I'm going to be in Iowa" (or Oregon . . . or Florida . . . or Maine . . .). In order to book an appointment, 90 to 120 days' notice is advisable! At the time of this interview in the spring of 1983, he was already working on his 1985 travel schedule.

There is a newer side to Lee, too, a side that was developing during this interview: Broadway playwright. There is no doubt he will be as accomplished at that as he is in all his other activities.

We met at his Westchester County, New York, home where he moved some years ago to escape living in New York City. He is close enough for a comfortable commute and just far enough to have a touch of rural living. As he says, he had been raised in cities all his life and needed the change. He was so new to a rural surrounding that he made the astonishing discovery that all birds were not city pigeons!

## THE INTERVIEW

J.R.     It seems pretty obvious to me that because of the nature of this book and the nature of some of the books you have done, we had better clear the air about *Books Are by People* and *More Books by More People*! Okay?

L.B.H.     I had the idea to do what you're doing. I started with Maurice Sendak and had done his interview as a prototype. When my editor, Mary L. Allison at Scholastic, got it, she said, "Look this is very good, but twenty-five[1] is not a good selling point. I think you should do one hundred." I almost dropped dead. I didn't even know one hundred authors then but I ended up doing one hundred and four.

I never used a tape recorder. I took notes instead. And I developed a very good questionnaire that covered everything from the moment the authors were born. I asked them to fill it in before I met them so as not to spend too long and also use it as a point of reference.

I have a file on every person I interviewed. It's unbelievable. It's like the CIA. Some of it, extremely important now, contains many personal letters and drawings from these people. Many of the people in *Books Are by People* are dead now. It's an unbelievable amount of material. At this point it's historical!

For the sequel, *More Books by More People*, I did sixty-five interviews. Since then I've done more interviews for magazines. But I don't do them anymore. That was another life. I've been asked to revise the books but I don't want to.

J.R.     There is a very warm introduction to *Books Are by People* by Charlotte Huck.[2] Did you know Charlotte well at the time?

L.B.H.     She had been, and is, my mentor! Oh, I lived with her *Children's Literature in the Elementary School* when I was teaching. It was my introduction to children's books. It is my Bible. I have two copies of it.

I studied her book and then got a chance to meet her. In '68 when I was at an NCTE[3] meeting and I didn't know who she was. I was with a friend at a cocktail party and said, "Who is Charlotte Huck?" He looked at me and said, "That lady in the green dress standing over there." So I walked up to her, introduced myself. She didn't know who I was. She may have heard of me because I was writing a lot of articles at that time, in '67 and '68. I introduced myself and told her I was doing a book of author interviews and said there was no one in the world I wanted more to do the preface than her. It was unbelievable.

At twenty-four, twenty-five years old to approach her. She's a mountain! She said, "Send me a couple. Let me see them." I sent her about seven that I had done. Within two weeks she had the introduction written, a beautiful introduction. It's as warm and personal as she is. This began a tremendous friendship between us. I love her.

J.R.　You have been intensely involved with children's books for quite awhile. Does that stem back to, possibly, a college level course on the subject?

L.B.H.　I had no interest in children's books when I started teaching. None. I had a course in college as an introductory course, which was needed for teaching elementary school. I didn't find it at all exciting. I found Charlotte's book so exciting that it led me to the books themselves!

But it was in '63 when Sendak was the Caldecott Medalist for *Where the Wild Things Are* when I really found books. I was then working with young children. Sendak's book was *magic* with them. It just did wonders. I never knew a book that could *happen* like that with kids. I wasn't up on the literature, I didn't read the magazines and journals. I didn't know of the controversy surrounding the book.[4] I didn't care. But I saw what it did to children and started to use children's books en masse. Mainly Caldecott-winning books. Some of them are still as good now as when they were published, like *Make Way for Ducklings*.[5]

I didn't know about publishing, publishers, authors, illustrators, or the library world. All that was foreign to me. But I quickly got into it once my interest was up. I became a children's literature groupie! It just sparked from there.

J.R.　Then, did that lead to your early involvement with the Council on Interracial Books for Children?

L.B.H.　I must back up. I had taught for six years in New Jersey and then went for my master's at Bank Street. I worked in five all-black West Harlem schools. Then I started to write articles for various journals on my use of poetry with children and on black history. It was the height of the Civil Rights movement and I was very involved.

There was a group of us who thought it was time to start to recognize black artists and illustrators. So we established the Council and started the establishment of the Interracial Book Council awards.[6] There are many people active today who started out from there.

J.R.　And your own writing began when?

L.B.H.　Mine started when Langston Hughes died in 1967. I naively got into children's books then.

I called Knopf and asked for the juvenile editor. I didn't even know her name. I got her on the phone and said there hadn't been a decent collection of Hughes' poems since 1932 when *The Dream Keeper*[7] came out. I said, "My God. All those pictures look as if the blacks just got out of the watermelon patch! It's the last thing I want to show my kids to develop self-concept."

So she said why don't you come in and we'll have lunch? So I went and it was Virginie Fowler.[8] We had lunch and *Don't You Turn Back* came from that. It was my first children's book. Ann Grifalconi did the woodcuts, which I think are among her most beautiful. The book was a 1969 ALA Notable Book.

J.R.    And from that you eventually formed the basis for the number of anthologies you have become so well known for. You seem to have a different approach than most. Why don't you talk about it?

L.B.H.    My anthologies aren't haphazard. They have a beginning, a middle, and an end to them. In a book like *A Dog's Life* it starts out from the puppy and goes right through the death of a dog in old age. The same with *My Mane Catches the Wind: Poems about Horses.* It starts with a foal and goes to the death of an old mare. They're life-cycle books.

J.R.    But how do you go about forming the basis of the book?

L.B.H.    Take *My Mane Catches the Wind,* which was my niece's idea. She is a horse freak and was thirteen at the time. She said, "Uncle Lee, you do all those nice books. Why don't you do a book about horses?"

So, to start, I get a theme. Then I begin to go through poems. There are about twenty-four poems in *Mane.* So that means I must have read several hundred horse poems from the body of literature. I work from my own library. There's little in the public library I don't already have.

I start by hitting the "old saws," Robert Frost, Carl Sandburg. Then the children's poets like Myra Cohn Livingston and Aileen Fisher, to see if they've done anything on the subject.

I always start from the original sources, the poets. After I've exhausted that I start going through anthologies. After I exhaust that I often go through the magazines I read—poetry and literature magazines. I like to encourage young poets because that makes for an exciting part of an anthology. It contains work that's never been anthologized before.

I try to maintain a balance. I want a balance of children's poets. If I can find an adult poet who fits, fine. But I want a balance of the old and new.

And the language has to flow. When I do a selection I may have a selection of one hundred poems. I look for poems where almost the last word of one poem flows into the first word of the next. That way a child is reading the collection as if it were a novel or a picture book. My anthologies are not just a bunch of poems put together. There's a beginning, a middle, and an end to all my anthologies. I feel there has to be some kind of flow.

When I was growing up anthologies meant a gigantic book with anything someone could find to throw into it. It's a different concept than what I use!

J.R.     Do reviewers see that?

L.B.H.     Most don't. It's incredible to me. Many reviewers don't know how to review anthologies.

I get annoyed when they say, "This is a collection of poems that can be found in other books." Well, of course they can! That's what an anthology is! That phrase pops up so often it drives me up a wall.

A lot of anthologies come about because I wish I had had them when I was teaching. For example, the holiday books. At the time Halloween is coming everyone has the same idea to share poems. They all race to the poor librarian. So I thought to put together a book of twenty-two good, solid poems by masters into one volume that a teacher could use all month.

J.R.     How long does it take to put an average-sized one together?

L.B.H.     At least a year. I'm not trying to cash in on the market. If I were, I'd do them a lot quicker!

You don't dare leave out one poem that really fits. It's a tremendous amount of work you have to research and an awful lot of memorizing.

You also need balance. There aren't that many major poets writing so you're limited to those who are. And I also try to have a balance of black poets. And I go all the way back. But I prefer contemporary poets and poems when I can find them.

J.R.     Why?

L.B.H.     Because I'm writing for today. There's an awful lot of dated verse that doesn't work anymore. I like the contemporary music of poetry. Someone like David McCord is unbelievable. And Myra Cohn Livingston, she taps in on today.

The first poem has to be very good and has to fit the collection. Sometimes I'll have a wonderful first poem that just doesn't fit, that doesn't go with anything else that comes before or after. So it's rejected.

J.R.     What was the most challenging anthology?

L.B.H.     *Surprises,* the first *I Can Read* anthology for Harper! Now, talk about work! Thirty-six poems. No poem could be more than thirteen lines, including the title. No line could be longer than thirty-eight characters, including punctuation marks and spaces. And I had to design a book that would appeal to a very young child. That took me well over two years to do.

I had to scour the body of literature. I set my typewriter at thirty-eight characters. When the bell went off I'd say, "I can't use this!" It was a tremendously exciting challenge.

J.R.     Certainly clearing permissions and paying permissions fees can be its own sort of challenge?

L.B.H.    Permission fees are rising so fast and so high that it almost doesn't pay to do an anthology.

A book like *Moments* has fifty poems, and permissions ran over two thousand dollars. You're talking about investing a lot of money and perhaps not reaping it back.

Not only that, permissions are incredibly difficult to do. No one realizes, once you've made the selections, how difficult tracking down permissions can be. Through agents, through families, estates. It takes over six months to clear up all those.

And I do my own. I imagine different people work differently but I only know what I do. I do all the permissions, all the clearances. They take me longer sometimes than it does the book.

The average teacher and many librarians don't realize how much work goes into the Acknowledgments page. That little type in front that everyone skips? *That* constitutes an enormous amount of time and up-front money.

For a book like *Moments* there were two thousand dollars in permissions, an advance to me and an advance to the illustrator. You're talking about six to eight thousand dollars before it moves from one side of the editor's desk to the next without even touching it! That's why books are hitting new price levels.

J.R.    How much say do you have in the selection of the illustrators for your anthologies?

L.B.H.    Now I often have a say. Now they ask me. I always tell them Maurice Sendak but I haven't gotten him yet! I have had some wonderful artists—Tomie dePaola, Michael Hague, Sam Savitt, Dirk Zimmer. I've had so many.

Sometimes I see the final art before it's printed. Sometimes I see a sketch and the editors ask what I think.

Fritz Eichenberg is wonderful to work with. Now he does only what he wants to do which is a wonderful stage of life to be at. Absolutely! When he got the Sandburg manuscript he was thrilled with it and wanted to do the book. He was eighty-one when he did it.

My niece suggested Sam Savitt for *My Mane Catches the Wind.* "There's only one person," she said, "Sam Savitt. He's the official artist of the U.S. Equestrian Team." So when I told my editor she laughed and called him up. He was, of course, terribly interested.

J.R.    Well, certainly one of the nice things about anthologies is they don't take much work for editors. There's certainly not much they can do, is there, with an anthology?

L.B.H.    Oh, I like editors to butt in. Editors are very important in the shaping of a book.

In *Rainbows Are Made,* Anna Bier[9] was instrumental in editing the book with me. We wanted something fresh on Sandburg but the problem was his two books for children were still available. He had done a fine job in selecting his poems for young readers from his complete works. That meant I had to go back into the complete works, too, which is over eight hundred poems including his epics.

We decided more than half the poems in my books would have to come from the complete poems and less from *Wind Song*[10] and *Early Moon*.[11] That took two and one-half years. I was dizzy at the end. I nearly went blind from reading! It was a tremendous challenge!

We had to keep out poems that were controversial because Sandburg was a controversial poet. He wrote in the vernacular when he lived and of the times. So Anna greatly helped shape the book idea for the necessary balance. She also made me do an introduction to give a perspective on Sandburg.

J.R.    Do you get very involved in the marketing of your book?

L.B.H.    Only in the sense that I do a lot of speaking nationally and when I go, publishers will sometimes have my books there. Certainly some books are often sold that way more than any other.

I don't talk about my work much. I talk about children's literature and how to get books into the lives of boys and girls in the classroom or in library programs. I may use one or two of my books as examples, but that's all.

Publishers haven't found a way to tap the teacher market yet. The average teacher does not get material. If they get a catalog in the mail it's often the only catalog they get. They will go to that catalog when book monies are available. They don't know there are a lot of other publishers around. They don't have the same access as librarians do.

J.R.    Don't you tire of saying the same things over and over again?

L.B.H.    I *never* say the same thing over and over again because I do different kinds of things.

When I do a two-hour session on poetry all I need is one index card. I don't use notes. The philosophy is the same but the activities change because I'm constantly thinking up new things to do. The poetry I read is always different because I'm always using new poems. Teachers know Shel Silverstein so I don't need to use him that much. He is important for light verse but I want kids to move along. They need to know N. M. Bodecker or X. J. Kennedy. They need to know Myra Cohn Livingston and Eve Merriam. I want the younger kids to know Mother Goose. I want kids to reach. They're not going to get to Shakespeare if they haven't had Seuss.

J.R.    With the travel schedule you have, you must do a great deal of writing in the air, on trains, in hotel rooms. Correct?

L.B.H.    No. I can only work at home. I can't work in hotel rooms. I can't work on planes.

Traveling gives me a chance to get away from my books because I work very intensely at home. I can put in twelve or fourteen hours a day and not know the time has gone. I work seven days a week. There are no Saturdays, Sundays, holidays. I could easily finish up a manuscript on Christmas morning before my family comes over! There's no time otherwise.

Also remember I don't have to get up in the morning to go to an office. I roll out of bed and I'm there. And I'm very decisive. I know what I'm doing. Once I get into a project I do it. I don't fool around.

J.R.       On top of your anthologies you manage to produce a substantial number of professional books and articles about children's books for teachers and librarians each year. Certainly those are done more for professional commitment than for money?

L.B.H.     I'm not worried about money. I never grew up with it. I have more than I need now. I don't spend it. I don't use it. What do you do with it after awhile? How much can you have? Another table? Another chair? Another book? I'm comfortable. It's a nice stage to be in.

Yes, I'm still very involved in the educational world. I do at least one article a year for *Language Arts,* the "Book Sharing" column for *School Library Media Quarterly,* and "Poetry Place" for *Instructor.* "Poetry Place" is great because the words are short and the sentences aren't very long! Seriously, it works more now, I think, in the media age than ever before because children are used to very short things. They have short attention spans and watch a lot of television. Good poetry is shorter than a commercial and lasts a lot longer.

Poetry has come into its own in the past few years. Nancy Willard winning the Newbery Medal for *William Blake's Inn,*[12] Shel Silverstein's *A Light in the Attic*[13] appearing on the bestseller list for over ninety weeks and being the first book of verse ever to win the William Allen White Award.[14] The establishment of the NCTE Poetry Award[15] is also very important.

J.R.       There is an area of writing we haven't discussed yet, your novels.

L.B.H.     I've done three novels, *Mama, Mama & Her Boys* and *Wonder Wheels.* Each of them are highly autobiographical, reminiscences of my growing-up years.

*Mama* is a love story about a wise, wonderful, very outrageous and outspoken working class mother who steals to provide her two young sons with what she thinks are the "better things in life." *Mama & Her Boys* continues the adventure.

*Wonder Wheels* is a story of love and loss based upon something I experienced when I was sixteen years old.

Writing these three books has led me on to other projects.

J.R.      Like what?

L.B.H.      Playwrighting.

You get to a certain age where you do think of your life. I'm at a wonderful place where I can afford to fail. I want to have that luxury. I don't have to worry if my plays don't get bought.

I've done two now. It's something I want to pursue. I know the limitations. I know how hard it is. I'm not naive. It's very difficult to get something produced on Broadway. But I love it. I've never done anything so exciting!

J.R.      Contrast playwrighting with book writing.

L.B.H.      It's easier and it's harder. Everything is dialog and you have 120 pages for it. You have to develop characters quickly.

I love writing plays. If it takes me twenty years to do it, I'm going to!

J.R.      With all your writing that you do, you still find time to review books for your workshops and for publication. Doesn't it get terribly draining?

L.B.H.      No. I love it.

I read all the reviews because I'm very involved with education. I think that's one thing I have that many authors don't. I'm very involved with the professional and educational end.

I get all the journals and read them all from cover to cover the minute they come in the mail. I have tremendous retentive memory so I can tell you exactly what's been reviewed. I receive some two thousand books from publishers each year, more with paperbacks, for my own reviewing. And I read them and I use them when I speak.

I think reviewers who only give space for bad reviews are doing a disservice to readers. Who wants to know only about the bad? Why don't we spend more time telling people who's good? If I were a parent I would want to know what to buy. I don't want to know of the ones that are lousy.

If I don't like a book I don't review it. Since I'm serving teachers and librarians I see no function to tear apart an author. If the book isn't good I don't review it. I want my small space to be devoted to fine books. Or if I can find a way to use a middle-of-the-road book I'll call attention to it.

J.R.      From the sounds of things you manage to keep your agent very busy!

L.B.H.      I love my agent. I've been with her forever. It's my version of a sexless marriage. I don't make a move professionally without her. She advises me on every facet of my career. We have a wonderful time!

J.R.      As I look around your room I don't see a word processor, which is something I would expect to see with the amount of writing you do.

L.B.H.      A kid asked me if I had a word processor. I said, "Yes. Here it is." [He holds up a pencil.] I said, "It's cheap. It's portable. It's light to carry around. It makes you think." The kid looked at me like I was crazy!

          I don't like word processors. I don't like computers. I'm appalled at the way this whole computer business is mishandled in education. It's like what happened in the 1950s and 1960s after Sputnik. The same craze. We'll survive this. It's a matter of time and money.

          I sometimes wish the computer revolution will disappear very quickly due to a worldwide massive power failure!

J.R.      What else is coming up after your plays, your books, your anthologies, your columns?

L.B.H.      Nothing much. It's a very quiet life!

## Notes

[1] Lee refers to an early idea in the development of this book in trying to decide what is a suitable number of people for a book of this type. Twenty-five was one of the numbers suggested.

[2] Charlotte S. Huck, professor at Ohio State University (Columbus, Ohio) and author of *Children's Literature in the Elementary School,* published by Holt, Rinehart & Winston (3d ed., 1976).

[3] National Council of Teachers of English.

[4] The controversy Lee refers to regarding *Where the Wild Things Are* is that many adults felt the book might give nightmares to children.

[5] Robert McCloskey, *Make Way for Ducklings* (New York: Viking Press, 1941).

[6] The Council awards were developed to promote and publish minority authors and illustrators.

[7] Langston Hughes, *The Dream Keeper and Other Poems.* il. Helen Sewell (New York: Alfred A. Knopf, 1932).

[8] Virginie Fowler, former editor-in-chief of children's books for Alfred A. Knopf.

[9] Anna Bier, editor of children's books for Harcourt Brace Jovanovich.

[10] Carl Sandburg, *Wind Song.* il. William A. Smith (New York: Harcourt, Brace & World, 1960).

[11] Carl Sandburg, *Early Moon.* il. James Daughtery (New York: Harcourt Brace & Co., 1930).

[12] Nancy Willard, *A Visit to William Blake's Inn: Poems for Innocent and Experienced Travelers.* il. Alice and Martin Provensen (New York: Harcourt Brace Jovanovich, 1981).

[13] Shel Silverstein, *A Light in the Attic* (New York: Harper & Row, 1981).

[14] The William Allen White Award is chosen by Kansas schoolchildren.

[15] The National Council of Teachers of English Award for Excellence in Poetry for Children is presented to a living American poet in recognition of his or her aggregate work.

## BIBLIOGRAPHY

### As Author:

*The Best of Book Bonanza.* New York: Holt, 1980.

*Books Are by People: Interviews with 104 Authors and Illustrators of Books for Young Children.* New York: Citation, 1969.

*Charlie's World: A Book of Poems.* il. Charles Robinson. Indianapolis: Bobbs-Merrill, 1972.

*Children's Literature—A Balanced Collection for Teachers, Preschool through Grade Three.* New York: Citation, 1972.

*City Talk.* photogs. by Roy Arenella. New York: Knopf, 1970.

*City Workers: Suggested Guide for Teachers.* New York: Watts, 1969.

*Creative Activities for the Gifted Child.* With Annette Frank Shapiro. Palo Alto, Calif.: Fearon, 1969.

*Do You Know What Day Tomorrow Is?: A Teacher's Almanac.* With Misha Arenstein. New York: Citation, 1975.

*How Do You Make an Elephant Float?: And Other Delicious Riddles.* il. Rosekrans Hoffman. Chicago: Whitman, 1983.

*I Loved Rose Ann.* il. Ingrid Fetz. New York: Knopf, 1976.

*Important Dates in Afro-American History.* New York: Watts, 1969.

*Kim's Place and Other Poems.* il. Lawrence DiFiori. New York: Holt, 1974.

*Let Them Be Themselves: Language Arts for Children in Elementary Schools.* New York: Citation, 1969; 2d ed., enlarged, 1974.

*Mama: A Novel.* New York: Knopf, 1977.

*Mama & Her Boys: A Novel.* New York: Harper & Row, 1981.

*More Books by More People: Interviews with Sixty-five Authors of Books for Children.* New York: Citation, 1974.

*Partners in Learning: A Child-Centered Approach to Teaching the Social Studies.* With Misha Arenstein. New York: Citation, 1971.

*Pass the Poetry, Please!: Using Poetry in Pre-Kindergarten—Six Classrooms.* New York: Citation, 1972.

*This Street's for Me!* il. Ann Grifalconi. New York: Crown, 1970.

*To Look at Any Thing.* photogs. by John Earl. New York: Harcourt Brace Jovanovich, 1978.

*Wonder Wheels: A Novel.* New York: Knopf, 1979.

_As Editor:_

_A-Haunting We Will Go: Ghostly Stories and Poems._ il. Vera Rosenberry. Chicago: Whitman, 1977.

_And God Bless Me: Prayers and Lullabies and Dream Poems._ il. Patricia Henderson Lincoln. New York: Knopf, 1982.

_Beat the Drum: Independence Day Has Come._ il. Tomie dePaola. New York: Harcourt Brace Jovanovich, 1977.

_By Myself._ il. Glo Coalson. New York: Crowell, 1980.

_Circus! Circus!._ il. John O'Brien. New York: Knopf, 1982.

_The City Spreads Its Wings._ il. Moneta Barnett. New York: Watts, 1970.

_Crickets and Bullfrogs and Whispers of Thunder: Poems and Pictures by Harry Behn._ San Diego, Calif: Harcourt Brace Jovanovich, 1984.

_A Dog's Life._ il. Linda Rochester Richards. New York: Harcourt Brace Jovanovich, 1983.

_Don't You Turn Back: Poems by Langston Hughes._ il. Ann Grifalconi. New York: Knopf, 1969.

_Easter Buds Are Springing: Poems for Easter._ il. Tomie dePaola. New York: Harcourt Brace Jovanovich, 1979.

_Elves, Fairies and Gnomes._ il. Rosekrans Hoffman. New York: Knopf, 1980.

_Girls Can Too!: A Book of Poems._ il. Emily McCully. New York: Watts, 1972.

_Go to Bed!: A Book of Bedtime Poems._ il. Rosekrans Hoffman. New York: Knopf, 1979.

_Good Morning to You, Valentine._ il. Tomie dePaola. New York: Harcourt Brace Jovanovich, 1974.

_Hey How for Halloween._ il. Janet McCaffery. New York: Harcourt Brace Jovanovich, 1974.

_I Am the Cat._ il. Linda Rochester Richards. New York: Harcourt Brace Jovanovich, 1981.

_I Really Want to Feel Good about Myself: Poems by Former Drug Addicts._ With Sunna Rasch. Nashville, Tenn.: Nelson, 1974.

_I Think I Saw a Snail._ il. Harold James. New York: Crown, 1969.

_Kits, Cats, Lions and Tigers: Stories, Poems and Verse._ il. Vera Rosenberry. Chicago: Whitman, 1979.

_Love and Kisses._ il. Kris Boyd. Boston: Houghton Mifflin, 1984.

_Me!: A Book of Poems._ il. Talivaldis Stubis. New York: Seabury, 1970.

_Merely Players: An Anthology of Life Poems._ New York: Nelson, 1979.

_Merrily Comes Our Harvest In: Poems for Thanksgiving._ il. Ben Shecter. New York: Harcourt Brace Jovanovich, 1978.

_Moments: Poems about the Seasons._ il. Michael Hague. New York: Harcourt Brace Jovanovich, 1980.

_Monsters, Ghoulies, and Creepy Creatures: Fantastic Stories and Poems._ il. Vera Rosenberry. Chicago: Whitman, 1977.

*Morning, Noon and Nighttime, Too.* il. Nancy Hannans. New York: Harper & Row, 1980.

*My Mane Catches the Wind: Poems about Horses.* il. Sam Savitt. New York: Harcourt Brace Jovanovich, 1979.

*On Our Way: Poems of Pride and Love.* il. David Parks. New York: Knopf, 1974.

*Poetry on Wheels.* il. Frank Aloise. Champaign, Ill.: Garrard, 1974.

*Pups, Dogs, Foxes and Wolves: Stories, Poems and Verse.* il. Vera Rosenberry. Chicago: Whitman, 1979.

*Rainbows Are Made: Poems by Carl Sandburg.* il. Fritz Eichenberg. New York: Harcourt Brace Jovanovich, 1982.

*Sing Hey for Christmas Day!: Poems.* il. Lauran Jean Allen. New York: Harcourt Brace Jovanovich, 1975.

*The Sky Is Full of Song.* il. Dirk Zimmer. New York: Harper & Row, 1983.

*A Song in Stone: City Poems.* photogs. by Anna Held Audette. New York: Crowell, 1983.

*Surprises.* il. Meagan Lloyd. New York: Harper & Row, 1984.

*Take Hold! An Anthology of Pulitzer Prize Winning Poems.* Nashville, Tenn.: Nelson, 1974.

*Thread One to a Star: A Book of Poems.* With Misha Arenstein. New York: Four Winds, 1976.

*Witching Time: Mischievous Stories and Poems.* il. Vera Rosenberry. Chicago: Whitman, 1977.

*Zoo!: A Book of Poems.* il. Robert Frankenberg. New York: Crown, 1971.

## AWARDS AND HONORS

*Don't You Turn Back*
   Notable Children's Book

*Girls Can Too!*
   Notable Children's Trade Book
   in the Field of Social Studies

*Mama*
   Notable Children's Book
   Notable Children's Trade Book
   in the Field of Social Studies

*Rainbows Are Made*
   Best Book of the Year
   Best Illustrated Children's Book
   Notable Children's Book
   Reviewer's Choice Book
   Teacher's Choice Book

*The Sky Is Full of Song*
   Best Book of the Year
   Book Show
   Children's Choice Book

*A Song in Stone*
   Notable Children's Book
   Teacher's Choice Book

*Surprises*
   Best Book of the Year

*Wonder Wheels*
   Children's Choice Book

Broadcast Media Award from the International Reading Association for the New York Public Library broadcast of *Moments*

Educational Leadership Award, Phi Delta Kappa

Honorary Doctor of Laws, Kean College (Union, New Jersey)

Literacy Award, from the Manhattan Council of the International Reading Association

Outstanding Alumnus Award, Kean College (Union, New Jersey)

## ADDITIONAL SOURCES

Commire. *Something about the Author.*
*Contemporary Authors.*
Ward. *Authors of Books for Young People.* Supplement.

Steven Kroll

## BIOGRAPHICAL NOTE

Born in New York City on August 11, 1941, Steven Kroll graduated from Harvard University in 1962. He was a reader-editor at Chatto & Windus Publishers in London and an acquiring editor through 1969 at Holt, Rinehart & Winston in New York; since then he has been a free-lance writer. Some of his manuscripts are in the de Grummond Collection.

## PRELUDE TO THE INTERVIEW

Steven Kroll is the perfect image of a New Yorker. He has the attitude of one who has been born and raised in the City: This is the best of all possible worlds and it's all mine!

The attitude is unique to those who are confident they have made the right choices. It was a chance comment that led Steven to children's books, and it was yet another right choice for him; so right that he has been steadily writing books for children since 1975.

Up until his decision to become a free-lance writer, he had worked as an editor and written novels in his spare time. He has the remarkable ability to see inside a large story to get to the smaller story, the one that has child appeal and humor. His writer's eye and voice get directly to the essence and the stories he creates are high in interest and eagerly read. More recently, that same ability has been finding its way into Steven's young adult novels, a new area of writing for him.

To leave a full-time position for a free-lancer's life is not an easy decision to make. For Steven, the security of a steady paycheck has given way to the freer style of making his own decisions and setting his own pace. It has worked for him.

For some people it may seem incongruous that a classically educated, urbane man writes stories for children. It is really not all that incongruous. It is more simply stated that he works in a field where incongruity is the norm—and that same incongruity allows a freedom and success of its own.

# THE INTERVIEW

J.R.    As is the case with many writers, you come from a strong publishing background. Why don't you fill in a few details?

S.K.    Well. I almost went to work for the *Paris Review* after I graduated from college in 1962.

When I was at Harvard I worked as a faculty aide at the Harvard University Press, which meant, curiously enough, that there were moments when I had to read manuscripts by my own professors. An interesting position for a student to be in.

When I got out of Harvard I had done two weeks as a summer reader at the Atlantic Monthly Press and met some New York publishing people, George Plimpton[1] among them. George gave me an unpaid job working out of the Paris office of the *Paris Review.* Supposedly I was to earn my money selling ads to Paris grocers. I wondered, since my French was not so great, how I was going to survive.

At that time I really wanted to be in London. So I stopped off in London on my way to Paris. I had with me a list of people to see. For three-and-a-half weeks I went in and out of people's offices, seeing London in my spare time. And I got myself a job as a reader at Chatto & Windus. I also became an associate editor of the *Transatlantic Review,* which was being edited in London at the time, and got myself assignments to review books for *The Spectator, The Listener,* the London *Magazine* and the London *Times Literary Supplement.*

By that time I was getting frantic telegrams from George. "Where are you? We're expecting you in Paris. Why haven't you shown up?" I finally called and said I was going to have to stay in London.

Shortly thereafter I started work at Chatto and met my future—now former—wife. We became the office romance.

J.R.    What was working in England like?

S.K.    My first day there was interesting. My ear was not familiar with English speech and the first day all my colleagues took me to lunch. There were Oxford accents, there were Midland accents, there were Cockney accents, there were West Country accents. I didn't understand anything anybody was saying! I don't know how I survived the lunch.

I was primarily a reader for Chatto. I read everything that came in, all the solicited as well as all the unsolicited manuscripts. I was reading five a day and loved it. After a while I got to do some editing. By the end I was both reader and editor.

The Chatto office itself is worth a story. The offices were built around this crazy courtyard. The people on part of the third floor had to go *through* one another's offices to get down the hall. So you'd be going in and out of doors saying, "Excuse me, excuse me. . . ."

And another wonderful story about Chatto. Ian Parsons, then the chairman, took me to a Society of Bookmen[2] dinner in honor of what was supposed to have been Alfred Knopf's seventy-fifty birthday. There were all these tributes for the occasion, and then Knopf got up to give his own speech and said, "I hate to tell you all this, but I'm only seventy!"

J.R.    Wonderful!
And from Chatto where did you go?

S.K.    I moved back to New York and worked at Holt[3] for three years. I was an adult trade editor there.

I had a kind of crisis of conscience at Holt, over a book of poems I wanted very much to publish. Everyone on the staff adored it, but my editor-in-chief said no—for various reasons of his own, most of them legitimate. That book, incidentally, was Lucille Clifton's first book of poems, *Good Times.*[4] Random House finally published it and it was named one of the best books of the year by the *New York Times.*

I realized at the time that life was like this in publishing. If you were an editor, even editor-in-chief, you would always have a boss and you would always have to abide by the decision of that boss, even if you didn't like it much.

I had always been interested in writing myself. At the insistence of my Harvard advisor, Walker Cowen, I had begun keeping a journal and writing fiction in London. I had even written a novel in London and another back in New York, but neither one was ever published.

During my crisis of conscience my agent said, "You shouldn't be doing this. You're too talented. Leave while you still can and go away and write." I was in a position where I hadn't grown too comfortable, too powerful, or too enmeshed to leave. If I were going to go, it was the right time.

So my wife and I decided to move to Maine.

J.R.    Why Maine?

S.K.    It was remote enough to avoid a deluge of weekend guests—and by accident we fell into a house to rent for eighty dollars a month. The decision was made for us.

So we saved our money for several months, moved all of our stuff to Maine, moved into the house and promptly blew all our savings on a cross-country trip driving to California. When we got back to Maine, we had next to nothing.

I began publishing book reviews in magazines and writing experimental adult short stories and novels. A couple of years later, my wife, who was then a children's book editor,[5] suggested I might try writing for children. I said, "Oh, no. I couldn't possibly. I don't know how to do that." And one night at a dinner party I got an idea for a children's story. I wrote it and it was bad.

But I discovered an important thing. I discovered that I liked doing it.

So, off and on for the next year or so, I did more picture-book stories for children. In the same way that nothing had happened with my adult books, nothing happened with my children's books. I began to despair, and my family began to despair of my ever earning an honest living again.

My wife and I finally agreed to move back to New York. Within a month of moving back I met Margery Cuyler[6] and we were off and running. I've been publishing with her ever since. And now I do two books a year for Holiday House and have done so since the fall of 1975. I have missed only one list since then.

J.R.   So you plan on a minimum of two books a year?

S.K.      Yes, at least two, usually more than two. I have had as many as six published in one year.

J.R.   How do you handle being edited by someone else since you are obviously capable of doing the same?

S.K.      I had some problems at first, but not anymore.

I also belong to a writing group of professional writers, some of whom are children's book writers and some not. We meet one evening every other week and read works-in-progress to one another. We've been doing this, with a slightly changing cast, for six years. The experience has been fabulous.

It's a support group and ever so much more than that. It's built up my ability to deal with criticism to such an extent that I no longer mind being reviewed and seldom mind dealing with editors.

When I read in the group, I bring a pad of paper and take notes on what everyone says. And then I go home with those notes and use them. What develops from the group is a fairly comprehensive picture of what you are doing right and what you are doing wrong. With that picture intact, it becomes possible to do whatever work needs to be done on the manuscript.

When I go to an editorial session, I do the same thing. I take notes on what's said and then go home and work.

My attitude toward constructive criticism is almost always positive. Mostly it becomes a tool for me to use. I'm always interested in what buyers, reviewers, anyone has to say about my work. I feel in some way I'll be able to use those comments in the future.

J.R.   Are you a very disciplined writer?

S.K.      Yes, because I like the good life too much.

When I'm working on something long, I work a schedule every day. I'm a slow starter, so in the morning I'll do all the things that are likely to interfere with writing: necessary phone calls, letters, appointments. Then I'll write all afternoon, usually about five hours. That's about as much as I can do and still be fresh. My best moments come about mid-afternoon. When I'm through, I'll usually go play squash or tennis and unwind.

On a very good day I'll do anywhere up to seven pages. Ordinarily it's about five or six. When I write my picture book stories, which are usually five or six pages total, I can do a draft in an afternoon.

J.R.     Do you suffer from the perennial writer's fear, writer's block?

S.K.     The short answer is no. The long answer is of course.

When it comes to isolation, I don't mind that. I love spending the day by myself, writing. My apartment is quiet, the phone bothers me sometimes but not much. I have the day to do my work, and most evenings and weekends I will spend with people.

As for "writer's block" itself, I don't suffer from it because I'm so accustomed to working with words and so accustomed to working as an editor. But I do suffer moments of anguish and doubt, particularly when I have just finished a project and feel I'm never going to have another idea and will never write again.

That, I suppose, is its own variety of writer's block.

J.R.     Don't you keep ideas in a file?

S.K.     I admire, I *adore*, those writers who say, "I have sixty-two projects going, I have enough ideas for the next twenty years." I say, "How is that possible?"

I get totally involved in what I'm working on. How could I have all these ideas for the next twenty years? Usually I will have a couple of ideas on tap. But they won't necessarily be ideas I've thought out and know I can work on next.

I've had to learn that that's part of the way I am as a writer. Yes, the well fills up again. Yes, there will be more stories to tell. It's a matter of being a little patient, getting some reading done, giving some talks, doing some thinking, relaxing. That next idea will be coming soon.

But I do have a tendency to panic and say, "Oh, I better go out and get a job." When I feel that happening, I tell myself it will be OK. But it's scary everytime. Deep down you really don't know if the well will fill up again. The panic never lasts more than a couple of weeks. But it lasts long enough to really drive me crazy.

J.R.     Well, you can always answer a backlog of mail during those dry spells. Do you get much?

S.K.     Lots. Unfortunately, much of it is of the "We've been assigned this class project in school and I've chosen you, please write back" variety. Sometimes I get a letter from a child who happens to love a particular book.

The best letter I ever got was from a first grader in Connecticut where I was going to speak the following week. This one read, "Dear Mr.

Kroll, My heart is beating because it's so anxious to see what you look like." The little girl was wonderful! She signed everything she wrote with her name and "Made in U.S.A."

I also get letters from adults who say they are organizing an exhibit. "Please send us a writing instrument." I say, "I'm sorry, but I cannot send my typewriter. It would be too expensive to mail." So I usually send a pen.

J.R.     How involved do you get with the art in your books?

S.K.     It depends.

I usually start with an idea that is a visual image for the first scene, what will, in fact, be the first picture in the book. Then I write from there. I might know nothing else when I start.

And if you choose the right artist with the right style for the story you have written, you know you will be getting what you see in your head. If I don't always choose the artist, I do approve my editors' choice of one. There have not been many instances when I have not been given that privilege.

Usually I see the dummy and go over the dummy with the editor. I do the same thing with the finished art.

J.R.     You certainly make things sound easy enough. Are they?

S.K.     When I first started writing professionally every day I sat down was agony. The act of writing was all agony.

A lot of people have tremendous difficulties finishing a book because they can never get it perfect enough. And there are also a lot of writers who find it very difficult to put words on paper.

I don't face those problems anymore. Writing for me is a joy. I know I can always rewrite if I don't like what I've got at the end.

We are taught in school how hard it is to write anything. Maybe it's unintentional, but we are given the impression that writing is going to be tough and we should approach it with a certain amount of trepidation.

That needn't be. When I teach kids writing I try to emphasize that writing is a natural act. And if we overcome the obstacles, it can become just that.

## Notes

[1] George Plimpton, a popular adult magazine editor and writer of sports and literary books.

[2] Society of Bookmen is a group of distinguished English publishers who meet for dinner once a month at Kettner's Restaurant in Soho in London.

[3] Holt, Rinehart & Winston.

[4] Lucille Clifton, *Good Times: Poems* (New York: Random House, 1969).

[5] Edite Kroll, formerly a children's book editor, now a literary agent.

[6] Margery Cuyler, editor-in-chief of Holiday House, also interviewed in this book on pages 51-58.

## BIBLIOGRAPHY

*Amanda and the Giggling Ghost.* il. Dick Gackenbach. New York: Holiday House, 1980.

*Are You Pirates?* il. Marilyn Hafner. New York: Pantheon, 1982.

*Banana Bits.* il. Maxie Chambliss. New York: Avon, 1982.

*Bathrooms.* il. Maxie Chambliss. New York: Avon, 1982.

*The Big Bunny and the Easter Eggs.* il. Janet Stevens. New York: Holiday House, 1982.

*The Biggest Pumpkin Ever.* il. Jeni Bassett. New York: Holiday House, 1984.

*The Candy Witch.* il. Marylin Hafner. New York: Holiday House, 1979.

*Dirty Feet.* il. Toni Hormann. New York: Parents Magazine, 1980.

*Fat Magic.* il. Tomie dePaola. New York: Holiday House, 1978.

*Friday the 13th.* il. Dick Gackenbach. New York: Holiday House, 1981.

*Giant Journey.* il. Kay Chorao. New York: Holiday House, 1981.

*The Goat Parade.* il. Tim Kirk. New York: Parents Magazine, 1982.

*Gobbledygook.* il. Kelly Oechsli. New York: Holiday House, 1977.

*The Hand-Me-Down Doll.* il. Evaline Ness. New York: Holiday House, 1983.

*If I Could Be My Grandmother.* il. Lady McCrady. New York: Pantheon, 1977.

*Is Milton Missing?* il. Dick Gackenbach. New York: Holiday House, 1975.

*Loose Tooth.* il. Tricia Tusa. New York: Holiday House, 1984.

*Monster Birthday.* il. Dennis Kendrick. New York: Holiday House, 1980.

*One Tough Turkey: A Thanksgiving Story.* il. John Wallner. New York: Holiday House, 1982.

*Otto.* il. Ned Delaney. New York: Parents Magazine, 1983.

*Pigs in the House.* il. Tim Kirk. New York: Parents Magazine, 1983.

*Santa's Crash-Bang Christmas.* il. Tomie dePaola. New York: Holiday House, 1977.

*Sleepy Ida and Other Nonsense Poems.* il. Seymour Chwast. New York: Pantheon, 1977.

*Space Cats.* il. Friso Henstra. New York: Holiday House, 1979.

*Take It Easy.* New York: Four Winds, 1983.

*That Makes Me Mad!* il. Hilary Knight. New York: Pantheon, 1976.

*T. J. Folger, Thief.* il. Bill Morrison. New York: Holiday House, 1978.

*Toot! Toot!* il. Anne Rockwell. New York: Holiday House, 1983.

*The Tyrannosaurus Game.* il. Tomie dePaola. New York: Holiday House, 1976.

*Woof, Woof!* il. Nicole Rubel. New York: Dial, 1983.

## AWARDS AND HONORS

*Amanda and the Giggling Ghost*
> Children's Choice Book

*The Tyrannosaurus Game*
> Children's Choice Book

## ADDITIONAL SOURCES

Commire. *Something about the Author.*
*Contemporary Authors.*
Ward. *Authors of Books for Young People,* Supplement.

Charles Mikolaycak

## BIOGRAPHICAL NOTE

Charles Mikolaycak was born in Scranton, Pennsylvania, on January 26, 1937. His acclaimed artistic career began after his graduation from Pratt Institute in Brooklyn, New York, in 1959, as an illustrator and designer in Hamburg, Germany. He went on to be a designer and picture editor at Time-Life Books until 1976, at which time he became—as he still is—an instructor at Syracuse University and a free-lance designer. Mr. Mikolaycak married Carole Kismaric in 1970. Some of his original art is held by the Kerlan Collection.

## PRELUDE TO THE INTERVIEW

Charles Mikolaycak* is considered by many to be one of the leading artist-designers at work in children's books today. His style is a sophisticated one, blending together unusual perspectives, styles, designs, and colors to a unified whole. His books, whether in color or black and white, stay in the mind long after they are closed.

When talking to him, it becomes apparent he is impassioned about what he does and how he does it. He has been involved with books and bookmaking for over twenty-five years and knows the profession intimately.

Chuck is continually at work, even while talking about it. His conversation refers to works-in-progress or those just completed, commenting on how a change here would do this or a change there would do that. He is a restless speaker, always in motion, whether folding and refolding a napkin, underscoring a comment with a cigarette drawing the invisible line in the air, or using silverware or glassware to form boxes to frame the image on the table as he speaks of it.

Even his conversational pauses are restless, preceding each with a measured, "Ah-h-h-h" before speaking. He is thinking, to be sure. What he is thinking is unknown. When it is said, whatever it is, it is not what has been expected.

---

*pronounced Mike-o-LAY-check

He brings to this interview an in-depth knowledge of all the art processes involved in bookmaking. A successful free-lance artist, he is as committed to excellence in the physical book as he is committed to art theory. Here, during the interview, is a glimpse of an artist at work, caught in the process of the considerations before the pen is set to the page.

## THE INTERVIEW

J.R.    Well, Chuck, shall we be "heavy," or "light?" What's your pleasure? Shall I ask leading questions?

C.M.    That's what I've been thinking about all day! *D'accord.* Go ahead. Shoot!

J.R.    Forget the leading questions. You don't need them. Let's just jump right in—you are now an artist, once a former art director. Describe what an art director does. Better yet, contrast the two.

C.M.    Hmm. OK.

Being an art director means getting what you want as far as design. And working with the illustrator to make the pictures, which is my realm, to live together.

I think the saddest thing of all is an art director who takes on the art direction of a project wishing that he or she were the illustrator. Because then it becomes picky.

As an illustrator I work with a couple of art directors who do very well by me—marvelous type, better than I thought of—but they don't say to me "Well, I wouldn't use that texture there." As an art director for Time-Life I was very careful to put myself back and say when I saw some artwork, "Well, it fits my space and my design, but I don't like the way this guy painted." I would never send the artist back and say "paint that sky over again to my specifications." It had to be his sky. It had to be painted the way he wanted it painted.

J.R.    Better explain that a little bit more.

C.M.    All right. If, in art for a book you look and see the sky is splotched or smudgy, and as an art director you wanted a clear, beautifully painted sky, smooth, smooth, smooth. In comes the art with brush strokes because the acrylics were drying out or the cat walked over it or something like that. And there is another illustration that follows. As an art director you say, "Let's see if the illustrator did the same thing. And on the one that follows . . . . If there is only one with smudges and splotches then you can say this doesn't match the others." But you cannot say "you did a smudgy, splotchy sky. I didn't want it that way. I didn't want the sky that the cat walked across."

J.R.    Well, why not? After all as the art director you are buying a look, an image, to fit a certain book.

C.M.    No. You're buying the artist for their feelings. If the art director wants to do the project, then he or she should do it. It's like teaching. You can tell someone how things should be done but if they're not done exactly the way you want them, don't blame it on the student. Go back and do it yourself because everyone will do it the wrong way. Provided they're sincere.

I think as an art director I was sincere. I'd say, "Here's what I have, this is the problem, and this is what we have to tell." And at Time-Life there was lots of didactic information to be told. If the artist came in with blue and green next to each other and I hated it, I wouldn't say, "Don't do that." Who am I to judge that? There are people who don't like polka dots, too.

I think there is a very fine line that has to be drawn between an art director-designer-illustrator. I despise illustrators who sit around and say this book is *mine* and I'm going to do what I want to do with it as much as I despise designers who say, "I will take your artwork and turn it into exactly what I want."

J.R.    Why? That's a terribly vehement thing to say.

C.M.    It's a joint venture. The illustrator wants a good-looking book. The art director wants a good-looking book. The editor wants a good-looking book. The publisher wants a good-looking book. So, the art director and the illustrator cannot want two different things.

J.R.    Then as an artist, what do you expect from the art director?

C.M.    Help me. Pick a typeface that looks good with my work. If I'm going off the end say, "Bring it back!"

The designer should talk to me about the surface of the picture. The editor should talk to me about the content of the picture.

J.R.    As a former art director don't you find yourself in conflict with the art directors that you work with?

C.M.    Well . . . I used to be rather presumptuous and give complete design and type specs and hand it in. Of course it completely alienated the designer and completely pleased the editor!

Now I try to say, "Look. This is what I'm trying to do. I want you, the designer, to make it look good as far as good type and so on. Editor, you look at this and say are you really telling me what the voice of the character is saying or what you want me to tell of this text?"

When that does happen I'm most happy. What I really want to do is work with three people to make really nice books—the editor, the designer, and myself.

J.R.    What about art designers who have much less experience than you in bookmaking?

C.M.    Let's put it this way.

I find it difficult working with them. In many instances it's them, not me. I have lots of credits as an art director and as a designer and I think some of those people know some of that and are therefore a little reluctant to say to me what they think.

The same way I, being in the position of an illustrator, don't necessarily want to enforce my role, my knowledge, as a designer on them because they are supposed to design. At the same time if they're doing some really bad stuff I wouldn't allow as a designer I have to say no. And all of a sudden I have to step out of my role as an illustrator and say, "That's not what I want. I don't like that."

J.R.    Isn't that somewhat of a pie-in-the-sky syndrome? I mean, for all intents and purposes your work is being bought for a reason, whether you like it or not.

C.M.    Well, I do enjoy having the freedom to do the whole book but I am not paid to do the whole book. I am being paid to illustrate.

And yes, I do have a problem working with designers because I've been there and I have some idea of what I want. I don't want to sit around saying which typographer to use. I'm not interested in the economics of the publisher I'm working with. I would like to say where to get the type but places I like are awfully expensive and publishers can't afford them. I *can* say I want such-and-such type and let it go at that.

I used to think about type and design before and not get paid for it. I'm not thinking about it anymore. I'm getting paid for the illustrations.

J.R.    I would say that most, if not all, of your books do receive that extra attention from publishers. They have that "designed" look that many don't have. You must be doing something right.

C.M.    I like to experience the incredible beauty that an illustrator feels when he is secure with a good art director.

J.R.    From the other side now, what do you do about an author who says to you about your art, "But that's not what I thought! Here's what I have in mind."

C.M.    Well I've had things like that, but not quite in that manner. I've been spared authors like that.

This is one of the main things I'm asked when I teach or talk, "How much does the author get involved in the pictures?"

Most people, even those in art classes, envision themselves writing books. So they're very presumptive of the fact that the author has all the say about everything. And I say, "No."

If the author doesn't say it in the text, then the author really doesn't have any say when it comes to the pictures. The editor is the marriage-maker, the match-maker. He or she will pick the illustrator he or she thinks will complement the text. That's probably the way it should be. Illustrators do not necessarily work well with authors because they have to work for themselves and they have to interpret their way. They're not there to transcribe someone else's visual ideas.

If the author says, "I simply love blue," there is no reason in the world the illustrator has to draw in blue unless the text says something is in blue. Then the illustrator has an obligation and a responsibility to do it in blue. But if the author does not mention blue in the text, and even while secretly loving blue, and the illustrator makes it in orange and the author hates orange, that is not a valid reason to turn down that illustration.

Do you realize what an illustrator does?

I draw the picture. You tell me the scene is "Betsy sitting down. She is thinking something." Period. I am going to have to illustrate that.

OK. We know Betsy is sitting down. We know how the body folds.

What is Betsy sitting on? A couch? In the living room?

Maybe earlier on you tell me what she looks like. What is she wearing at this point?

What time of day is it?

What's behind the couch? A picture window? A framed series of prints? And if so, of what?

What kind of things are on the floor?

What kind of lamp is in that room?

What things are next to Betsy?

What I'm adding up to is the whole feeling of what Betsy is thinking. If the details are not in the text, I, as illustrator, have to complete all the details.

Is it spring? Summer? Fall? Winter?

Is it dark? Light?

Is it a big couch? Does she feel small?

Is it a small couch? Does she feel big?

I don't know any of this. As an author you're not telling me anything except, "She is sitting down and thinking." And as an illustrator I have to visualize Betsy thinking.

I have to give a whole lot of things to flesh out the one sentence you gave. And not just flesh it out. But add to it. Illustrators add to things.

I'm afraid we've become very literate in reading sentences. We're not literate in reading pictures. We don't know how to read pictures.

J.R.     "We?"

C.M.     Adults. I think kids can read pictures easier than adults can. I think adults screen a lot. We've got so much going that we don't go back to the base for something. I think there is a whole level of post-adolescence syndrome of looking at pictures only on the surface. The same way you look at a movie. It simply goes by.

Whereas as a child or as a maker of pictures you have a tendency to "read" pictures. You look *into* pictures. You see this versus that. You see that little thing in the corner. You see that looming shadow on the wall. That's what pictures are about.

When I think of a thirty-two page picture book I think of a picture grabbing you, not as something that passes your eyeballs as you turn the page.

J.R.   Your work, as far as I'm concerned, certainly doesn't fall in that passing-by-your-eyeballs syndrome. The ones that stand out most in my mind are richly detailed and very sensual. One book that comes to mind that is indicative of your rich, sensual style is *I Am Joseph*. There have to be stories about it!

C.M.   Oh, yes!

I remember taking it into Dorothy[1] and saying, "Here it is." She just sat back and looked at it for about twenty minutes at which point my handkerchief was dripping from wiping myself. Actually, I wiped myself with my hat. She said, "Chuck. I love it. We're going to have problems with it." All I heard was, "I love it." The problems with it? Well, let's work with them later on. I was satisfied because I had worked for my editor and I satisfied the bond we both had.

I think it will be one of my major books. I'm at that point in life that you start thinking about your obituary and they only have room for three books. I think *Joseph* is going to be one of them. If I die tomorrow they will also mention *The Great Wolf and the Good Woodsman*. The rest will be forgotten.

But I won't die tomorrow. I don't have that third book yet!

J.R.   Talk some more about *Joseph.* There is no question it is a stunning book, a brilliant book.

C.M.   When I did it one reviewer chose not to review it right away. Dorothy was told by the reviewer, "I'd rather be turned on by *Playboy.*" She said thank you and hung up. She called me to tell me it wasn't going to be reviewed in that journal because of the seduction image.

So I got an eight year old, very normal. I read through the whole book with him. He didn't bat an eyelash at the seduction scene. He listened all the way. At the end he turned to me. He said, "Well, I have two things to say. First of all when Joseph was thrown into the pit by his brothers, why isn't he more bloody? Second, that scene where Joseph is with the naked lady. She's a fool. She's much too old for him." This rather technical eight-year-old kid is not at all concerned about the fact that Joseph is naked.

The point is, to get to any child you have to go through a barrage of adults.

And I was asked once to speak on morality in children's books. Of course they wanted me to talk about *Joseph*. I said to myself, "I've no reason to defend it. It is what it is. There are certain areas where you want to touch the figure because it almost comes out and touches you. I don't want to go into that. I don't want to spend another hour defending the book. There's nothing to defend. The book just is."

Reviewers from the Catholic and Jewish communities hate it because of what the text says and they love it because of what the text says. Some talk about being too naked. Some talk about not being naked enough. You can't please everyone. You just do what you do.

All I can do is sit down and say I just wish that book was reproduced better. The originals are beautiful. The book is a little bland as far as reproduction is concerned.

J.R.    Do you consider yourself an illustrator of books or an illustrator of children's books?

C.M.    For *Joseph* I went back to reading Thomas Mann's quartet[2] and for about two weeks read those books, making notes in the margins. He had done fantastic research. There's an awful lot in *Joseph* on how people treat each other, what conditions were like in prison, what pets people had. That is not necessarily there in the children's book. It is Mann's embellishment I'm using in Cohen's text. Is that a children's book? I don't know. But it is an illustrated book.

I sometimes now question talking about illustrating children's books at all. I'm not sure I do children's books. I do do illustrated books. *The Highwayman,* with all its blood and gore and lust, is my gothic for teenage girls! Is it a children's book? I don't know. I just am pleased by the fact that the format of children's books give me the opportunity of making an illustrated book on the subject.

J.R.    Since you're working primarily in a picture-book format or, rather in a format that is usually identified as a children's book, do you think about the child reader at all?

C.M.    I knew you would ask me that! Do I think about the kids?

Initially, no. It's all me at first. I think about myself. Doing what I want to do, exorcizing what I can't do, figuring out what my hands will permit me to do. There are things I cannot draw or design as well as I want to, which I work for all the time. I work more and more to improve my drawing and designing.

Once I've got the text in hand and the editor gives go-ahead approval with the pictures, I read through the book again. Initially I think of making a good picture, a good graphic, a good spread, basically building on another good spread that basically should make a good graphic book.

Then when I get into it, minor changes such as a kick of the leg one-eighth inch higher happen. I don't have to show that to an editor. That is maybe when I think of the person who will be looking at it, which is probably children.

I feel a certain responsibility to the child reader. But that's a difficult question because I don't know the kids who will be reading this book. But I do feel the responsibility in the sense that I'm wanting them to have the same kind of high I get from an illustration. Or I may want them to see the same point of view I'm making my illustration from. I obviously feel it is important or else I wouldn't have gone through a lot of thumbnails[3] and thoughts and decided on that point of view.

J.R.    Let's back up a bit. Talk about how you work.

C.M.    It's like this. If I'm reading a good book I've got two choices. One is to absolutely stop all work and read exactly five hundred pages, get it over with and get it out of my life. And then I can get down to work. Or, I can dole out the five hundred pages and read twenty pages a night, a chapter a night or something like that.

Well. I can't do a book of drawings over a weekend. I just can't. I mean, physically I can't.

If I could I might want to rush it through and say, "Wow! You're through!" What I do is dole it out to see how it's going. I want to like it as I go along. If I don't like it, I change to the next point. I get more into the next drawing than I did in the last one, and into each successive drawing of the book.

I plan each book so much in the beginning up here [taps his forehead] and on paper and in my heart. There is so much in the master scheme that what changes occur from the thumbnails to the finishes[4] can be few, like an actor on the stage where one night there's a slight nuance if you light your cigarette one way or another and the next night you pause before you light the cigarette. The art has to remain slightly living while I'm doing it. If I do the thumbnails and the editors say, "fine," I then do very complete sketches.

That's the way I work it. And that's what I like. When someone is marching through a field, it matters to me whether the knee is raised one-eighth inch or not.

What I do is give very complete sketches to the editor and art director so when I bring in the finishes whatever slight modifications or embellishments on my part have occurred are not so major and everyone is not completely thrown. I mean the figure hasn't moved from the left-hand side of the page when it was planned for the right-side of the page. But the knee has been raised or lowered one-eighth inch.

J.R.    What if you have a change of heart after you have shown something in an early stage of development—something that you haven't warned them about or shown them?

C.M.    Ah, then I go ahead and do it! I keep very much in mind all the comments that have been made and the efforts the art director has made in placing type. And I build the picture around the grid or format.

I've never really changed anything that radically. What I show them is not my first impressions. I *angst* a long time over thumbnails and little small sketches. I jump this way and that way. I try point of view. It's not my first impressions that I turn in.

My first impression is what I get when I first read the story. I make little marginal notes on the outside of the manuscript. Those are not important.

The notes that follow in the second, third, fourth, fifth rereading of the story and to the point when I clear my desk and get working are important. I draw them up on about a three-by-five card size, vaguely recognizable so someone can read them.

J.R.     How many sketches do you plan for in a thirty-two page picture book?

C.M.     I don't know. Sometimes you get thirteen pictures for a thirty-two-page book. Four or five will remain basically what I think the first feeling is what you get from the first reading of the book. The others you make changes in. Then on the second and third reading you evaluate what happens in the change from one to two to three. Will image one and two be alike because that's what happens when you're reading quickly. So image one, image three change a little bit. Image two, you've got to find a way of melding it from image one to image three. Sometimes not much happens. Change the point of view. Get up, get down. Get closer. You start making a movie.

J.R.     Why do you care so much about all this?

C.M.     Because . . . because it's all I've got. I've been the route of designer. I've been the route of art director. Those were very nice things to do. But I chose to be an illustrator and I enjoy it.

J.R.     But from an art view, isn't the concept, the form, of a book just another means of graphic expression?

C.M.     No, no, no! If it was just that it becomes a single means of expression that doesn't have anything to do with the concept of a book.

A book is not bound images. It is not a tablet. It is not a calendar. I can take sixteen images from sixteen different sources and as a graphic designer make the most magnificent calendar you can buy. I will whip that material into shape. I will force it all into the medium of a bound calendar. That is not a book. It is a bound calendar of sixteen images.

A book is not sixteen graphic images. A thirty-two page book is sixteen images that somewhat fold into each other, blend, meld with each other. You can draw, design, sequence. It is the crossing, the latticing of everything all the way along that line that makes it, I think, a book.

I've not always made great books. I've made some good books and I think I've made one or two great books. They work. I'm still looking, still finding. There is no formula.

J.R.  Name one of the books you've done that stands out in your mind.

C.M.  *The Binding of Isaac* moved me very much because it was all about sacrifice. The very final picture, the sacrifice, when Isaac was saved by his father and God.

Off into a corner there was a lot of smoke from the burning ram. There were pictures up there of Auschwitz and Jewish children with the yellow star. That was not seen by any reviewer. It was seen by a couple of people who write children's books. And when it has been pointed out, some people still don't see it. And it's not like an upside-down picture book or an optical illusion. They just don't see it. They cannot read pictures.

This is extraordinary to me. The eye can see the whole of it. And if it's there and pointed out to you, you can see it. You usually hear, "Oh, I see it now." Or, "What are you talking about?"

J.R.  But do others see it?

C.M.  Yeah, and ask about it. Which that picture was meant to do. It was meant to provoke something. It was meant to make the adult around ask, "What is that?"

J.R.  You have done a good number of books but have you managed to produce one book each season, in the spring and the fall, yet?

C.M.  No, no. It's very hard. I can no longer predict how long a book will take. Ideally, yes, one should do a book a season. But I can't because some take me six months or more to do.

I find my books being ganged, two in the fall, nothing in the spring, two more again in the fall. Ganged by circumstances because that's the way I turn them in. Some publishers can turn them over quicker and get them into production faster than others can. So I usually say to myself on the basis of being on time one, later on another, they have to decide to make it a spring or fall book.

It's not that I'm too slow, but it's just the way it is. Right now I'm about a year and a half behind on my contracts. The books are taking me longer and longer to do.

J.R.  Is it because of the nature of the your art and the books?

C.M.  Yes, I think it's that. I think, more, it's the nature of myself. I like doing it. I prolong it. I get more into it. I just love doing it.

With all of its *angst* and all of its horribleness in doing it, which is terrible at times, I like prolonging it. Is it a love affair? I don't know.

J.R.  Given your choice, what books would you like to illustrate?

C.M.  I'd like to do *Anna Karenina*,[5] *The Magic Mountain*,[6] Jean Genêt's *Our Lady of the Flowers.*[7]

But to correct you. When you say can it be illustrated you really mean, "Can you interpret it?"

There's a German book called *Children's Stories* and I'd love to do about six of them.

J.R.    From conversations I've had with other artists, you have a reputation as being "one of the most important children's book artists working today." You seem to be developing a very strong cult following.

C.M.    That's interesting because this is the first I've heard of it. But that's OK with me. I don't mind being a cult person as long as I'm with a good author. But when I hear an editor who says you and X cannot work together because your work is going to be stronger and will cancel out his or her text, I don't know what that means.

J.R.    What do you do to keep yourself interested in the work at hand? Do you have any little quirks?

C.M.    Well, I work with music an awful lot. Sometimes program music, sometimes not. I'll play a mass or a requiem when I want something solemn. Or if I'm finishing and I'm working too heavily, I'll put on an operetta or show tune.

The music doesn't really get me going. The music accompanies me when I am going. I block it out earlier. Because when I'm doing a drawing my attention is focused there. Sirens on the street? I don't hear them. Once I get the image blocked out I know where I'm going. In the heat of the drawing there is nothing else.

J.R.    But aren't you at least somewhat conscious of the musical background?

C.M.    I guess I am *somewhat* conscious of it, yes. There must be a consciousness but it doesn't interfere or apply. If I'm drawing blood from Oedipus' eyes and Offenbach is on the soundtrack, I don't hear it. I'm focused right where the blood is coming from in the eyes. Once that's done I can program the image. If it's a sad picture I'll put on something sad.

This is a new thing for me. I used to shut out music all the time.

J.R.    Has music particularly influenced any one of your books?

C.M.    *Peter and the Wolf!* For it I listened to seventy tapes of the music and I want more! I have it in all different languages. That's the librarian in me. The words are the same, the music is the same, but I'm still collecting and will continue to collect all the versions. They're all tapes of people reading the story, all recorded versions, some with music.

J.R.    There has to be a story behind that.

C.M.      There is.

J.R.      Which is?

C.M.      One day a long time ago someone called me and said come to my party. I said I couldn't because I was thinking of *Peter and the Wolf*. This fellow was working with records then that were going to be sold to the mass market. So he said he'd send me a recording of *Peter and the Wolf*. And he sent me Alec Guiness reading with the Boston Pops Orchestra. When I started working on the book I pulled the record out and started drawing.

I listened to it for about four days and decided I was getting bored with Alec Guiness. So I went out and bought Basil Rathbone and listened to that.

From there I went to collect other versions. And now Radio Moscow, Radio Budapest—all these people—are sending me recordings! I got these fantastic tapes from them.

I called everyone I knew from Time-Life, all the stringers in Finland or wherever and they all bought for me records and tapes. I now have seventy of them.

Now I'm working on getting it in Portuguese and other languages. It's not so crucial now that I'm finished with the book. And I can wait until I find someone going to Chile or wherever to fill in the gaps.

How did I get them? I called. At three o'clock in the morning I called Radio Budapest. And within two weeks they sent me a record.

My phone bill was horrendous!

They're wonderful to have, really.

Eleanor Roosevelt did one on a 78, which I'm looking for. And Joan Kennedy did one with the Boston Pops I'd love to have. I want people who have them in their attic to give them to me. I'll kiss them, but I won't give them a picture!

J.R.      Your *Peter and the Wolf* is a strong book for you. And it was the first to come along in many years. How did you come to do it?

C.M.      I was asked to do it. And when first asked I said, "I cannot do any better than Chappell's version.[8] I love what he did."

Then I made a presentation. I told the editor, Linda Zuckerman,[9] what I wanted to do, and how I felt about it, and off I went. I was overwhelmed that some of the reviewers thought my version was better than Chappell's. The fact that someone says it was better makes me think, "What does that mean?" My version is not better, it is just different. There's nothing wrong with being better if someone says you're better than someone you think is good. I don't think it's applicable in this case.

J.R.      Other than the books you mentioned earlier, what else would you really like to be doing?

C.M.      What I'd *really* like to do, I guess, is not very different from what I think I'm doing, illustrating books. I'm very pleased because I'm illustrating books. I've been very lucky to have been given some books with very heady themes or ideas.

As a child I spent more time with the pictures because I knew the story once it was read to me. I could look at a book fourteen, fifteen, sixteen times, but I kept looking at the pictures without asking my mother or father to read it to me again. I would pick out where the choice words were and I could go back and look at the pictures. I started reading the picture more than I started reading the text.

This was very crucial, I think. This was a time when there was no television. There was sound. Radio made me make my own pictures. There was the sound, there was the narrative, and there was making the pictures come in one's head.

## Notes

[1] Dorothy Briley, editor-in-chief of Lothrop, Lee & Shepard Books.

[2] Thomas Mann, *Joseph and His Brothers* (1934), *The Young Joseph* (1935), *Joseph in Egypt* (1938), and *Joseph the Provider* (1944). All translated by H. T. Lowe-Porter and published in the U.S. by Alfred A. Knopf.

[3] "Thumbnails" are artists' preliminary sketches, short for "thumbnail sketches."

[4] "Finishes" is short for "finished" or "final art."

[5] Leo Tolstoy, *Anna Karenina,* the classic Russian novel, first published in the U.S. by T. Y. Crowell in 1875.

[6] Thomas Mann, *The Magic Mountain.* tr. H. T. Lowe-Porter (New York: Alfred A. Knopf, 1927).

[7] Jean Genêt. *Our Lady of the Flowers.* tr. Bernard Frechtman. intro by Jean-Paul Sartre (New York: Grove Press, 1963).

[8] Serge Prokofieff, *Peter and the Wolf.* il. Warren Chappell. foreword by Serge Koussevitzky (New York: Alfred A. Knopf, 1940).

[9] Linda Zuckerman, then editorial director of children's books at Viking-Penguin, Inc.

## BIBLIOGRAPHY

*As Reteller/Illustrator:*

*Babushka: An Old Russian Folktale.* New York: Holiday House, 1984.

*As Adapter/Illustrator:*

*The Boy Who Tried to Cheat Death.* With Carole Kismaric. From a Norwegian tale by Peter Asbjornsen and Jorgen Moe. Garden City, N.Y.: Doubleday, 1971.

*As Illustrator:*

*The Binding of Isaac.* By Barbara Cohen. New York: Lothrop, Lee & Shepard, 1978.

*The Brothers Karamazov.* By Fedor Dostoevski. Tokyo: Kawade Shobo, 1967.

*Captain Grey.* By Avi. New York: Pantheon, 1977.

*A Child Is Born: The Christmas Story.* Adapted from the New Testament by Elizabeth Winthrop. New York: Holiday House, 1983.

*Children and Books,* 6th ed. By Zena Sutherland, Dianne L. Monson, May Hill Arbuthnot, Dorothy Broderick. Cover and part opening. il. Charles Mikolaycak. Glenview, Ill.: Scott, Foresman, 1981.

*The Christmas Spider: A Puppet Play from Poland; and Other Traditional Games, Crafts, and Activities.* By Loretta Marie Holz. New York: Philomel, 1980.

*The Cobbler's Reward.* By Barbara Reid and E. M. Reid. New York: Macmillan, 1978.

*Crime and Punishment.* By Fedor Dostoevski. Tokyo: Kawade Shobo, 1966.

*Delta Baby and Two Sea Songs.* By Richard Kennedy. Reading, Mass.: Addison-Wesley, 1979.

*A Fair Wind for Troy.* By Doris Gates. New York: Viking, 1976.

*The Feast Day.* By Edwin Fadiman, Jr. Boston: Little, Brown, 1973.

*The Feral Child.* By Eric Sundell. New York: Abelard-Schuman, 1971.

*The Gorgon's Head: A Myth from the Isles of Greece.* By Margaret Hodges. Boston: Little, Brown, 1972.

*The Great Wolf and the Good Woodsman.* By Helen Hoover. New York: Parents Magazine, 1967.

*Grimm's Golden Goose.* By Jakob Ludwig Grimm and Wilhelm Karl Grimm. New York: Random House, 1969.

*The Highwayman.* By Alfred Noyes. New York: Lothrop, Lee & Shepard, 1983.

*How the Hare Told the Truth about His Horse.* By Barbara K. Walker. New York: Parents Magazine, 1972.

*How Wilka Went to Sea and Other Tales from West of the Urals.* Tr. Mirra Ginsburg. New York: Crown, 1975.

*I Am Joseph.* By Barbara Cohen. New York: Lothrop, Lee & Shepard, 1980.

*In the Morning of Time.* By Cynthia King. New York: Four Winds, 1970.

*Johnny's Egg.* By Earlene Long. il. with Neal Slavin. Reading, Mass.: Addison-Wesley, 1980.

*Journey to the Bright Kingdom.* By Elizabeth Winthrop. New York: Holiday House, 1979.

*Little Red Riding Hood.* By Jakob Ludwig Grimm and Wilhelm Karl Grimm. Norwalk, Conn.: Gibson, 1968.

*The Man Who Could Call Down Owls.* By Eve Bunting. New York: Macmillan, 1984.

*Mourka, the Mighty Cat.* By Lee Wyndham (Jane Lee Hyndman). New York: Parents Magazine, 1969.

*The Nine Crying Dolls: A Story from Poland.* By Anne Pellowski. New York: Philomel, 1980.

*On Leadership.* By Carole Kismaric. Armond, N.Y.: IBM, 1974.

*The Perfect Crane.* By Anne Laurin. New York: Harper & Row, 1981.

*Peter and the Wolf.* By Serge Prokofiev. Tr. Maria Carlson. New York: Viking, 1982.

*The Pretzel Hero: A Story of Old Vienna.* By Barbara Rinkoff. New York: Parents Magazine, 1970.

*Russian Tales of Fabulous Beasts and Marvels.* By Lee Wyndham (Jane Lee Hyndman). New York: Parents Magazine, 1969.

*Shipwreck.* By Vera Cumberlege. Chicago: Follett, 1974.

*Signs and Wonders: Tales from the Old Testament.* By Bernard Evslin. New York: Four Winds, 1981.

*Sister of the Birds and Other Gypsy Tales.* By Jerzy Ficowski. Nashville, Tenn.: Abingdon, 1976.

*Six Impossible Things before Breakfast.* By Norma Farber. Il. with Tomie dePaola, Friso Henstra, Trina Schart Hyman, Lydia Dabcovich, and Hilary Knight. Reading, Mass.: Addison-Wesley, 1977.

*The Surprising Things Maui Did.* By Jay Williams. New York: Four Winds, 1979.

*The Tale of Tawny and Dingo.* By William Howard Armstrong. New York: Harper & Row, 1979.

*The Tall Man from Boston.* By Marion Lena Starkey. New York: Crown, 1975.

*The Three Wanderers from Wapping.* By Norma Farber. Reading, Mass.: Addison-Wesley, 1978.

*Tiger Watch.* By Jan Wahl. New York: Harcourt Brace Jovanovich, 1982.

*The Twelve Clever Brothers and Other Fools: Folktales from Russia.* Ed. and adapt., Mirra Ginsburg. New York: Lippincott, 1979.

### *As Designer/Picture Editor:*

*The Battle of Britain.* New York: Time-Life, 1976.

*Blitzkrieg.* New York: Time-Life, 1976.

*On Leadership.* By Carole Kismaric. Armonk, N.Y.: IBM, 1974.

*Prelude to War.* New York: Time-Life, 1976.

# AWARDS AND HONORS

*Babushka*
    Best Illustrated Children's Book

*Fair Wind for Troy*
    Library of Congress list

*Feast Day*
    Book Show

*The Great Wolf and the Good Woodsman*
    Book Show
    Brooklyn Art Book for Children

*The Highwayman*
    Fanfare Book
    *Parents Choice* Award

*How Wilka Went to Sea*
    Library of Congress list
    Notable Children's Book
    Notable Children's Book, 1971-
        1975

*I Am Joseph*
    Notable Children's Book

*The Perfect Crane*
    *Parents' Choice* Award

*Peter and the Wolf*
    Library of Congress list
    *Parents' Choice* Award

*Shipwreck*
    Book Show
    Showcase Book

*Tale of Tawny and Dingo*
    Book Show

*Tiger Watch*
    *Parents' Choice* Award

*Three Wanderers from Wapping*
    Notable Children's Trade Book
        in the Field of Social Studies

*Twelve Clever Brothers*
    Book Show

Gold Medal for Art Direction, Society of Illustrators

# ADDITIONAL SOURCES

Commire. *Something about the Author.*
*Contemporary Authors.*
Kingman. *Illustrators of Children's Books: 1967-1976.*
Ward. *Illustrators of Books for Young People.*

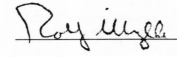

Rolf Myller

## BIOGRAPHICAL NOTE

Rolf Myller is an architect who was born in Nuremburg, Germany, on October 13, 1926. He graduated from Cornell University in Ithaca, New York, in 1951. In 1956 he married his wife, Lois, and they have two daughters, Elise and Corinne. Mr. Myller has also been published under the pseudonyms Rolf Milonas and David Smith. The de Grummond Collection holds some of his original work.

## PRELUDE TO THE INTERVIEW

Rolf Myller is the "Renaissance Man" personified. He is conversant and interested in all matters, whether they are financial, artistic, philosophical, scientific, or of general interest. He has seemingly achieved what many writers strive for: he is completely at ease in his world, continually amused and amazed by it, and moves easily within it.

His background in publishing includes selling books. He is able here to address bookselling, buying, and selling questions. He knows the buyer's language.

Rolf's books for children are unique. Drawing on his architectural background, they address complicated issues in meaningful and readable ways, making the difficult accessible. His ability in translating complex information has found another outlet in his puzzle and game books, which have enjoyed popular success. And beyond the books, he is also a game inventor. His studio is filled with various inventions and games created solely to amuse and entertain.

We have had to meet twice. Only part of the first tape is transcribable due to a mechanical breakdown of my tape recorder. The second interview builds on the first and is interrelated here.

# THE INTERVIEW

J.R.      How did you come to involve yourself in writing, especially with an architectural background?

R.M.      As an architect, I am totally preoccupied with "design." To me, writing and illustrating a book is just another form of design; words and pictures are tools with which to express an idea or a mood and to communicate a message—just as in architecture, where our tools are wood, sticks, and stones.

My wife Lois is now, as she was some thirty years ago, in publishing. Our relationship first brought me face to face with the making of books. I got turned on by the challenge; it was just another form of creativity, which to me implied making something from nothing. Well, not exactly . . . I should say, converting an abstract idea and packaging it so that others can appreciate it. For example, my first book idea came from a Dutch architect who had just come to the states. Having been used to the metric system, she quite logically but naively asked, "How big is a foot?" My answer, which involved relativity, became the subject of the book and her question, the title.

J.R.      You imply that when you work on your books, you are also concerned with design?

R.M.      Indeed. My stories always evolve graphically. In children's books as well as in my "how to" books such as *The Design of a Small Public Library,* the format, the type, the relationship of the illustrations to the text and even the layout of the consecutive pages all have been given consideration from the earliest drafts on. With that, I feel that I can get a visual equivalent of a tone of voice, build up suspense, and set up rhythms almost as in poetry. Yes, call it visual poetry. But to me this differs little from the coordination and integration of the many elements that make up a beautiful building.

J.R.      But with books, isn't that the responsibility of the publisher?

R.M.      To a large degree it is; or better, it should be. Personally, I have worked with houses that have been efficiently coordinated and are able to translate the manuscript into a handsome product and distribute it well. I stress distribution, since this is a most important aspect that requires just as much imagination and skill as any other part of publishing. But to my horror, I have worked with more houses that are staffed with amateurs and lack sensitivity, imagination, and knowledge. Just to mention a specific case, on one of my books (that no thanks to the publisher sold about a hundred thousand copies), the person in charge for promotion discussed the marketing program, without once having looked at the book! But let's not get into the proverbial complaining that all authors do, though I feel more qualified than most others because I had the chance to see the workings of the publishing process from the inside. You see, I once took a couple of years' sabbatical from my real life to write a novel. Meanwhile, to help pay the rent, I became a sales representative for a small, prestigious publisher. The job required but a few weeks work a season, which left me time for writing, but did give me the opportunity to witness the anachronistic state of the field, and to see how many potentials were lost or wasted.

J.R.    "Potential" is the key word, don't you think? Book sales, in general, have never been much to jump up and down about. There are all sorts of theories on why books don't sell in larger numbers and why distribution isn't better. What's yours?

R.M.    Partly, it's because of so little communication between the departments at the publishers. Different disciplines in the same office.

It's just like there is so little communication between architects and engineers. When I was teaching at Pratt, the interior designers didn't talk to the architects who didn't talk to the engineers. Even in the faculty dining rooms people of different specialties sit at different tables and don't talk to each other.

The same at a publishing house. To the best of my experience, most publishers don't have the necessary coordination among marketing, sales, and editorial. Very often, the left hand doesn't know what the right is doing.

J.R.    Certainly the lack of communication inside a publishing house can adversely affect your potential income via your royalty check. Or can you really make that much money from a single book, regardless of how it's marketed?

R.M.    Of course, it *all* depends on the book and how it's marketed. As you well know, even a bum book can make it if properly backed. Mind you, I didn't say *will* make it, or that a good book *won't* make it on its own merit, because there are always exceptions. Flukes. But a business can't depend on that. And if a writer and illustrator is doing his thing for a living, it is a business, which means he or she has to get royalties, which incidentally doesn't mean that the creative process isn't any less satisfying or less painful or the product less good, unless of course he compromises his work to please the market.

But in answer to your question I think a book's success depends on the subject, the mood of the times, the quality of the book itself, of course, and other variables. It doesn't take genius to figure out for example that my *Fantasex* which is about erotic games, sold better than my book on Community Mental Health Centers. Incidentally, the research and writing of the former was a lot more fun.

J.R.    What about the novel you mentioned? Where is that now?

R.M.    It's a historical story that combines events from the Bible and Herodotus. The manuscript has been rejected by many and is now resting on the shelf. I will go over it again because I suspect that the editors may be right and that there is room for improvement.

It may be of interest to mention that I used a graphic approach in the planning of this work of fiction. I started by plotting the story on a ten-foot-long tracing paper, juggling the interplay of the characters back and forth in relation to the overall picture and working with overlays. I fiddled events and relationships around to achieve well-balanced chapters. Before starting to write, I had a complete road map for the book.

J.R.    Were you able to follow that outline?

R.M.    To an extent only. Once I began writing, the characters took on a life of their own and zap! they went all over the place, fell in love with the wrong people and that sort of thing, and it was hard to get them back into line. But I did it gently and with respect to their idiosyncracies.

J.R.    I understand you helped build a library. What is the story behind that?

R.M.    It started in the army where I served on garbage details, kitchen police, and demolition teams and then, via the hospital, ended up in the military government in Japan. Here I was assigned to organize a library, which I did by begging, borrowing, and stealing books from the various army posts, many of which received cartons containing books of the same titles. By going from company to company in a jeep, I swapped duplicates and assembled a comprehensive collection which, as far as I know, became the nucleus of the first American-style library in Japan.

It did give me a wonderful chance to see the country the way it was before it became westernized.

J.R.    After the dropping of the bomb, that must have been a difficult situation for you there.

R.M.    It was interesting. Personally, however, I was lucky never to have had to do any killing. But I don't think that any one of us there and then fully understood the horrors of the atomic bomb. The numbers who died and the destruction of the conventional warfare had been so overwhelming that we were unable to isolate the atomic tragedy and assign to it the proper horror quotient.

But I was struck by the waste, the poverty and hunger. The Japanese were polite but never shared with us their feelings, though they made me comfortable and accepted, probably because of my commitment to their library.

I would love to return to Kyoto, though I am sure that I won't recognize the place. I experienced that century jump of change that took place in a ten-year span, in Greece. I lived there before the war, and when I returned I couldn't even find the house I grew up in.

J.R.      You lived in Greece? When?

R.M.      I lived there from the age of eight to fifteen. I was born in Germany, a Jew, and when one day in 1934 my dad was tipped off that the Nazis were going to arrest him he escaped that very night to Greece, where the family followed him some time later. Again, in 1941 when the Germans invaded Athens we got out in time and via Palestine, Egypt, East and South Africa, Brazil, and Trinidad, I ended up in Cleveland Heights, Ohio, at the age of sixteen, wearing short pants, the last, an experience as traumatic as being strafed by a Stuka dive bomber.

There was a report when we left Greece that our ship had been torpedoed and some bodies had been identified as my Dad and me. Years later, in the cafeteria at Cornell I met an old classmate from Athens, who stared at me with disbelief. Holding on to his tray for support he gasped, "You are Rolf Myller . . . and you should be dead." Fortunately, he was only part mistaken.

J.R.      We became sidetracked . . . finish telling me about your involvement with libraries.

R.M.      Oh yes, sorry. Years ago when Lois and I were camping in Maine, we ran out of toilet paper. We approached our nearby lean-to neighbor, who was kind enough to share his roll. He was Sam Prentiss, a librarian, who that night, over the camp fire, spoke of his dream for a much-needed book on the subject of the design of small libraries. We exchanged ideas, and when Sam became commissioner in New York State in charge of libraries a few months later, he commissioned me to do the book.

J.R.      Terrific. What about the children's books?

R.M.      Well, nothing much exciting. I've got the *Maze* books with Pantheon, the *Bible Puzzle* with Harper & Row, and the *Symbols,* the *Very Noisy Day* and some others with Atheneum/Scribner, and I am always working on one or two new ones. I do them for the fun, for love, but unfortunately not for profit. For me, financial reward for the time invested in writing and illustrating kids books, not counting the completed unpublished ones in the drawer, comes to an hourly wage below the figure that the government considers minimum. You really have to be a prolific, dedicated pro who is consistently good to be successful. But isn't that true with everything else?

J.R.      By training you are an architect. What sort of things have you done as an architect?

R.M.      As with my books, as an architect I have been a generalist. My work has ranged from design of furniture to the planning of towns for tens of thousands. My office produced the master plan for New York State

College at Geneseo with most every type of building on it, an office building in Ethiopia, low-cost housing for Israel, systems for industrialized housing, schools, monuments . . . .

J.R.     Monuments?

R.M.          Yes, I was one of the finalists in the competition for the Memorial planned for Franklin D. Roosevelt in Washington. That was some time ago, and I even had the honor of being invited for tea at Mrs. Roosevelt's, who sent to Hyde Park a photograph of my sculpture, part of the design. I was told that the original is someplace in the basement of the White House. Anyway, you see the work ranged all over the ballpark. It was a fun office.

J.R.     Are you still practicing?

R.M.          No more. My partner, Henryk Szwarce, who had been one of the Marines whom they made trot across the Yucca Flats in Nevada in the wake of the atomic tests—he got cancer a few years ago and died at forty-six. And me, I stupidly got a stupid dose of Parkinson's disease, which knocked out my drawing hand, so I opted to switch to a new and exciting career. At this time I am harnessing all my creative efforts to the marketing of Danfoss thermostatic radiator control valves—and don't ask me what that is, we don't have the space for that here. And most recently, I am doing the same with Runtal, which is the world's most beautiful radiator!

J.R.     Some switch. But are you still writing?

R.M.          Is there a cat that doesn't like fish? Of course I am. I can still sort of type, and am looking forward to the acquisition of a word processor. And I illustrate with paper cutouts and collages. I can even draw by overdosing on the little yellow pills, which I have to do sparingly because one of the side effects is hallucinations. In my case, these take the form of little white rabbits hopping around when I work. And my wife, Lois, doesn't mind, because the bunnies seem to be well-behaved and house broken.

# BIBLIOGRAPHY

## As Rolf Myller:

*Automobile Dealerships.* Detroit: Ford Motor Co., 1965.

*The Bible Puzzle Book.* San Francisco: Harper & Row, 1977.

*Community Mental Health Centers.* Washington, D.C.: HUD, 1966.

*The Design of the Small Public Library.* il. Lewis Silverstein. New York: Bowker, 1966.

*From Idea into House.* House designed by Rolf Myller and Henry Szwarce. il. Henry Szwarce. New York: Atheneum, 1974.

*How Big Is a Foot?* New York: Atheneum, 1962.

*Mazes: 60 Beautiful and Beastly Labyrinths with Solutions.* New York: Pantheon, 1976.

*New Mazes: 60 Beautiful Yet Rotten Labyrinths with Solutions.* New York: Pantheon, 1979.

*Rolling Around.* New York: Atheneum, 1963.

*Symbols and Their Meaning.* New York: Atheneum, 1978.

*A Very Noisy Day.* New York: Atheneum, 1981.

### As David Brown:

*Someone Always Needs a Policeman.* New York: Simon & Schuster, 1972.

### As Rolf Milonas:

*Fantasex.* New York: Grosset & Dunlap, 1975; new ed., Perigee Books, 1983.


## AWARDS AND HONORS

*From Idea into House*
>Library of Congress list
>Notable Children's Trade Book
>>in the Field of Social Studies
>Outstanding Science Trade Book
>>for Children

*Symbols and Their Meaning*
>Library of Congress list
>Notable Children's Trade Book
>>in the Field of Social Studies


## ADDITIONAL SOURCES

Commire. *Something about the Author.*
*Contemporary Authors.*
Ward. *Authors of Books for Young People.*

_Elise Primavera_ (signature)

Elise Primavera

## BIOGRAPHICAL NOTE

Elise Primavera was born on May 19, 1954, in West Long Branch, New Jersey. In 1976 she received a bachelor of fine arts degree from the Moore College of Art in Philadelphia, and has continued to study at the Arts Students League in New York City. From 1976 through 1979 she was a free-lance fashion illustrator and since then has been a free-lance book illustrator.

## PRELUDE TO THE INTERVIEW

Elise Primavera is relatively new to children's book illustration. At the time of this interview she had published five books, anticipating a bright future of more to come.

She brings to her interview a freshness of view and purpose that is characteristic of someone entering a new career.

Elise didn't intentionally start out in children's books. After an attempt to be a professional equestrian, she changed her plans midway. She now raises horses as an avocation rather than a vocation. And even then it wasn't straight to children's books; she made a detour in fashion illustration first. She is now comfortable with books and intends to stay a while.

Elise is overwhelmed—and pleased—with the unlimited possibilities that book publishing offers an artist. Unlike the high-pressure, committee-oriented world of commercial art, she finds publishing a welcome relief and a chance to explore her talent and ideas.

As she grows in her craft she sees new horizons. Next to the actual creation of the art, that is one of the more exciting aspects of publishing for her. Because of her prior experiences she appreciates these horizons more than many people who directly enter the field. Options that are granted to artists are generally few, but in publishing one is expected to utilize a full range of talent. And that pleases Elise more than anything else.

## THE INTERVIEW

J.R.    Moving from fashion illustration to children's books has—or at least, must be—quite a change. How do you like working in books so far?

E.P.    On the whole I'd have to say that I like illustrating children's books. I guess what I like is the freedom that I'm given. My only limitations are the number of pages, the amount of text, the size of the book and whether the art is preseparated, full color, or black and white. Aside from that I'm on my own.

And it's been my experience so far that editors are more than happy to let me do the books in the most imaginative and creative way that I can.

J.R.    Are you learning as you go along or have you, to your way of thinking, found your style?

E.P.    I'm definitely learning as I go along. I was, as you know, a fashion illustration major in art school, and although I learned a lot about figure drawing and composition, I left school with very little knowledge of color theory or printing or reproduction processes such as how to do color separations. And I had no knowledge of how one went about illustrating a book.

As far as having found a style I'd have to say that my style presently is that I have none! Each book I've illustrated so far looks different. I like to fashion a style to fit the mood of the book. I consider it part of the whole creative process of illustrating the book.

J.R.    What is the difference between fashion illustration and book illustration?

E.P.    Fashion illustration is more commercial than book illustration. It's actually a form of advertising. Many times being a fashion illustrator means working on quick sketches or doing finished art from the layout artist's sketches.

I worked as a free-lance fashion illustrator for about three years. I did catalogs and some newspaper work. I eventually stopped doing it because I found it to be unfulfilling to me creatively.

J.R.    Was there an actual turning point for you in making the switch from fashion illustration to children's books?

E.P.    At the end of three years of free-lancing I found myself doing catalog work for *Seventeen Magazine*. I felt very restless doing this type of work and I wasn't making very much money. I had always had an interest in children's books but I didn't have the confidence in my ability to pursue the field. However, more and more I could see that what I was doing was going nowhere for me.

So I went to an illustrators' workshop and felt very encouraged after three weeks. I spent the summer of 1979 putting a portfolio together to show publishers. At the time I had an agent who took my work around to fashion people. I decided to leave her and take my children's book port-folio around myself.

J.R.   Yourself? Wasn't that a bit risky?

E.P.   Yes, but this time I was a lot more knowledgeable as to how to go about it than I was with my fashion portfolio. I was organized and relent-less! I saw everybody and anybody who would give me an appointment and once I got in the door I'd always ask if there was anyone else that could see me while I was there.

J.R.   What was the first break?

E.P.   A book jacket for Harper & Row. A few months later I got a pic-ture book from Margaret McElderry[1] and in my going around I heard of, and met, and began to work with Dilys Evans,[2] who has been my agent since 1980.

J.R.   Are there any outside influences that led you to children's books?

E.P.   I've always admired the artists associated with Howard Pyle and the Brandywine School.[3] I love the way children's books were illustrated in the early 1900s. I especially like N. C. Wyeth,[4] Jessie Wilcox-Smith,[5] and Charlotte Harding.[6] I became familiar with these artists from visiting the Brandywine Museum in Chadd's Ford, Pennsylvania. I lived in that area for about three years because I was a serious competitive equestrienne and the Unionville-Chadd's Ford area offered excellent training facilities for me.

J.R.   A long shot question. Are there any similarities between training to ride horses and training to illustrate books?

E.P.   Yes. I feel there are many similarities between any demanding sport and art.

To be an athlete or an artist requires discipline, sacrifice and some sort of vision of what one is trying to accomplish, be it the way one believes books should look or the way one believes she can make a horse perform or her body perform.

J.R.     You mentioned earlier a lack of confidence in your art. Are you gaining it as you go along?

E.P.     Yes. More and more I am. I think I have more confidence in myself as an artist than I did as a rider. But I feel that my struggle has been more in trying to decide what is more important to me—the art or the riding—rather than trying to gain confidence in either.

I've always felt incredibly torn between the two. So I've led a sort of schizophrenic life, dividing myself between the rider and the artist. Consequently, I've excluded everything else simply because the two are so consuming and demanding. But more and more my priorities are with my artwork, and the horses have become my enjoyment rather than a competitive thing.

J.R.     Do you have some sort of local support group to discuss your work with?

E.P.     I take classes at the Art Students League in New York. I talk to my agent, Dilys, and whichever editor I happen to be working with at the time. And if that's not enough I always have my unarty friends out here in New Jersey. They're all involved in horses but they suffer through the traumas of whichever book I'm working on at the moment with me.

J.R.     You're getting exposed to a number of editorial styles. What do you look for in an editor?

E.P.     Someone that I can have a rapport with. Who will give me plenty of room to explore all areas. Someone who I believe has good taste that I can trust so that when they say something doesn't work I can believe them.

J.R.     What's your work day like?

E.P.     I start early, usually around seven o'clock. I work straight through until three o'clock or so. Then I go look after my horse and run. And then do errands. That's pretty much the day for me.

As far as my work time goes I spend much of it working out the sketches and dummy and the "look" of the book. I try to capture its mood through an appropriate style. This takes a good deal of time because I'm not always comfortable or facile in a particular style. So I spend a lot of time not only on sketches, composition, and characterization (and the dummy in general), but also on the finishes because sometimes I have to work out technical problems because I'm working in an unfamiliar medium. This brings us back to me learning as I go along. I hope I'll be able to speed up this process in the future!

J.R.     Do you ever pretest your ideas on children?

E.P.        No.
         In so far as being a writer-illustrator I do what interests me and hope
         that kids will find it entertaining as well.

J.R.     How aware are you of your ultimate audience—children—when working
         on your books?

E.P.        I find it impossible to understand what kids will find funny or
         interesting! The one thing I do keep in mind is to make the most bizarre
         thing seem possible and real to the reader. It's sort of like watching a
         good magician perform: you know he really can't be pulling that rabbit
         out of the hat, but it all looks so real that for a moment something magical
         really is happening. This is the response that I try to work for through my
         illustrations.

J.R.     Where do you see yourself in five years?

E.P.        I see myself doing basically what I'm doing now but working more
         on my own projects and being able to pick and choose which books I
         illustrate. It's difficult for me to say which direction I'll go in because I'm
         interested in many different aspects of art from portrait painting to
         animation. I enjoy writing as well as illustrating other people's work and I
         can work alone. But I can see myself collaborating at some point. I feel
         that right now I'm in a state of transition and that all I can do is keep
         working and leave myself open for other opportunities that might present
         themselves.

## Notes

[1] Margaret McElderry, director of Margaret K. McElderry Books, a division
of Atheneum Publishers.

[2] Dilys Evans of Dilys Evans Fine Illustration.

[3] The Brandywine School takes it name from the Brandywine section of
Pennsylvania, near Chadd's Ford, where Howard Pyle taught his students.

[4] N. C. Wyeth, illustrator of many twentieth-century children's classics,
including *The Boy's King Arthur, Sir Thomas Malory's History of King Arthur
and His Knights of the Round Table,* edited by Sidney Lanier (New York: Charles
Scribner's Sons, 1918), and *Robin Hood* (Philadelphia: David McKay, 1917).

[5] Jessie Wilcox Smith, one of Howard Pyle's more noted students, also an
illustrator of many twentieth-century children's classics including *Little Women* by
Louisa May Alcott (Boston: Little, Brown and Co., 1922), *Dicken's Children* (New
York: Charles Scribner's Sons, 1912) and *The Jessie Wilcox-Smith Mother Goose,
a Careful and Full Selection of the Rhymes* (New York: Dodd, Mead & Co., 1914).

[6] Charlotte Harding was also a student of Pyle's and illustrated *Verses for Jock and Joan* by Helen Hay (New York: Fox, Duffield & Co., 1905), among others.

## BIBLIOGRAPHY

*Always Abigail.* By Joyce Saint Peter. Philadelphia: Lippincott, 1981.

*Basil and Maggie.* Philadelphia: Lippincott, 1983.

*The Bollo Caper.* By Art Buchwald. New York: Putnam, 1983.

*The Giant's Apprentice.* By Margaret Wetterer. New York: Atheneum, 1982.

*The Joker and the Swan.* By Dorothy Crayder. New York: Harper & Row, 1981.

*The Mermaid's Cape.* By Margaret Wetterer. New York: Atheneum, 1981.

*Santa and Alex.* By Delia Ephron. Boston: Little, Brown, 1983.

*The Snug Little House.* By Eila Moorhouse Lewis. New York: Atheneum, 1981.

*Surprise in the Mountains.* By Natalie Savage Carlson. New York: Harper & Row, 1983.

*Uncle George Washington and Harriot's Guitar.* By Miriam Anne Bourne. New York: Putnam, 1983.

_Ellen Raskin_ (signature)

Ellen Raskin

## BIOGRAPHICAL NOTE

This talented and beloved children's book author-illustrator was born in Milwaukee, Wisconsin, on March 13, 1928. Ms. Raskin died in New York City on August 5, 1984. She attended the University of Wisconsin through 1949 and then began her thirty-year career as an illustrator and designer. She married Dennis Flanagan in 1960 and had a daughter, Susan. Her original work can be found in the Cooperative Book Center, the Kerlan Collection, and at Rutgers University.

## PRELUDE TO THE INTERVIEW

Ellen Raskin and I had to reschedule our first meeting because of a major blizzard that hit New York City. Our roofs, with too much snow on them, had to come first. When we did get together it was in the spring, when the leaves were new and fresh.

She is relaxed during the interview, being no stranger to them. Her responses are immediate. It is when she begins talking about her work that she slows and becomes more considered.

It was Ellen's sense of innovative design and graphics that brought her to public attention in 1966 when she published _Nothing Ever Happens on My Block._ It was apparent then that here was a new voice, indeed; the problem was the voice was so new that it tended to confound people in the beginning. Since that book, Ellen Raskin has come to be known for her typographical, design, and text surprises. Even more difficult is that she has maintained a fresh and highly original voice with each publication.

Each of her books is a logical progression that can be calculated mathematically. An astute businesswoman, she has devised her books in an unobtrusive systematic way, using numerical precepts. Nothing ever happens accidentally in an Ellen Raskin book: it is intentional and it is there for a reason, including the exact spot where a page breaks or where a graphic element is to appear. Hers is a unique ability and one for which children's books have become all the richer.

Ellen is also a restless writer, rewriting manuscripts until the right mood, the right tone, the right character is met. By nature she is a quiet person, preferring the closeness of a few to a crowd. It is in her books that we see the blossoms of her solitude.

## THE INTERVIEW

J.R.     You have managed to work your way up the publishing ladder to the top. An Ellen Raskin book has come to mean certain things to buyers, so in a sense you've become a "brand-name product." How does it feel?

E.R.     Oh, that's the last thing I want. The last thing I want is for people to think all my books are the same. I want them to be surprises. Each of the books is of itself. That's what's so nice about doing books.

J.R.     Was there a beginning to all this?

E.R.     I was trained in fine arts, but that's no way to make a living. So I got a job in an art studio to learn the mechanical processes.

Then I bought myself a printing press and some type and learned about type that way. I printed woodblocks with type in experimental forms, made up a sample book, and started showing them around to art directors.

I had only two hundred dollars in the bank at the time. As luck would have it, I got one thousand dollars of assignments the first week! I had no trouble starting and was never without work after that.

I did calendars, pharmaceutical ads, magazine illustrations, posters, and over one thousand book jackets. That was about 1953-1956. It was strictly commercial work and I decided I had to do something else.

J.R.     Which was books?

E.R.     Yes. I decided to take a month off, not accepting any assignments, to see if I could do a children's book. It took about *three* months! Also, I ended up doing two books at one time.

Earlier Doubleday called me to do a jacket for a book called *Improvisations in Music.*[1] As a child I wanted to be a musician so I studied piano and became a fine artist! But all I could do was read notes, I never really played. This book opened it all up for me.

I sat down and started improvising. It was great! So I took Blake's *Songs of Innocence* and started writing music to it. I happened to mention it to the art director at Doubleday who mentioned it to the children's book editor. The art director asked me to show the editor a sample, which I did.

At the same time I roughed out an eighteen-page dummy of *Nothing Ever Happens on My Block* and submitted it to Jean Karl[2] at Atheneum.

I was so dumb then. She explained to me that a book had to be either twenty-four or thirty-two pages. She had to *tell* me that!

But she sent me a contract anyway.

And Doubleday sent a contract.

So then I took off six months and did both of those books.

I kept asking myself the whole time why I was doing *Nothing Ever Happens on My Block* because it was so cartoony and the Blake book was very arty.

J.R.    That's a nice way, though, of breaking into what is considered a tough field.

E.R.    But then I went back to taking assignments because I had to make money.

About six months later I asked Jean if there were any reviews on the book. "There is," she said, "but I don't think you want to hear it." I told her I did. That review would decide if I would keep publishing books or go back to free-lancing. I asked if it was "important." She said, "Very." The book had a short review which said basically, "a boring book, not recommended."

What happened, it seems, is that one person *read* the text to a library selection committee and no one looked at the pictures where all the action is.[3]

I thought at the time, "OK, I'll go back to my other stuff." I wasn't devastated because I had a career in illustration.

J.R.    You obviously didn't go back for very long. What happened?

E.R.    A week later Jean called back and said, "Congratulations! You won the *Herald Tribune* Award for the best picture book of the year!" So I decided, "Well, maybe I'll try another book."

Then the *Herald Tribune* went on strike and the review was never published! Even the awards party was postponed. They did send me the winner's check, though.

But I kept taking assignments until book royalties started coming in.

J.R.    So that got you started in illustration and picture books. How did the novels come about?

E.R.    I had lunch with Ann Durell.[4] I had done some illustrations for books she published by other authors. She said, "I want you to do a book for me." I said, "I'd love to, Ann, but I'm with Jean." Then she said, "A novel." "A novel?! But I'm an illustrator," I said. "Well, write about your childhood," she said. "About your childhood in Milwaukee during the Depression."

I started writing, and writing, and writing, and out came a novel that had nothing to do with my childhood in Milwaukee, *The Mysterious Disappearance of Leon (I Mean Noel)*.

J.R.      What followed that?

E.R.        *Figgs & Phantoms.*
          I put so much of myself in that book, I really did. I thought I had sold my soul. And if no one understood it, I figured I always had my picture books to fall back on. As an illustrator you get used to being rejected so I was steeled for whatever might happen.
          I said to Ann, "I know it's not going to get the Newbery, but this has to be an honor book. I put so much of myself into it, that it has to be." Ann said, "Please don't get your hopes up. It's too strange. You know that."
          I repeated, "It has to." And sure enough, it was. There were four honor books that year, and *Figgs & Phantoms* was one of them.

J.R.      Was the reaction the same to *The Westing Game*, your Newbery Medal book?

E.R.        Actually, when I handed it in to Ann, I said, "This is definitely *not* a Newbery Medal book. It's too much fun. But *next* time . . . ." She sighed and said, "All right, next time."

J.R.      Did you intentionally set out to write a Newbery Medal book?

E.R.        Not really, but I had set up the Newbery as a goal for myself. But when most of the reviews and recognitions are so great, the hope builds up and you start to think, "Maybe I can."
          I remember the day the medal winner was to be chosen. My husband had asked me why I washed and set my hair. And I answered, "In case the phone rings!"
          We are usually in bed by ten o'clock. The phone didn't ring. We stayed up until midnight. It still didn't ring. My husband was so tired and kind. He said, "I really want to see you win."
          We finally went to bed at one o'clock, with me repeating to myself Ann's words: "Next time."
          At two-thirty the telephone rang. I was going to hold out for three rings but I got it on the first!
          Pat[5] said, "Congratulations!" And I asked, "Is it an honor book?" She said, "No, it's the Medal." My husband broke open a bottle of champagne at three o'clock in the morning.

J.R.      How much of yourself comes out in your books?

E.R.        Everything in my books has to have a happy ending. I hated being a child in the Depression. I was very shy, sheltered, and doted on, and I was so very unhappy. I mean, I was Angela in *The Westing Game*. But more so, I wore glasses, I was a Jew with very few friends, poor much of the time, and all those awful woes of childhood.

J.R.     You have created picture books, illustrated novels, and have written your own novels, most of them using humor. Do you prefer one form over another?

E.R.     What's so nice about a picture book, unlike a novel, is it doesn't confront you.

I can't take myself very seriously. I am too harsh of a self-critic to think I can write a profound, deeply-moving book. In spite of that arrogance about "I should win an honor or a medal," I am really quite humble about myself and my work.

Humor is not difficult to write. Either it works or it doesn't work. I don't think of myself as a humorist, though I know other people do. I never grew up to be one. I don't think any writer should have to work at humor. What you work for is good timing. And everything is funny if it's made that way. Not quite everything. Social inequity isn't funny. Nuclear war isn't funny. At least I wouldn't even try to make it funny.

J.R.     And your other characters? Are they based on people you know?

E.R.     I don't know who the characters are. Some of them are nobody and, yes, some are based on people I know. But they always change. Some don't work out, sometimes I'll divide one into two. But after working two years on a book all my characters are people I know very, very well.

J.R.     How about your illustrations? I would imagine working a picture over many times can be draining.

E.R.     Well, they're not always what I want them to be. That's just the way they come out.

My illustrations are very masculine, which is why I used to sign myself "E. Raskin." When I was working for Young & Rubicam, the advertising agency, some of their clients wouldn't employ a woman. Easily enough, I became "E. Raskin." No one knew any differently.

J.R.     Your books, all of them, have a very designed look to them. Is this intentional on your part?

E.R.     I work very hard on them to make them look easy so children won't have to read too much at one time. That's why I break up the paragraphs the way I do. And when I see the galleys, I make sure everything breaks on the page just the way I want it to or else I have it changed until it's right.

My books are easier for slow readers. Adults read much too quickly and miss a lot. Slow readers get everything.

I get letters from adults saying, "It's the first time so-and-so has ever read a book all the way through." That's great!

J.R.     Your novels are very complicated. Do you go through a lot of rewrites?

E.R.     I always write five times as much as I have to and then cut and cut, and make everything readable.

The most important things for me are the first few words, the first line to catch the reader. You can always start over again. I do. I write too much as it is.

And, before you ask, I never know the ending. If I do know the ending by the second draft, I don't want to write the book. The ending is my reward for doing that book. So maybe on the fourth draft when I type out the ending I love it! I always have happy endings, too, because I write children's books and I do them specifically for children. And I never make fun of people. I'm very sensitive to that. Perhaps because I was made fun of as a child by other children; or perhaps because I love my characters too much.

J.R.     Do you go back to the books when they're done or do you walk away from them?

E.R.     When a book is done, it's done. But the characters stay with me for a long, long time.

When I wrote the music for *Songs of Innocence,* I started playing the piano again. It was a dream in all my life to do. After I was finished with the book, I stopped, and didn't touch the piano for seven years.

That's something I've done all my life. When I'm done I move away from it.

J.R.     Maybe it has something to do with your Karma?

E.R.     Oh, that's funny. Things happen to me all the time!

Once a librarian at a convention asked to look at my aura. I don't know if I believe in that stuff or not. I thought I would hear some nice fairy tale.

Instead she saw me in the seventeenth century, looking sad. I was a Spanish peasant in a red dress, very fat, and was waving onions while doing a dance.

I don't know what to make of *that*!

J.R.     Did she say if you had an audience or not? Maybe it was a prelude to your Newbery speech?

E.R.     Ah! That Newbery speech. I had to have it finished a month ahead of time. And you can't ad lib at all because it's taped ahead of time for giving away.[6]

The very worst speech I ever had to make was at an ABA[7] meeting in California. I was running a fever of $104°$, my bronchitis was acting up and I was the first speaker at this breakfast. There had been a terrible airplane crash the day before and I was supposed to "wow" them after a minute of silence.

Schools are hard, too. Often you think you're going to give one speech and it ends up being five. Plus the kids are unprepared, teachers haven't read the books, and meetings are scheduled while you're there.

I've found the bigger the audience, the easier it is for me. I have a hard time in front of ten people. They think I'm cracked.

But the worst! The worst is fifteen minutes before the speech. I psych myself up and run around looking for the bathroom. I *have* to know where it is before I start.

J.R.     I imagine you must have a lot of people ask you questions like, "How do you learn how to write?" How do you handle that?

E.R.     Well, I always avoid formulas. I don't think you get very good books from that.

And I'm always reading. For anyone who writes or wants to write, that's necessary. I don't see the need for writing courses. For illustration and art, yes, but not for writing.

I tell them to *read*! You can even learn from bad books.

## Notes

[1] Dorothy Price Wollner, *Improvisations in Music* (Garden City, N.Y.: Doubleday & Company, 1963).

[2] Jean Karl, editor-in-chief of children's books for Atheneum Publishers.

[3] What Ellen is referring to here is that *Nothing Ever Happens on My Block* is, for all intents and purposes, a wordless picture book where action all takes place in the background, hence the difficulty of "reading" the book to a selection committee.

[4] Ann Durell, publisher of children's books for E. P. Dutton.

[5] Patricia Cianciolo, head of the joint Newbery-Caldecott Medal committee for the year Ellen won the Newbery Medal.

[6] Ellen refers to the pretaping of the acceptance speeches of the Newbery and Caldecott Medalists. These tapes are handed out as mementos to the audience the evening of the ceremony.

[7] American Booksellers Association; the speech Ellen is referring to was presented at the annual meeting in 1979 in Los Angeles.

## BIBLIOGRAPHY

*A and The; or, William T. C. Baumgarten Comes to Town.* New York: Atheneum, 1970.

*And It Rained.* New York: Atheneum, 1969.

*Books: A Book to Begin On.* By Susan Bartlett. New York: Holt, 1968.

*A Child's Christmas in Wales.* By Dylan Thomas. New York: New Directions, 1959.

*Circles and Curves.* By Arthur G. Razzell and Kenneth George Oliver Watts. Garden City, N.Y.: Doubleday, 1968.

*Come Along!* By Rebecca Caudill. New York: Holt, 1969.

*D. H. Lawrence: Poems Selected for Young People.* ed. William Cole. New York: Viking, 1967.

*Ellen Grae.* By Bill and Vera Cleaver. Philadelphia: Lippincott, 1967.

*Figgs & Phantoms.* New York: Dutton, 1974.

*Franklin Stein.* New York: Atheneum, 1972.

*Ghost in a Four-Room Apartment.* New York: Atheneum, 1969.

*Goblin Market.* By Christina Georgina Rossetti. New York: Dutton, 1970.

*Happy Christmas: Tales for Boys and Girls.* ed. Claire H. Bishop. New York: Daye, 1956.

*Inatuk's Friend.* By Suzanne Stark Morrow. Boston: Little, Brown, 1968.

*The Jewish Sabbath.* By Molly Cone. New York: Crowell, 1966.

*The King of Men.* By Olivia Coolidge. Boston: Houghton Mifflin, 1966.

*Lady Ellen Grae.* By Bill and Vera Cleaver. Philadelphia: Lippincott, 1968.

*Mama, I Wish I Was Snow; Child, You'd Be Very Cold.* By Ruth Krauss. New York: Atheneum, 1962.

*Moe Q. McGlutch, He Smoked Too Much.* New York: Parents Magazine, 1973.

*Moose, Goose, and Little Nobody.* New York: Parents Magazine, 1974.

*The Mysterious Disappearance of Leon (I Mean Noel).* New York: Dutton, 1971.

*Nothing Ever Happens on My Block.* New York: Atheneum: 1966.

*A Paper Zoo: A Collection of Animal Poems by Modern American Poets.* ed. Renee Karol Weiss. New York: Macmillan, 1968.

*Piping Down the Valleys Wild: Poetry for the Young of All Ages.* ed. Nancy Larrick. New York: Delacorte, 1968.

*Poems.* By Edgar Allan Poe. ed. Dwight Macdonald. New York: Crowell, 1965.

*Probability: The Science of Chance.* By Arthur G. Razzell and Kenneth George Oliver Watss. Gafden City, N.Y.: Doubleday, 1967, c1964.

*A Question of Accuracy.* By Arthur G. Razzell and Kenneth George Oliver Watts. Garden City, N.Y.: Doubleday, 1969, c1964.

*Shrieks at Midnight: Macabre Poems, Eerie and Humorous.* Ed. Sara and John E. Brewton. New York: Crowell, 1969.

*Silly Songs and Sad.* New York: Crowell, 1967.

*Songs of Innocence.* By William Blake. 2 vols. Garden City, N.Y.: Doubleday, 1966.

*Spectacles.* New York: Atheneum, 1968.

*Symmetry.* By Arthur G. Razzell and Kenneth George Oliver Watts. Garden City, N.Y.: Doubleday, 1968.

*The Tattooed Potato and Other Clues.* New York: Dutton, 1975.

*This Is 4: The Idea of a Number.* By Arthur G. Razzell and Kenneth George Oliver Watts. Garden City, N.Y.: Doubleday, 1964.

*Three and the Shape of Three.* By Arthur G. Razzell and Kenneth George Oliver Watts. Garden City, N.Y.: Doubleday, 1969.

*Twenty-Two, Twenty-Three.* New York: Atheneum, 1976.

*We Alcotts: The Story of Louisa May Alcott's Family as Seen through the Eyes of "Marmee," Mother of Little Women.* By Aileen Fisher and Olive Rabe. New York: Atheneum, 1968.

*We Dickinsons: The Life of Emily Dickinson as Seen through the Eyes of Her Brother Austin.* By Aileen Fisher and Olive Rabe. New York: Atheneum, 1965.

*The Westing Game.* New York: Dutton, 1978.

*Who, Said Sue, Said Whoo?* New York: Atheneum, 1973.

*The World's Greatest Freak Show.* New York: Atheneum, 1971.


## AWARDS AND HONORS

*And It Rained*
> Best Book of the Year
> Library of Congress list
> Notable Children's Book

*Books*
> Book Show
> Library of Congress list

*Come Along!*
> Best Book of the Year
> Library of Congress list

*Ellen Grae*
> Best Book of the Year
> Fanfare Book
> Library of Congress list

*Figgs & Phantoms*
> Best Book of the Year
> Best of the Best Book
> Library of Congress list
> John Newbery Medal honor book
> Notable Children's Book
> Showcase Book

*The King of Men*
> Best Book of the Year
> Best Book of the Best Book
> Notable Children's Book

*The King of Men*—continued
> Notable Children's Book, 1940-1970
> Spring Book Festival award, *New York Herald Tribune*

*Moose, Goose, and Little Nobody*
> Children's Choice Book
> Library of Congress list

*The Mysterious Disappearance of Leon*
> Best Book of the Year
> Library of Congress list
> Notable Children's Book
> Notable Children's Book, 1971-1975
> Showcase Book

*Nothing Ever Happens on My Block*
> Best Illustrated Children's Book
> Brooklyn Art Book for Children
> Library of Congress list
> Notable Children's Book
> Notable Children's Book, 1940-1970
> Spring Book Festival award, *New York Herald Tribune*

*Songs of Innocence*
>Best Book of the Year
>Book Show

*Spectacles*
>Best Book of the Year
>Best of the Best Book
>Best Illustrated Children's Book
>Book Show
>Library of Congress list
>Notable Children's Book

*The Tattooed Potato*
>Best Book of the Year
>Library of Congress list
>Notable Children's Book

*Twenty-Two, Twenty-Three*
>Notable Children's Book

*We Alcotts*
>Fanfare Book
>Library of Congress list

*We Dickinsons*
>Library of Congress list

*The Westing Game*
>American Book Award finalist
>Best Book of the Year
>*Boston Globe—Horn Book*
>Award
>Fanfare Book
>Library of Congress list
>John Newbery Medal
>Notable Children's Book

*Who, Said Sue, Said Whoo?*
>*Boston Globe—Horn Book*
>Award
>Brooklyn Art Book for Children
>Library of Congress list
>Notable Children's Book
>Notable Children's Book, 1971-
>1975
>Showcase Book

## ADDITIONAL SOURCES

Bader. *American Picturebooks.*
Commire. *Something about the Author.*
*Contemporary Authors.*
de Montreville and Hill. *Third Book of Junior Authors.*
Kingman. *Illustrators of Children's Books: 1957-1966.*
_____. *Illustrators of Children's Books: 1967-1976.*
Kirkpatrick. *Twentieth-Century Children's Writers,* 1978 and 1983.
Ward. *Illustrators of Books for Young People.*

Pat Ross

## BIOGRAPHICAL NOTE

Born in Baltimore, Maryland, on February 4, 1943, Pat Ross graduated from Hood College in Frederick, Maryland, in 1965. That year she began a distinguished career in publishing at *Humpty Dumpty's Magazine*. Ms. Ross is now the owner of Sweet Nellie—A Country Store in New York City. With her husband, Joel, she has a daughter, Erica. Her manuscripts are in the Kerlan Collection.

## PRELUDE TO THE INTERVIEW

Pat Ross, whose children's books have increased in popularity with the publication of the *M and M* books, was one of the key figures in the development of the nonsexist attitudes toward children's books in this country.

One of the founding members of the Feminists on Children's Media[1] in the 1970s, she has led an active campaign for the accurate and positive portrayal of women and girls in children's books. It was not a challenge she took lightly. In addition to the overall stance she took to the children's book industry, she carried the same into her own writing in the *M and M* books and others, as well as into the editing (and later publishing) of many for Alfred A. Knopf and Pantheon Books.

At the time of the interview she was vice president and editor-in-chief for Alfred A. Knopf and Pantheon. Since the interview, she has left the field of publishing to pursue another lifelong interest. She is now the owner of a "country store," Sweet Nellie, on Madison Avenue in Manhattan. The store allows her the time to indulge her passions for antique quilts, traditional weaving, and finely crafted objects in the American folk art tradition.

Though she is not actively in an editorial role, she continues to write for children. The pressures of meeting editorial deadlines have been replaced by purchasing deadlines—and, of course, deadlines of getting her new children's books in on time. These days, they are pressures she enjoys! Deciding to watch Pat in the beginning of her new career, I telephoned her and have inserted her comments following the main interview.

## THE INTERVIEW

J.R.    You are one of a very small minority of writers who are also editors. Let's start with your editorial side first. Many people who come into publishing generally come from another industry or didn't really intend to enter publishing for a long time. What's your story?

P.R.    I was always very single-minded about wanting to go into publishing and I suppose it all started rather early. Even in kindergarten I was thrilled when the teacher would read my stories to the class! Later, I was active on my school paper. The yearbook prophecy for me was: "Editor of *The New York Times*." The closest I've gotten to that is a review or two, and being misquoted on a number of occasions! Then in college I wrote a number of stories for children for an independent project. Now when I look back on those stories, it's almost embarrassing . . . inanimate objects coming to life, and all the other traps. I even showed them when I interviewed for jobs in New York!

    The first job I had was as assistant editor of *Humpty Dumpty's Magazine* when they were still in New York. There were only two people actively working on the magazine—an art director and an eager me—with supervision. I quickly moved up to managing editor since there was no one ahead of me. Seriously, it was a wonderful first job. Arnold Lobel was submitting and having published delightful stories about frog characters in *Humpty Dumpty*. I kept saying how great they'd be in a book, and now look at those frog stories.[2] Not that my suggestion was ever heeded by the right people, but it's always been fun to consider those beginnings.

J.R.    So when did you actually begin your publishing career?

P.R.    Right out of college, in 1965. I remember those interviews as though they were yesterday, too. I wore a blue linen suit and, are you ready? white gloves. And I debated whether or not to wear a hat!

J.R.    You remember all that?

P.R.    Perhaps I remember the shoes best. They were very high and very thin and most uncomfortable. And my skirt was very chic, a mini. I had to be very careful how I sat during interviews. After college graduation, I'd attended a summer business school at Radcliffe, so I was well versed in job interviews.

J.R.    Was it hard to locate that first job?

P.R.    Yes, but probably not as difficult as it is for kids today coming out of college and hoping to break into publishing. At least people would see me, and I felt that I had half a chance. However, the way I landed my first job was a bit ironic. I'd had excellent journalism experience in school, but that's it. And, yes, I was wide-eyed, eager, and enthusiastic. (Years later, someone I knew in my first year of publishing ran into me and commented that now I looked as jaded as everyone else.) But I was not all that qualified for a magazine job. About a year later, I learned that the *Humpty Dumpty* assistant editor job had been between me and another young woman who was indeed more experienced. However, she was apparently rather heavy, and the boss decided he might have to requisition a special chair for her. But secondly, I had better legs! So sex discrimination got me my first job.

Then after three years, I made a transition into children's books at David White, then to Knopf.

The magazine was the best way to start. I had a chance to edit, to meet many people including authors and illustrators, and to write, too. At that time I was writing magazine pieces as a free-lancer.

J.R.    From that first experience you came to the forefront of social activism, promoting nonsexist children's books and organizing Feminists on Children's Media, helping shape the literature to what it is today. Now with your increased responsibilities as a department head, a family, and other pressures, are you still as vocal or as active as you were?

P.R.    Over the years, the stance I've taken as a feminist has had to change with the changes in my own life. When we started Feminists on Children's Media I was able to devote a great deal of time to everything from licking stamps to traveling around with the audio-visual presentations on sexism in children's books that we had worked very hard to prepare to turn heads and change minds. This was before my daughter figured into my life. Erica was born most appropriately during Children's Book Week in 1972 and while the second *Little Miss Muffet Fights Back*[3] was in the works. My group gave me a baseball glove as a baby present.

Then I had a child, a husband, a career, not always in that order, and things did change. There were only so many hours in the day. There have been times over the past years when I've been guilty about being so inactive publicly. I comfort myself by thinking that at least I'm living the message, if I can no longer shout it.

J.R.    When do you find the time now to write and still keep pace with your job?

P.R.    I like to get to the office early, by seven-thirty, have my coffee and use the quiet time before nine to do paperwork and organize myself for the day. I try to keep the long business lunches at a minimum, which means I work through lunch with a sandwich in one hand and the telephone in the other. By five, I'm ready to head for my health club, or home, or maybe even out to dinner. I'm skeptical about people who tell you they work a twelve-hour day. Few people can keep up a meaningful productivity for that long a span.

I find that my writing comes in productive spurts. I'll connect with a character or a good idea, and then just go with it. In the evenings, on weekends. I'm not very consistent about my writing. I have to go with it when the spirit moves me. I don't spend very much time looking at blank pages. That's not my style.

J.R.     Taking over the department was, of course, a major professional step up for you. That sort of move does create its own problems, doesn't it?

P.R.     Taking over the department was a substantial change for me. I went from being a senior editor and working very much on my own to being a vice president and administrator. I'd never taken a course in business school on how to run a department, and suddenly I had some eleven people depending on me. There was much support, but still it was an enormous adjustment. I soon realized I couldn't do the job and keep writing, at least not the way I had before, so my writing took a back seat. For the first year, my family took a back seat, too. I thought I was doing a terrific job of covering all my bases, but my daughter, then seven, straightened me out on that account.

J.R.     How so?

P.R.     We were taking a relaxed walk and she said, "You look pretty today." I thought, "Wow, I haven't had a compliment from Erica in months." Then she went on to say, not unkindly at all, "I hate to tell you this, but you really looked ugly for about a year." It was at that moment of truth that I realized I must have looked—and been—very ugly indeed for that year of baptism by fire.

J.R.     I assume that things have settled down by now.

P.R.     Of course, there's always a period of adjustment. So many parts of the job that were totally new are now routine. The people I work with are all talented and intent on pulling together. That's a wonderful feeling.

J.R.     We haven't talked much yet about your specific books. What about the *M and M* books? Are they based on your daughter's experiences?

P.R.     Yes, she was my inspiration for the books. As you know, the friends in the *M and M* books, Mandy and Mimi, are five or six. I never say exactly. When Erica was very young, I wasn't all that inspired to write books about the way she was. I just didn't connect with that very early childhood period in that way. As a mother, I found the earliest years rather trying and exhausting so perhaps I was just too spent to see all the great opportunities for stories.

Whatever, when Erica was about four going on five, I became especially fascinated by the social behavior of that age group. I used to hide behind her door and listen to her and her friends play. It's marvelous the way children that age will take adult rules of behavior and apply them to fit their unique situations. For example, in one of the *M and M* books, I have the two girls in Mandy's room playing the "Haunted House Game." The lights are off and things are getting pretty scarey. Mimi tells Mandy to turn on the light, which involves crossing the dark room to get to the switch. And Mandy tells Mimi *she* should do it because, "You're the guest and the guest always goes first." That sort of thing.

J.R.    Do you have a routine when you write?

P.R.    The books begin with an idea about something that Mandy and Mimi will do together. They have "funny troubles," as the catalog copy said of one of the books. Once I had them shopping alone for the very first time. In another book, they babysat twins. During the adventures, the two friends experience their share of conflicts, trying to work things out. And because they're such good friends, things do work out.

J.R.    In the books, Mandy and Mimi look very much alike. In fact, they call themselves twins. How do you keep them straight?

P.R.    They may look alike but they're two very different personalities. Mandy is the more conservative child, playing it safe and generally acting in a more reasonable way. Mimi is gutsier, a bit of a slob, and more inclined to initiate mischief. She's also the first one of the two to run the other way at the sign of getting caught! Their personalities dovetail nicely. And I think that's true with adults, too. You know, the theory of complementary personalities. . . .

J.R.    Where are the adults in your books?

P.R.    There are adults in my *other* books. I keep parents out of the *M and M* books on purpose. Children that age like to think of themselves in independent terms. It's nice for them to read a book where some grownup doesn't bail them out, or punish them (moral message books!) or even praise them. Mandy and Mimi are on their own. But in a book like my *Molly and the Slow Teeth,* the parents are essential, and their support role is important to Molly as she loses her first tooth and important to readers.

J.R.    How do you find the time to write?

P.R.    With difficulty! If I have to write with interruptions, I turn into an ogre. If I sit down to my typewriter on a Saturday and have to keep saying to my family: "Please keep quiet. I'm trying to write," I work myself up into such a frenzy, I can't write. It's hard for me to sit down with a three-ring circus going around me and get anything done. Or with somebody saying, "What's for lunch? We're out of apple juice."

So I'll block out quiet time for myself—an afternoon behind closed doors, a week alone in the country. And then when I get down to it, I can write for sixteen hours a day! Then time goes by very quickly. I generally draft a section or a chapter and then make changes in pencil until the page looks like a roadmap. Then I'll retype and change as I go along. I redraft and redraft, and keeping running them through. People tell me I'm a good candidate for a word processor, but I think I would miss the *process* of thinking in pencil, too.

I have creative spurts when I'm able to turn out a tremendous amount of, well, good stuff. And then it goes so quickly. If it starts well, it goes well. If I have trouble with a piece and don't have time without interruptions (*days,* I mean) to rethink character and plot, for example, then I might as well put that piece in a file drawer and wait for another life to finish it!

J.R.    Do you think it's necessary to have children to be able to write children's books?

P.R.    No, not at all. But in my situation, it's certainly been a catalyst.

J.R.    As an editor how do you handle that persona of author and editor? It must be difficult sometimes.

P.R.    Sometimes. When I attend a writers' conference, I generally attend as an editor. But it gets tricky because I'm a writer, too. Often it's helpful for me to tell the group that I've been rejected, too. Then they feel more comfortable somehow.

During conventions, my identity in the booth can be confusing. I'll be standing there with my corporate name on my button when someone will walk up and say, "Didn't you write thus and such a book?" Then they'll mention that they didn't know whether or not they should say something. I'm always glad they do!

J.R.    What's your best book?

P.R.    Since I've done different types of children's books, I find it hard to choose. But I'll stick my neck out and say I think *What Ever Happened to the Baxter Place?* is a book of substance and a subject dear to my heart.

J.R.    How is that?

P.R.    The book is about the disappearance of a way of life, the small farm life. I grew up on the Eastern Shore of Maryland and have watched those lovely fields and woods turn into shopping centers. That's essentially what happens to the 'Baxter' family in this book. Before they know what's happened, their small farm is gone. Of course, they've made some money, but money can't replace their lost way of life.

J.R.    Some people see that as development and progress.

P.R.         Yes, but I'm a traditionalist and have another point of view in this book. I like the old things that endure in my books and in my life. When everyone else was into "minimal" decorating, I was reupholstering the living room furniture in chintz. Once I went to someone's elegant new apartment, totally redone with built-ins. It was exceptionally well done, airy and clean and tasteful. But when we were headed home, I was seized with a sense of panic. I turned to my husband, Joel, and wondered, "If we lived there, where would we put my grandmother's desk?" The things I live with mean a great deal to me. I don't like things that self-destruct, like the shopping center in *Baxter Place.* The late Roger Duvoisin, who illustrated the book, felt the same way. Now the book is out of print after a good life, but it's still sad to see it go.

J.R.       As an editor, do you find yourself looking for new writers or do you tend to use the same people over and over again?

P.R.         We still read the slush pile as thoroughly as possible. And agents know we enjoy the adventure and challenge of publishing first-time writers. That's the exciting part of publishing. Of course, it's becoming more and more impossible to publish literary fiction, my favorite area, and do well with it. The hardcover sales on those books, especially the YA novel, are sluggish. And the rights market has practically dried up. A weeding-out process is always useful, but I think things have gone a bit too far now.

        On the whole I think everyone's a lot more cautious than they used to be. Money is tighter and those big advances are not parted with so easily anymore. I feel that both as an editor and writer. Not that my advances were ever in the heavy-hitter category, but everyone feels the crunch.

J.R.       You're reading reviews for the books you edit as well as your own books. Does that present any conflicts?

P.R.         Again, my double life. . . .

        One day I received two reviews on the same book. One said, "This original, sprightly text is somewhat reinforced by the artwork" and the other said "the exuberant drawings redeem the overworked text." Or something like that. All this on the same day! I just keep reading them, looking for some sense to the process.

J.R.       What do you enjoy most about your own books?

P.R.         The humor. I'm pleased when I can read my own books and find the fun in them.

J.R.       What are you working on now?

P.R.         I've just finished the fifth and sixth adventures of the *M and M* characters. In one, the friends go to the Natural History Museum for the new mummy exhibit. But they're a week early, so they treat themselves to a sneak preview. In the other, which resembles *Meet M and M* in its friendship aspects, Mandy and Mimi don't have a clue as to what to get for each other for Christmas, until Santa helps them out unwittingly.

J.R.    Is Erica still inspiring you?

P.R.    Erica is almost a teenager, but, thankfully, I'm still time-warped at age six with Mandy and Mimi. And that's a nice age to be.

----

## (Telephone interview follow-up)

J.R.    After eighteen years in publishing, you decided to pursue a new career. How did that decision come to be made?

P.R.    It certainly was not an easy decision, but I'd come to the point that I really wanted to run my own business. I'd been a part of a large corporation for many years, and felt I understood the pros and cons of that situation and it was just time to change. The experience as a manager was invaluable to me, as you can imagine. When you have your own business, you do *everything.* It's very exciting to make things happen that way. I love the independence and taking responsibility for both my losses and my gains.

J.R.    Why a country store?

P.R.    I grew up in Maryland among antiques and folk art, and I became more and more interested in making that a part of my present life. Then I began to collect vintage quilts, and it was like an addiction. My quilt collection grew out of the blanket chest and, suddenly, there were more quilts than beds or chests. My husband said jokingly, "You're going to have to start selling these." And that's when the idea began. Joel has his own business, in venture capital, and soon we were talking about *my* being in business on my own, too. We celebrated the incorporation of Sweet Nellie on my fortieth birthday.

J.R.    Do you have time to write now?

P.R.    When you have your own business, you never *stop* working. It becomes a way of life. But, yes, I do have slow seasons and perhaps my new career will give me more of that uninterrupted time that I need to write more. I hope so.

J.R.    Do you miss publishing?

P.R.    Of course I do. It was a part of my life for eighteen years. But I still manage to keep in touch with the people, and that makes me feel that I'm still involved in some small way. And I'll keep on writing, but now I'll just have that one hat to wear.

## Notes

[1] Feminists on Children's Media described itself as a "collective of people interested in upgrading the portrayal of girls and women in children's literature and other media," in the 1970s and first published the landmark bibliography, *Little Miss Muffet Fights Back: Recommended Non-Sexist Children's Books about Girls for Young Readers* in 1971.

[2] Pat refers here to Arnold Lobel's *Frog and Toad* series published by Harper & Row.

[3] As above, 1974.

## BIBLIOGRAPHY

*As Author:*

*Gloria and the Super Soaper.* il. Susan Paradis. Boston: Little, Brown, 1982.

*Hi Fly.* il. John Wallner. New York: Crown, 1974.

*M and M and the Bad News Babies.* il. Marylin Hafner. New York: Pantheon, 1983.

*M and M and the Big Bag.* il. Marylin Hafner. New York: Pantheon, 1981.

*M and M and the Haunted House Game.* il. Marylin Hafner. New York: Pantheon, 1980.

*Meet M and M.* il. Marylin Hafner. New York: Pantheon, 1980.

*Molly and the Slow Teeth.* il. Jerry Milord. New York: Lothrop, Lee & Shepard, 1980.

*Trouble in School: A Portrait of Young Adolescents.* New York: Avon, 1979.

*What Ever Happened to the Baxter Place?* il. Roger Duvoisin. New York: Pantheon, 1976.

*Your First Airplane Trip.* With Joel Ross. il. Lynn Wheeling. New York: Lothrop, Lee & Shepard, 1981.

*As Compiler:*

*Young and Female; Turning Points in the Lives of Eight American Women: Personal Accounts Compiled with Introductory Notes.* New York: Random House, 1972.

## AWARDS AND HONORS

*M and M and the Big Bag*
Children's Choice Book

*Whatever Happened to the Baxter Place?*
Notable Children's Trade Book
in the Field of Social Studies

*Young and Female*
Notable Children's Trade
Book in the Field of Social
Studies

_Marilyn Singer_

Marilyn Singer

## BIOGRAPHICAL NOTE

Marilyn Singer was born in New York City on October 3, 1948. She received a bachelor of arts degree from Queens College in 1969 and a master's degree from New York University in 1979. Before devoting her full time to writing, Ms. Singer was a teacher in the New York City schools from 1969 to 1974. She married Steven Aronson in 1971.

## PRELUDE TO THE INTERVIEW

Marilyn Singer is a teacher-turned-writer which is not all that unusual. What is different in Marilyn's case, however, is that once she made the decision to leave teaching she automatically turned to writing—having _never_ published a word! Her only writing activity had consisted of lesson plans and poetry she had written for her own enjoyment. Once the decision was made, it didn't occur to her for one minute that she couldn't make it work.

Since that time she has produced an enormous amount of work including study guides, filmstrip commentary, educational film scripts, and, of course, picture books and novels. It is in the latter two categories where she is the most comfortable, being free to explore her ideas in whatever manner she chooses.

Marilyn is as much an enthusiastic speaker as she is an eager listener. A conversation with her includes a healthy give-and-take, each one expressing ideas and passing on bits of information either for discussion or just to think about. She has a kind of lively energy about her, the kind that shows a listener that she is involved with the conversation and what is being said. She is quick to ask questions of questions; she is quick to laugh and match joke for joke. While she decidedly takes her work and her books seriously, she is also able to see the more humorous side of the publishing industry—as a writer should—and keep a healthy perspective on it all. It is only when she is not treated as the professional she is that she becomes concerned, as expressed in this interview. Her interview touches upon some of the problems she has had as a writer. Although they are by no means unique, they testify to her perseverance—a major trait of the professional writer.

# THE INTERVIEW

J.R.    As it happens, you, like so many writers, have a background in working with youth. You left a secure situation to join the ranks of the insecure. Want to fill in the details?

M.S.    Oh, I was an English teacher in the New York City school system. The department got a new head, we took one look at each other and it was, immediately, *bad news.*

We got into a political discussion, somehow, and she told me about a teacher who wore a black armband on Moratorium Day.[1]

I thought it was a great idea. She didn't. She said, "I can see his point of view but I don't think that politics and teaching have anything to do with each other." And I said, "You teach what you are. And whatever your views are affect what you do."

So we started off on the wrong foot and stayed on the wrong foot for three years. Although she couldn't fire me she made my life very unhappy. She observed me frequently, she wrote up lousy reports on me. Finally she gave me an "unsatisfactory" rating that the principal supported, and that I appealed. It was a real Catch-22 situation because when you appeal it's to a committee of other principals. It was a big hassle situation.

So I decided to quit teaching to write. I did some substitute teaching just to pay the bills. And I came up with a few ideas for proposals, which I sent around.

J.R.    Had you written anything for publication up to then?

M.S.    No. Just poetry for myself.

J.R.    Had you published?

M.S.    No.

J.R.    Did you have any kind of income?

M.S.    No, but my husband did hire me to do some program notes for a film, you know those inserts to tell teachers how to use a film with kids.

I liked doing them and saw new possibilities for a career with them. So I started contacting film companies like Phoenix Films and Time-Life.

Eventually I got quite a bit of work from Time-Life, including doing all the study guides for *The Ascent of Man.*[2] That was thirteen full booklets! And I didn't have a background in science, which made that project interesting for me. Luckily, I am a very good researcher and I did a lot of research for those booklets.

Time-Life gave me a lot of work because they really liked my writing. When the man who'd hired me left, I worked for his replacement until she left. Then I pretty much stopped writing for them altogether. By then I was tired of that and wanted to make some money from the books I'd started writing.

J.R.    How did you start writing children's books?

M.S.    I got a job doing both notes and catalogs for a bunch of films from the British Arts Council that the American Federation of Arts wanted distributed in this country. So I went to England for a month in 1974. I had some problems there not related to the work. I came home rather agoraphobic. To help deal with my problems, I started to write fiction.

I don't think it was a conscious decision.

One day I just sat down and started writing stories. I drew on characters I made up when I was eight years old. Talking insects!

Nothing came of it but I loved writing about those insects. It was like getting in touch with that little child part of myself, you know. I wrote a bunch of stories and kept reading them to my husband. He encouraged me to continue.

Then I signed up for a writing class that was going to take a year, but it got cancelled. The instructor mentioned a free workshop at Bank Street College.[3] This was in 1974 or 1975. So I sent Betty Boegehold[4] some samples. She called me up and said, "You know, you may be a talent."

I went to the workshop and Betty really encouraged me, too.

I want to add a lovely piece of irony here. The insect stories didn't sell when I wrote them, over ten years ago. But recently, my husband, who, as you can tell, has probably been more instrumental in my career than almost anybody, suggested I show them to Meredith Charpentier[5] at Macmillan. He knows her and felt she would know how to turn the stories into a book. He was right. She will be publishing *The Lightey Stories* as a book!

J.R.    Were you doing any other types of writing in the mid-seventies?

M.S.    I was still writing teacher's guides, program notes, and catalogs. Later on, I did some filmstrips for a company that had to teach me how to do it.

They taught me mainly about form. I'd turn in something and then they would tell me to rewrite. They hired me because they looked at my resume and said, "You've written everything else so you might as well learn to write this." Really!

I've been writing full-time since 1976.

J.R.    Because you do so much varied writing, do you have an agent who keeps things straight for you?

M.S.    I had one. I don't have one anymore, for a couple of reasons. One, she sold only two books for me; two, I'd already been published by several major publishers and didn't feel I needed her help with them; three, she was no help in an impossible situation I had with one publisher. That's a long, terrible story.

J.R.    Go ahead.

M.S.        Well, I was asked to do this one book, which shall remain nameless, through my agent. I wrote the proposal as I was asked to do. The editor loved it. The book was accepted. Then the editor left the company.

The next editor had me do more work on it. She and I got along well but she did no editing on it. None. And, I wrote a long book when what they were expecting was a short book. I turned it in and it went to copyediting.

The copyeditor missed twenty-five of my typos and misspellings! A taxonomist friend who was reading the manuscript to check the botany caught all of those. On top of it the copyeditor changed some of the text and many of the sentences that I started with "and" or "but" to "in this case." She didn't like my style.

So I complained to the editor, whose response was, "I'm older and wiser than you." I went to her office and showed her what I meant. She agreed to have the manuscript recopyedited. The new job wasn't too bad but there were a number of mistakes in the galleys. So I had to go over the galleys with them.

Then, a new editor came in. The *third* editor! The book was ready for indexing and the publisher agreed to get someone to do it and to have it paid for from my royalties.[6] An enormous index was turned in with all sorts of extraneous things. The bill was something like six hundred dollars, I can't remember for sure.

I had been talking to my agent all along about the mess. She hadn't done anything. Finally, over the index business, she said it would be better if I tried "to straighten things out with the editor because the editor won't deal with me."

So I called the editor and told her I wasn't pleased with the index. At this point the editor started screaming at me and hung up the telephone.

It was finally settled that I would pay for half the index. But I had to sit down with it and make the cuts. I may as well have done it myself in the first place.

When the book finally came out, it was a beautiful production. It looked absolutely gorgeous.

But it didn't sell. Other than the initial catalog entry, I saw almost nothing on the book. Only one or two reviews. It never got into the stores. I don't know what they did with it. They sold just about zero copies.

When I asked my agent what was going on, she basically said to forget about the book because that's what the publisher was doing. In fact, the book went out of print in less than two years.

Since then, I haven't worked with that publisher or agent. I've never been so humiliated. Degraded is a better word.

Luckily most of my editors aren't like that!

J.R.     That's quite a story and admittedly more severe than most. Are you a difficult author?

M.S.        No. In fact, I've been told I'm good to work with. I do changes very quickly and I usually don't have any problems with the changes the editors want.

I feel that editors should be tough if they know their business. If they tell me to do something there's a reason for it, and nine times out of ten they're right. So I really respect them.

In some ways writing is a partnership between an author and an editor. I like it. I like somebody going over my work with a fine-toothed comb—as long as what she or he does is subject to my approval. I really mean that. Editors are there to help make the book better. Not necessarily more saleable, but better.

In *The Course of True Love,* for example, Liz Gordon[7] said about the last chapter, which has a bit of sex in it, "I'm not going to tell you whether to take it out or not. I just want you to think about it and decide what you want." She said the book would probably be more saleable without it but if it was artistically important to leave it in to do so. It stayed in.

J.R.    How do you handle rejection?

M.S.    I just do.

I figure there are editors who want books to be perfect so they don't have to do much editing. They turn down imperfect ones. Mine are rarely perfect at the beginning. Others will see something in a book and are willing to work with it until it's right.

I did a book set in a hospital once and the editor wrote back, "This is too much of a downer. People don't want to read about hospitals, number one. And number two, your character doesn't learn as she goes along."

I thought, "Uh-huh. That's your opinion. Then I gave it to another publisher who read it and said, "This is good, but it needs some work."

This is not quite the same thing you asked but when someone sends a manuscript for me to criticize I ask if they want me to say if I like it or don't like it or if they really want me to criticize. Let me tell you, it's tough. Actually, though, I find most people want to be criticized.

If *I'm* going to be rejected, I prefer rejection with criticism accompanying it.

J.R.    As a professional writer what is, to your thinking, a mandatory prerequisite?

M.S.    Professional conduct.

It has to do with being prepared and disciplined. It has to do with listening to other people's ideas and meeting deadlines. If you say you're going to do something, you do it.

There are a lot of professional writers without professional conduct. Both parties must respect each other. That's why I have such a good relationship with one of my publishers, Harper & Row—mutual respect. Their attitude toward me is you are a talent and you're going to get better. Their attitude is, "We're going to nurture you."

For example, Liz called me up one day in between books and said, "What are you doing these days? I haven't seen anything from you. Come in and let's talk. I want to hear what's on your mind." And I think, "What a difference that makes."

My feeling is to give them things they want to publish. I want to be a professional. I want to do the work. I don't want to get into ridiculous unnecessary arguments. I don't like getting on a high horse. That's nonsense. There's no such thing as something that can't be worked out. That's absurd.

J.R.     Let's back up for a minute. I'm unclear on one point. Did you start publishing books because of the Bank Street workshop?

M.S.     Actually, yes. In that workshop, I read a story about a dog who thought he was a person. The group liked it. So I sent it around. I didn't even know enough then to send it to one publisher at a time. So I sent it to three and I got a letter from Ann Durell,[8] who took it.

She took another two of my books very quickly including my first novel, *No Applause, Please,* which is one of those semi-autobiographical things about growing up on Long Island.

So I sent her another one. And she didn't want it. I sent it to Harper. I had met Liz at an SCBW[9] conference at Bank Street. I really liked her a lot so I just walked up and introduced myself. She turned the book down, too, but said, "If you have anything else, just send it to me." So I sent her *It Can't Hurt Forever,* which I think has probably been my most successful novel to date.

J.R.     So much for loyalty to a publisher?

M.S.     Oooo, that's a tricky question. Yeah, I think loyalty is a good thing. But. . . .

J.R.     I know, I know. It's also an unfair question. Let's get safe. Go through your day.

M.S.     I get up very late because I go to sleep very late. It depends how many projects I'm working on. I usually don't start writing until three or four o'clock in the afternoon and then I write for two, three hours. I get a lot done in those hours. I spend so much time thinking before I sit down to write it, the idea is in good shape. Also, I find after writing for two or three hours I'm absolutely bonkers. It's invigorating to write but if I do it too long I don't do it as well.

When I write, I write linearly—first chapter, second chapter, et cetera. I go straight through. I never used to outline because frankly I hate to. I prefer watching the story unfold before me along the way. But lately I've been selling books before I write them. What I mean is, I guess I'm well known enough so that if I give a publisher a proposal and sample chapter, the publisher will give me a contract without having to see the finished work. So, sometimes I now outline.

J.R.      As you are writing, how aware are you of trends and topics?

M.S.      I think a lot of books have a proper timing. Sometimes I'll write a book because there seems to be something in the air that tells me to. It fits right. If the book comes out too much later, it misses the timing. If it comes out too early, readers may not be ready for it. But to be just early enough is to be on the vanguard.

When I wrote *The First Few Friends,* which is about growing up in New York in the turbulent late '60s, I was on the vanguard. There weren't many '60s books around. But I suspected there soon would be. And, in fact, several showed up after mine came out.

But the book didn't sell well. I don't know exactly why. I got good reviews on it and even some fan mail. But now I wonder if I wasn't too early after all. Or maybe it's the present "moral" climate in this country that accounted for the poor sales. The book has some rough language in it, which was appropriate to the '60s, but that seems to bother a lot of people now. It also has sex, drugs, and rock and roll. Basically, it's a borderline young adult-adult book, and that may have had something to do with its inability to find a niche.

J.R.      But was it successful?

M.S.      Financially, no. Artistically, yes.

J.R.      How?

M.S.      Because it was genuinely exhilarating to write. And because when I pick it up even now I still feel a sense of wonder that I managed to get all that stuff down on paper.

## Notes

[1] Moratorium Day was nation-wide protest held in October 1969, to demand an end to American involvement in Viet Nam.

[2] *The Ascent of Man* was a British Broadcasting Corporation/Public Broadcasting Service television series on many scientific topics, hosted by Jacob Bronowski.

[3] Bank Street College, New York City, sponsors writing workshops for would-be and established writers.

[4] Betty Boegehold, organizer of the Bank Street workshops, also an author.

[5] Meredith Charpentier, formerly editor of children's books at Frederick Warne and Macmillan, is now editor of children's books of Four Winds Press, a division of Macmillan Publishing Company.

[6] It is a common publisher practice to have authors pay indexing costs for any indexing done to books, either directly or by having it deducted from their royalties.

[7] Elizabeth Gordon, publisher of children's books for Harper & Row.

[8] Ann Durell, publisher of children's books for E. P. Dutton.

[9] Society of Children's Book Writers, an organization for people involved in the writing or publishing of children's books.

## BIBLIOGRAPHY

### As Author:

*The Case of the Sabotaged School Play.* il. Judy Glasser. New York: Harper & Row, 1984.

*The Course of True Love Never Did Run Smooth.* New York: Harper & Row, 1983.

*The Dog Who Insisted He Wasn't.* il. Kelly Oechsli. New York: Dutton, 1976.

*The Fanatic's Ecstatic Aromatic Guide to Onions, Garlic, Shallots, and Leeks.* il. Marian Parry. Englewood Cliffs, N.J.: Prentice-Hall, 1981.

*The First Few Friends: A Novel.* New York: Harper & Row, 1981.

*The Great Fido Frame-up.* il. Andrew Glass. New York: Warne, 1983.

*It Can't Hurt Forever.* il. Leigh Grant. New York: Harper & Row, 1978.

*Leroy Is Missing.* il. Judy Glasser. New York: Harper & Row, 1984.

*No Applause, Please.* New York: Dutton, 1977.

*The Pickle Plan.* il. Steven Kellogg. New York: Dutton, 1978.

*Tarantulas on the Brain.* il. Leigh Grant. New York: Harper & Row, 1982.

*Will You Take Me to Town on Strawberry Day?* il. Trina Schart Hyman. New York: Harper & Row, 1981.

### As Editor:

*A History of the American Avant-Garde Cinema.* New York: American Federation of Arts, 1976.

*New American Filmmakers.* New York: American Federation of Arts, 1976.

## AWARDS AND HONORS

*The Course of True Love Never Did Run Smooth*
  Best Young Adult Book of the Year

*The Dog Who Insisted He Wasn't*
  Children's Choice Book

*The Great Fido Frame-Up*
  *Parents' Choice* Award

*It Can't Hurt Forever*
  Children's Choice Book
  Lovelace Award

## ADDITIONAL SOURCES

*Contemporary Authors.*

# William Sleator

William Sleator

## BIOGRAPHICAL NOTE

Havre de Grace, Maryland, is the birthplace of William Sleator. He was born on February 13, 1945, and graduated from Harvard University in 1967. Since 1970 he has been writing children's books, along with a career as a rehearsal pianist for the Boston Ballet Company, from 1974 through 1983.

## PRELUDE TO THE INTERVIEW

William Sleator* happens to be in New York on a tour with the Boston Ballet and his publisher, knowing I am looking for people to interview, arranges a meeting for us. Being on tour is an especially crowded time with generally inflexible schedules, and I am appreciative of efforts made so the two of us are able to meet in an unhurried atmosphere.

A writer's life is generally a stress-filled one when working on a manuscript; Bill's has been compounded because of his rehearsal-pianist position with the Ballet. But it hasn't slowed down his production or ability. One normally thinks that nights alone in a hotel room are conducive to writing; they are not. Most writers have certain requirements in order to write, whether it be in a special corner, a certain type of paper, a certain time of day. Bill has managed to overcome some of that and does spend time when he is traveling on his writing. The writing becomes a release for him from the pressures on the road.

After this interview was transcribed, he left his position with the Boston Ballet. There are undercurrents in the interview to this move, which were expressed this way in a letter to me:

"Recently I quit my job of nine years as a rehearsal pianist with The Boston Ballet Company. Partly it was because I wanted to spend as much time as possible on my writing. But my departure was also due to a growing discomfort with the way ballet companies operate. I no longer wanted to be part of an organization that needlessly abuses people the way a ballet company does."

He is now writing full-time for children and young adults. It is exactly what he wants to do. He finds the new arrangement quite to his liking!

---

*pronounced SLAY-tir

# THE INTERVIEW

J.R.  You are not only a writer but also a pianist for the Boston Ballet Company. Don't you find the kind of schedule you must keep between the two hectic?

W.S.  Not really. Before I worked for the Ballet, my day was: I would get up, have a cup of coffee, walk across the room and write. It could get kind of boring. Now, the way it works most of the time is I play for class from 10:00 to 11:30 in the morning, which is a short walk from my house, so I have my coffee while I'm playing, and waking up! By doing this I can be with other people and get involved with all the gossip and interaction. By 11:30 I'm revved up enough so I can go home and write. That leaves me five to six hours in which to write.

J.R.  With a background in music, how did you come to write for children and young adults?

W.S.  I took piano lessons when I was a kid. And I went to Harvard and started majoring in music until the music department suggested I major in something else. So I majored in English, which of course is fun, but you really don't learn a skill and just read books you'd read anyway.

I've always been involved with music in some way. As a kid and in college I wrote music for films and plays. One thing I'd love to do is write music for films. I like working within limitations and the length of films scenes is *absolute!* You have to write music to the precise second.

One film I did music for was *Why the Sun and Moon Live in the Sky.* Blair Lent, the illustrator, and this filmmaker worked on it together. It was really fun. They made these cardboard figures that they moved frame by frame. The fun thing about it for me was doing sort of pseudo-African music.

But to answer your question of how I got into books. I was friends with Blair Lent. And I wanted to be a writer. Emilie McLeod[1] wanted him to do for a long time a book about Indians. And he gave me this big break. He said, "Do some research and do a story I like and adapt it to a picture book, and in a way Emilie will like, then I'll illustrate it." And that was my big break in the field.

J.R.  Well, that seems simple enough. Just find an established person to help you get in!

W.S.  One of the biggest hurdles is to get in at all. I was very lucky. And then keeping at it.

You really have to discipline yourself. That's my biggest problem. It would be much easier if someone were forcing you, putting you on a schedule, forcing you to write X number of pages a day.

I consider I've done all right if I write five pages a day. I don't feel guilty that way. When I'm really going and going well, I've written as many as eleven. That's nothing in comparison to some people. Joyce Carol Oates[2] writes forty *routinely!*

J.R.　Because part of your time is spent touring with the ballet company, don't you find that going on the road interferes with your writing schedule?

W.S.　People think it's so glamorous to travel. But it isn't that much fun. The thing that isn't fun about it is that you have to work. You're working under bad conditions. At home or in the studio you set things up to be right for you. But when you're on the road you're doing your job but you have to take the situation you're thrown into. And a lot of time you're tired and sick.

I usually bring a typewriter with me everywhere, but I don't use it that much. You can't type when you're on a bus for eight hours with exhausted dancers asleep all around you. Instead I'd scribble down all the events in a notebook, where we went, what it was like, what the theater was like, who was going with whom, what happened during the performance, that sort of thing.

Touring does interfere with my writing. I have hundreds of pages of journal notes about tours, which someday I'll figure out how to use. The most interesting tour was five weeks of two-night stands doing outdoor theaters in Europe.

But I can't write books on tour. I've tried and tried. I never have enough time.

J.R.　It seems to me with your music and dance background that there will inevitably be a book set against it someday.

W.S.　*Fingers* was a book about a child prodigy traveling in Europe, so it's a sign that that part of my life has crept into my writing.

I've written several versions of a book about ballet, and because ballet itself is so melodramatic and blood, sweat, and tears, on paper it comes out sounding like soap opera.

Dancers are always being told what to do. Their whole lives consist of being told what to do from the time they start taking ballet as little kids. And there is an incredible amount of pressure and tension on them. There's a certain amount of tension to being a writer in that you worry if you're going to keep coming up with ideas. But it's not stressful in the way it is for dancers because you don't have to go out in front of an audience and be judged constantly.

Being a writer has a lot of problems that most people don't recognize. They think you're a free-lance writer making a living, wow! You don't have a boss. You have your own hours. But there are a lot of problems of trying to make yourself work, the tediousness of it, and having to never stop or else you won't have any money. But that's why it's so wonderful to have a job with the Ballet because I see how terrible the Ballet life is and it makes me appreciate being a writer and the solitude of it, with no one telling you what to do. You're not just a vehicle for someone else.

J.R.     Then how do you keep yourself going, working away at a manuscript?

W.S.     One of the things that keeps me writing—the fun part for me is not the actual work. The fun part is when the day is over and after dinner I can sit down and read what I've written.

One of the frustrating things about writing is that you're sitting there alone all day, slaving away. It's very hard for me to work and I don't work particularly fast.

I like to look at things in terms of behavior modification sometimes because I think it makes a lot of sense. They say if you get rewarded for something you'll repeat it. In writing the rewards are way, way off in the future and you don't know if you're even going to get a reward. You're sitting there writing but you don't know if you're even going to get paid, get published. That's one of the big problems. How are you going to reinforce yourself to do this thing? You have to establish artificial rewards for yourself because you don't know if you are going to get published or not.

Some writers make graphs of the pages they write per day. And if the graph goes down and continues for a long period of time, they feel bad. If the graph goes up, they feel good. It's a simple kind of reward.

Some people make contracts. They won't let themselves have a drink or something like that if they don't write five pages. I can't do that. I've never been able to establish a contract like *that!*

I have a friend who writes adult novels. She writes the first draft out on legal pads by hand. Then she takes that, tears it up and throws it away. Then she sits down at the typewriter and writes the second draft. She'll write about five drafts. And only then she'll send it to the editor. By that time there isn't much for the editor to do.

I can't work that way. I need feedback and I need it early. What I usually do is just send my first draft. This is how I work with Ann Durell.[3] Most of the time she doesn't offer a contract at that point. What she does is make a lot of suggestions and give me feedback. The book then goes through several drafts.

J.R.     You don't have an agent who sends things around for you?

W.S.     No.

It's a funny experience sending manuscripts around. It's a weird experience. I always send my manuscripts with a self-addressed, stamped envelope and a cover letter explaining who I am. You don't get published solely on the basis of your name. I'm sure some people do, but I'm not in that category.

I've always had good feelings about my publishers. They're very careful to explain to me why they want changes in my books. One gripe I'd have though is this business of getting royalties every six months. It really can be painful not to have a salary and get paid once every six months. It's very hard to live that way. You really have to be careful and budget and I'm not good at that. So I frequently run out of money before the six months is up!

J.R. That would then give you impetus to combat any feelings of writer's block in that you have to keep the rent paid.

W.S. Yes and no. There are some days I just can't write. I just sit there and hate myself. Maybe I'll write a page or two. And after while I'll give up and do something else. I don't have writer's block in the sense of not having ideas for stories. I just can't seem to organize myself to concentrate.

What I've learned to do is to have two books going at once. So if I'm trapped, get stuck on one, I can put it aside and work on the other one. It helps.

Another reason I write two books at a time is that I'll send one off to the publisher, that may be the first half of a book. It takes the publisher at least a month to respond. And I don't want to sit there doing nothing for that month. So I'll start writing something else. By the time I hear about the first book the other will be started.

J.R. You made a reference to keeping journals earlier on. Do you still do that?

W.S. Not really. I used to. When I was at Harvard, which I hated, I was depressed all the time. I kept a journal then. It was like a psychiatrist for me. It's hundreds of single-spaced pages. I tried to keep it up, but mostly I don't.

Now when I write letters I save carbons of them. I keep them in a notebook, chronologically. Those function as a sort of journal. A lot of notes I've kept from traveling around are in the form of letters.

But in the daily course of my life there aren't too many events that are particularly strange or peculiar or noteworthy. When I get an idea for a story I write it down and keep it. When I'm trying to find a particular thing that happened I go through my letters. But I hate reading my old journals from college. Most of it is such drivel, all whiny and complainy. Friends who have read them think they're hilarious so maybe there's some material there about a depressed college student. But that book has been done a million times.

J.R. Let's go back a little bit. Have you ever had formal writing classes?

W.S. The only classes I took were for a couple of years at Harvard and that was creative writing. We had to write forty pages a semester. The best thing about that class was you wrote. You learn writing by writing and by reading other people's work.

J.R.      You have written for all ages from picture books through adult books now. Are there any forms that are particularly difficult for you?

W.S.      Probably a picture book. A picture book is a five-page manuscript that goes through a lot of revisions. It is different from a novel. There are so many fewer words. It's almost more like a poem. Every word you have needs to be exactly right because there are so few. You have to have an idea that's so clear and so right in every way, and is so simple and so elegant. Everything has to fit right together. It's like a puzzle.

I feel I express myself better in a novel format.

J.R.      Your first novel was . . .

W.S.      *Blackbriar.*

After I graduated from college I spent a year in London where I studied musical composition privately and also worked as a pianist at the Royal Ballet School. The novel is about a lot of the experiences I had in England. A lot of it is really true. It's a strange book.

The house in the book is a pesthouse where people were sent when they had the plague. Very isolated, with no plumbing, no electricity, nothing. And I did spend almost every weekend when I was in England in a house exactly like that.

One of the things that made the book work was Ann Durell, who did a huge amount of work on it to put it together. She does a lot of work on all of my books.

One of my problems was my characters were not too clearly delineated. That was one of the major revisions I had to go through over and over again. Solidify the characters and make them stronger.

One of my tendencies is to have the plot be a plot and let my characters get pushed around by it. That's lazy. The characters have to determine the plot.

J.R.      But that's certainly not the case in *House of Stairs.*

W.S.      That book was unusual in that there were only five characters. They were put in this weird environment and the whole book was about how they related to each other and how they were manipulated by the experiment they were in.

For that book I did sit down and map out each character way ahead of time and figure out who each character was.

J.R.      Then you don't normally work from a formal outline?

W.S.      No.

When I first started writing I threw everything into the books, without knowing how they were going to end, and with whatever seemed interesting. I ran into a lot of problems with that. I'd get to the end and none of it meant anything! It ended up taking longer to write books without an outline.

Then there was a time when I was really broke and had this idea about two kids having the same dream. I had written a short version of it which was rejected. So I sat down and brainstormed for a couple of days and wrote out an outline. The plot developed from that. Then I sat down and did the actual writing. The whole thing went much faster.

Now that's what I try to do. I don't have a formal outline but when I get an idea I think is strong enough I'll spend several days typing and writing out everything I can think of. That usually ends up becoming the plot.

As I go along the characters make themselves. While I'm brainstorming I begin to figure out who the characters are.

J.R.     From your view, what is the most satisfying book you've done yet?

W.S.     *Tycho.* It was amazing. I got the idea, I figured out the plot, and I sat down and wrote it in a month. Everything fell into place. Ann, who's very picky and makes me do things over and over and *over* again, only made one little suggestion to change one scene and the book was done!

There isn't too much that is wrong with that book. It's not that I'm bragging but I think it came out very well. I'm very happy about that book.

And I said when I finished, "Oh, I've finally learned how to write books. And from now on every book I write will be this easy." But of course it hasn't turned out that way.

*Fingers* was another good book for me.

J.R.     In what way?

W.S.     It's very different and much more sophisticated, concentrated in plot, spookiness, and suspense. And to a certain extent, character. I think with that book I finally began to establish a style, a tone, that is sort of mine.

J.R.     You have done one collaboration. Do you think you'll do more?

W.S.     I don't know. That book[4] came about because of research I had to do for *House of Stairs.* I wanted it to be accurate so I showed it to a friend of mine who's a behavioral psychologist. He gave me some very good ideas for the book. Then he wanted to write a book about behavior modification because it gets so much bad press. So he said, "Why don't we do a book together?" He was the expert and I was the professional writer. And we got it published though it never did particularly well.

We had a lot of fun working on it. But I wonder how successful collaborations can be.

J.R.     What do you mean?

W.S.     I don't really feel that it was my book. I feel it might have been if I had done it on my own. But then I would have never written that book on my own because I didn't know enough about the subject.

I find my most successful books are me and the editor and nobody else. And I guess what I'm really best at is writing young adult books. That's somehow where it all clicks, where it all comes together.

J.R.    How do you define "young adult book"?

W.S.    I think I know the answer.

I say to myself sometimes, "I'm writing at this sophisticated level, doing the book any way I want, so why don't the kids read Dickens then? What are they reading me for? What's the sense? Why do my books exist?" One of the answers to that is that I think YA books are about adolescence, about teenagers and told from their point of view.

I think my books are generally positive even though they have a lot of ugly things in them. They usually have endings that are happy. Also, personally, and this may be childish of me, I don't like books to have horrible endings. I don't enjoy them as much. I think it's more fun to read a book where maybe a lot of horrible things happen and at the end something good happens. And when you close the book you have a feeling of satisfaction.

J.R.    So at some level you are keeping the ultimate reader of your books in your mind?

W.S.    To some extent. But when I start out writing a book I just write it in the best way to tell the story. I don't try to write down or make it particularly easy unless I'm writing a book aimed for younger kids.

J.R.    Are you planning more picture books?

W.S.    Only if I get more ideas that are appropriate for them. My feeling is that you have to have an idea that is right. An idea you can tell in a picture-book format. That it can be concise enough.

One of my easy-to-read books[5] is about a compulsive liar. It was one of the best ideas I've ever had. Everybody knows somebody like that. My idea that I thought was good was to convince the reader that she was a compulsive liar, and then to have it end that everything she said was true. And it worked. Stephen Kellogg's pictures are wonderful. That didn't start out to be an easy-to-read book. I wanted it to be a picture book. Anyway, my mother says it's my best book!

J.R.    How much do you draw from your own life for your books?

W.S.    Let's see. *Blackbriar* and *Run* were based on houses I actually lived in. *House of Stairs* was an attempt to get away from where I've been and it has a totally different setting. *Fingers* takes place in hotel rooms. Because of touring I've seen many of them!

*Tycho* is named for my youngest brother. In that book each kid is named after a famous person their parents would like them to be like when they grow up. Tycho doesn't know what he wants to be so he's a misfit. Tycho was for Tycho Brahe, a famous astronomer. And it makes for a good title!

J.R.  Back to drawing from real life.

W.S.  A lot of my characters are based on real people. That can sometimes be a problem. I try to disguise them enough so they won't be recognizable. I tend to focus on relationships, how people treat other people. I've done some things where an editor has said, "It's too far-fetched," and it had really happened. If you're going to have the reader believe, you've got to make it convincing—even if it's true.

J.R.  Every writer has a turning-point book, a book where everything finally comes together, style, characters, dialog. What's yours?

W.S.  *Tycho* again. I think it's a funny book. I don't know if kids see it as funny or not. That was the book when I really loosened up from the experience of having written X number of books already. And I outlined it so I knew what was going to happen!

That book I felt free with. I pulled myself together. I felt I could write, that I had potential.

My brother-in-law read it in manuscript and thought it was hilariously funny. I thought it was funny. Then it got published and the reviews said, "grim, spine-chilling horror." And I thought what is wrong with me if I think it's so funny and they think it's horrifying?

J.R.  Do you follow your reviews closely?

W.S.  Of course I believe good reviews and feel bad reviews are just wrong. The short ones from schools[6] can be really irritating. A lot of unpleasant things happen in my books. People are not nice to each other, but I think that's the way it is. And you have to have conflict in a book or there is no plot, no suspense.

The funny thing is you get these criticisms from schools and they say this book is unpleasant or nasty or "ugh." I don't know what they expect. I don't know what they want to read. Books that are "nice"? A lot of picture-book reviews must be so irritating to illustrators because they talk mooshy about stories and then say, "pictures are very pretty in pastel hues" and the pictures are at least fifty per cent, if not more, of the book.

J.R.  Characterize your style.

W.S.  Slightly cynical and black humorish. I tend to be too wordy and overdescribe things and draw on details that aren't too important. And I have a feeling my books won't be produced as movies because they are too cynical or dark or because people are too nasty to each other.

J.R.      You've shifted from writing in third person to first person in your novels. Why is that?

W.S.      *Fingers* was the first book I did that in. It was fun to do so I'm going to continue it. In a certain way I like it because somehow it seems more real to me. A third person story is told by the omniscient observer. It's too easy to just *tell* things rather than show them.

      I didn't think I'd be comfortable with first person because you have a lot of problems in telling the story from one point of view. How do you solve the problem of letting the reader know things the first-person narrator doesn't know? And the character may see things in a way that is slightly distorted and you have to be able to get that across. You try to get the characters to say one thing but somehow indirectly tell the reader something else.

      I think it's much more effective and better writing to have the reader learn those things from observing events and from what people say to each other. I think it's better education for the kids reading it, too.

J.R.      Better education than what?

W.S.      Better than just telling, and where it's all fed to them and where you don't have to think as much. In a first-person book they have to think things out for themselves and to look beyond the words to see what's happening.

      I was surprised at how young kids in the sixth or seventh grade were reading *House of Stairs* and understanding it. I was really impressed. You hear all this stuff about how kids are so illiterate but I'm impressed by how much they read.

J.R.      What appears to be your most successful book with kids?

W.S.      It seems to be *Into the Dream.* It's about ESP and has sold more than any other book of mine. When I first wrote it I sort of imagined that I might write a sequel, that I might use these characters again. I tried twice and the manuscripts were rejected with reason. They didn't work. I don't think I'll ever do that because I got tired of it. Kids write to me and beg me for a sequel to the book but I'm really not interested. It's hard enough to write something I'm interested in. But if the work bores me, forget it. I just can't do it.

      By the time my books are published I am bored with working on them. I rarely sit down and read my books after they're published. I get a feeling of satisfaction of seeing it there with the nice jacket art, flipping through the pages. And it's even more satisfying when you get a good intelligent review, when somebody sees what you're trying to do. The satisfaction is weird. It's not easily defined.

J.R.     You don't get that feeling of letdown that some writers get when you're finished?

W.S.    No, I don't get depressed!
I feel *relief*. It's done. The editor finally likes it. And now I can work on something else.

## Notes

[1] Emilie McLeod, former editor-in-chief of children's books for Atlantic Monthly Press, was also an author of children's books.

[2] Joyce Carol Oates, a contemporary playwright, poet, essayist, and short story writer, author of *Bellefleur* (New York: Dutton, 1980), *Invisible Woman* (Princeton, N.J.: Ontario Review Press, 1982), *Angel of Light* (New York: Dutton, 1981), and many others.

[3] Ann Durell, publisher of children's books for E. P. Dutton.

[4] *Take Charge.*

[5] *Once, Said Darlene.*

[6] Sleator refers here to reviews that are sent to publishers directly by schools and public libraries. These are usually staff-written reviews, written for in-house use, and sent to publishers as a courtesy to allow for a "grass-roots" feeling about individual books. Many are very short and to the point.

## BIBLIOGRAPHY

*Among the Dolls.* il. Trina Schart Hyman. New York: Dutton, 1975.

*Angry Moon.* il. Blair Lent. Boston: Little, Brown, 1970.

*Blackbriar.* il. Blair Lent. New York: Dutton, 1972.

*Fingers.* New York: Atheneum, 1983.

*The Green Futures of Tycho.* New York: Dutton, 1981.

*House of Stairs.* New York: Dutton, 1974.

*Interstellar Pig.* New York: Dutton, 1984.

*Into the Dream.* il. Ruth Sanderson. New York: Dutton, 1979.

*Once, Said Darlene.* il. Steven Kellogg. New York: Dutton, 1979.

*Run.* New York: Dutton, 1973.

*Take Charge: A Personal Guide to Behavior Modification.* With William H. Redd. New York: Random House, 1976.

*That's Silly.* il. Lawrence DiFiori. New York: Dutton, 1981.

# AWARDS AND HONORS

The Angry Moon
> Boston Globe-Horn Book Award
> honor book
> Randolph Caldecott Medal
> honor book
> Fanfare Book
> Library of Congress list
> Notable Children's Book
> Notable Children's Book,
> 1940-1970

Fingers
> Best Book of the Year

The Green Futures of Tycho
> Best Book of the Year

The House of Stairs
> Best Book for Young Adults
> Best of the Best/YA
> Best Book of the Year

Into the Dream
> Children's Choice Book

Interstellar Pig
> Best Book of the Year

# ADDITIONAL SOURCES

Commire. Something about the Author.
Contemporary Authors.
Science Fiction and Fantasy Literature.

Jovial Bob Stine

## BIOGRAPHICAL NOTE

Jovial Bob (a.k.a. R. L. Stine) Stine was born on October 8, 1943, in Columbus, Ohio, where he attended Ohio State University, graduating in 1965. His magazine publishing career began in 1968 at Scholastic Magazines, after which he spent nine years as editor-in-chief of *Bananas Magazine.* Since 1984 he has been the editor-in-chief of *Maniac Magazine.* Mr. Stine married Jane Waldhorn in 1969 and they have one son, Matthew.

## PRELUDE TO THE INTERVIEW

Jovial Bob Stine, who, as I said, is also known as R. L. Stine, is like most humorists. His public personality as author and editor of children's books and magazines is a madcap one. His private side is one that is calm and orderly, unlike his printed work. When asking a question and expecting a humourous answer, you get reflection. As with most humorists, his wit is reserved for his writing.

He has hit a nerve with children. His books and magazines are improbably funny and wild in their approach and strike the right balance between satire and truth. These are things many children look for in their "funny" books and magazines and things that many adults who purchase books for children sometimes question. As a humorist, it has created a sort of no-win situation for Bob, which is discussed here.

Bob has been associated with Scholastic, Inc. since the beginning of his career as the editor of some of its most successful magazines. It wasn't until he created *Bananas*—in its time the number one magazine in circulation for children—that he unleashed the full range of his talent. Since this interview, *Bananas* has given way to *Maniac,* his newest creation.

Appearing briefly here is Jane Stine, his wife and sometimes co-author. Jane was formerly associated with Scholastic and is now co-owner of Parachute Press, a children's book packager in New York. She was very helpful throughout the interview in bringing out a side of Bob that could very well have remained closed.

# THE INTERVIEW

J.R.     The past in children's books is littered with Aunt Janes, Grandma Lucys, Cousin Whomevers, and Uncle Whosits. And now there's Jovial Bob. What's the story behind the name?

J.B.S.     Well, I always tell people that I came up with the name Jovial Bob because my *real* name is inappropriate to the type of kids' books I write.

Then they ask me what's my real name, and I say, "Norman Mailer."

Actually, there's no good story behind the name at all. When I was a student at Ohio State, I was editor of the humor magazine, *The Sundial.* To help sales, I decided to create some kind of persona. So I called myself Jovial Bob.

Not much of a story, I'm afraid.

The name confuses some kids. I get mail to "Dear Mr. Jovial" or "Ms. Jovial Bob."

But there are at least forty-eight other Bob Stines or Steins in publishing in New York, so I keep my Jovial.

J.R.     Well, I did think there would be a funnier story behind it. Oh well. Were you always interested in doing magazines?

J.B.S.     From the time I was nine. I've had such a single-minded life. When I was nine I discovered an old typewriter up in the attic and I started typing up little joke books. Now it's thirty years later and I'm still sitting at a typewriter, typing the same jokes, most likely.

I've been writing humor ever since. When I was in high school, my parents would say, "Why don't you get a summer job?" and I'd say, "I can't this summer. I'm writing a novel." I can't believe I got away with it, but I did. I never worked a day my entire childhood.

J.S.     He was a real Jewish prince at twelve!

J.B.S.     I'd spend the entire summers typing. I hate to think what dreadful stuff I was turning out!

J.S.     He's kept it all. If he read it today, he'd probably still think it was hilarious!

J.R.     Were you one of those kids who secretly faced east to New York every day, thinking that someday it'll be all mine . . . the lights, fame, fortune, all that?

J.B.S.     That's what you do when you live in Ohio. You plan how you're going to get out.

I always knew I'd come to New York because I figured that's where writers lived. And I always figured that somehow I'd have my own humor magazine. I'm still amazed, though, that it all really happened.

But when I was a kid in Ohio, I had this huge, powerful radio, and I used to spend all of my time trying to tune in New York stations. I'd spend hours and hours in front of this radio. At night I could get Jean Shepherd on WOR. I'd listen to his fabulous stories and know that I had come to New York.

J.R.     What or whom were other big influences on you when you were a kid?

J.B.S.     Ernie Kovacs. Bob & Ray. Max Shulman. Sid Caesar.
And *Mad* Magazine.
I discovered *Mad* comics one day when I was eleven or twelve in the barbershop. They absolutely blew me away. I couldn't believe anything could be so funny.
I wasn't allowed to bring them home. My parents said they were trash, and wouldn't let them in the house. So I used to get a haricut every two weeks—just to make sure I didn't miss an issue of *Mad.*

J.R.     Well, when you finally got to New York, you took sort of a roundabout way of getting a humor magazine of your own, didn't you?

J.B.S.     Yes.
I ended up at *Junior Scholastic* in 1968 writing news and history articles. It was great! I was working on an actual magazine. And I was getting one hundred and twenty-five dollars a week. That seemed like *big* money!
Three years later, everything was reorganized and we started a new magazine called *Search,* which was for kids in junior high school but who read on a fourth-grade reading level. I was the editor of that. It was the first magazine I was the editor of.
When I was in school I hated social studies, I had no interest in it. So it was a real challenge for me to be the editor of a social studies magazine! And it was perfect for the readers because they didn't like school and couldn't read well.
It was a very creative magazine. We did all kinds of things in disguise, interviews, simulations, that sort of thing.
We had tremendous mail responses from teachers saying the kids loved it. But it was a little weird for Scholastic. Their other magazines, *Junior Scholastic, Senior Scholastic,* were very straight, and here we were doing all these strange things.
I got in trouble once by going too far. I did something called "Medical Care: Is It a Horror Show?" with a girl on a doctor's bed and the doctor as a werewolf. It turns out there are a lot of doctors and American Medical Association people on school boards! We got a *lot* of mail. It was not the wisest thing I ever did. But it was a great cover!

J.R.     From there you went to *Bananas?*

J.B.S.     Just about.

        *Dynamite Magazine* came in about 1974. Overnight it became the largest children's magazine in the country. It broke a million circulation with the very first issue and got bigger after that.

        The woman who started it, Jenette Kahn, left, and my wife, Jane, took it over. It became even bigger. *Dynamite* was so big that Scholastic wanted to duplicate it in some way for teenagers. *Dynamite* was for the fourth and fifth grade. And we wanted to appeal to teenagers. We figured the thing that united them all was television and humor. So we created *Bananas.*

        I ended up doing *Bananas* and *Search* together. It was a tough, hard year. But really exciting. Then I had to choose one. I took *Bananas.* It was what I really wanted to do from the time I was nine years old. I was thirty-two and I'd achieved my life's ambition! I was a very happy person.

J.R.     What's the single hardest thing in creating a magazine like *Bananas?*

J.B.S.     The hard thing is knowing who's going to be "in" six months in the future. Who's going to be popular; who's newsy.

        I spend half my life, *half*, trying to figure out who's going to be on the next cover. That's the biggest decision I make for each issue.

J.R.     Isn't it difficult to keep coming up with fresh humor material?

J.B.S.     Sure. We try real hard not to repeat ourselves. But I don't have any hobbies and I don't really work all that hard. I'm lucky. Writing comes very easily to me.

J.R.     What kind of humor do teens like best?

J.B.S.     Recognition humor. Things they recognize from their own lives. We had a feature called "It Never Fails!" For example, "It never fails when you get in the shower, the phone rings." "It never fails that when the teacher asks the one question you don't know, she calls on you." "It never fails that when you hit a ketchup bottle, ketchup comes out all over the place."

        They love this kind of material.

J.R.     What about the theoretical side of humor for children and teens? What are your views here?

J.B.S.     The whole problem with doing humor for children comes from adults. A lot of people seem to think that if a book or magazine is just funny, it's trash.

        Adults have their right to read or watch trash. Adults have their right to pick out a book that's just for entertainment, nothing else. But many adults seem to feel that every children's book has to teach them something, has to be uplifting in some way.

My theory is a children's book doesn't have to teach them anything. It can be just for fun. I'll sit down and watch some TV program, some garbage, just for entertainment. I have that right. Kids somehow don't have that right.

It seems to me they should. There's nothing wrong with something that's just for fun. The great thing about *Bananas* is that it doesn't offer any socially redeeming value. It's just fun.

J.R.        Did you run into problems, then, with the humor in *How to Be Funny*, your first book?

J.B.S.        Absolutely! No one knew where to put it.

It was my first book and I was really excited about it. I'd look for it in stores and people would ask me if they could find it under "theater arts." Where *do* you put a satire on how-to books?

There's one main reason why you can't sell humor to kids. Everyone says they want it—bookstores, librarians. They all say, "This is what we need, this is what the world needs." But it doesn't sell. And I think the main reason humor for kids doesn't sell in bookstores is because there isn't a shelf for it.

Think about children's departments in any bookstore. There is a place for young adult fiction, younger fiction, and picture books. But there's never a shelf called humor. No one knows where to put those books.

A lot of librarians were confused by it, too. Remember it's a satire on how-to books. It was called, in one instance, "a dangerous book." Another said, "If this book gets in the hands of kids, the kids will try some of the things in it. This will be a world of tears, not a world of laughter. Not recommended." Another said, "This was the kind of thing that was behind the Viet Nam war." I was even blamed for *that!*

Of course, I thought all this was hilarious.

J.R.     What's the worst publishing story of your career?

J.B.S.       It involves a book I wrote called *How to Do Everything.*

J.R.     I don't know that one.

J.B.S.       You shouldn't. It was never published. It's a shame. It was the ultimate how-to book. It covered everything, nothing was left out.

The editor loved it, but she wanted to change the title to *How to Wash a Duck.* I said, "But you bought this book for the title, *How to Do Everything.*" She had changed her mind. She said she now thought the title was too *dry.* She preferred *How to Wash a Duck* because "Ducks are funny and we try to get as many ducks as we can on our covers"! So we compromised and called the book *How to Wash a Duck and How to Do Everything Else.* And they put a picture of a duck in a shower cap on the cover. But they never published the book.

J.R.  How come?

J.B.S.  It was a "business decision." Maybe it was the humor? Maybe it was the ducks? I don't know.

J.R.  You and Jane have been doing a number of books together. How do you manage to do this? I think it would be difficult.

J.B.S.  It's very hard to work together, to collaborate. We always swear we'll never do it again.

We work very differently. I have to work from the beginning from the first word on the first page and right through. I don't like to revise at all. I'm too self-satisfied. I always think if it's typed, it's a masterpiece, it's perfect. So I don't change a word.

Jane *loves* to revise! She writes the back and thinks about it. Then she writes the middle. Then the introduction. She goes back and forth all the time. It drives me crazy. Consequently the books get better. But she's right, of course. There is something to be said for revision.

J.R.  Outside of getting involved with publishing in the first place, what is the biggest mistake in your career?

J.B.S.  An autograph party promoting *How to Be Funny* at a bookstore.
It was a Saturday afternoon and I was in the children's department.
To promote being "funny" I sat there with bunny ears on my head.
So there I was sitting there with these ears on my head. A grown man! No one would come near me! We didn't sell one book. The entire afternoon's stack just stayed there. I think I terrified a lot of kids. They'll never go near a bookstore again!

J.R.  How about a really terrific thing that's happened to you?

J.B.S.  I got a conference call one time from a fifth-grade teacher in Wichita, Kansas. She had read *How to Be Funny* to her class. A really *great* teacher!

Each kid had a question to read to me. This one little voice said, "Mr. Stine, where do you get your ideas?" So I gave her some vague answer. The next kid, "Mr. Stine, do you write all your own jokes?" The next kid, "Mr. Stine, where do you get your ideas?" They were all the same questions! It was an hour of answering the same questions. It was terrific!

J.R.  What have you been working on lately?

J.B.S.  Well, I just finished *Jovial Bob's Computer Joke Book.* This was a tough one to write. The way you usually write joke books is to get a bunch of joke books together, pick out some jokes, and put them into your joke book. But no one has written a computer joke book. There weren't any jokes to steal! I ended up having to write about eighty or one hundred original computer jokes.

J.R.     Do you have any complaints?

J.B.S.     No, not really. I still can't believe people actually pay me money to write the things I write. I feel as if I'm getting away with something, as if I should be paying them!

## BIBLIOGRAPHY

*The Absurdly Silly Encyclopedia and Flyswatter.* il. B. K. Taylor. New York: Scholastic, 1978.

*Bananas Looks at TV.* il. Sam Viviano. New York: Scholastic, 1981.

*The Beast Handbook.* il. B. K. Taylor. New York: Scholastic, 1981.

*Blips!* New York: Scholastic, 1982.

*Bored with Being Bored! How to Beat the Boredom Blahs.* With Jane Stine. il. Jerry Zimmerman. New York: Four Winds, 1982.

*The Complete Book of Nerds.* il. Sam Viviano. New York: Scholastic, 1980.

*The Cool Kids' Guide to Summer Camp.* With Jane Stine. il. Jerry Zimmerman. New York: Four Winds, 1981.

*Don't Stand in the Soup: The World's Funniest Guide to Manners.* il. Carol Nicklaus. New York: Bantam, 1982.

*The Dynamite Do-It-Yourself Pen-Pal Kit.* il. Jared Lee. New York: Scholastic, 1980.

*Dynamite's Funny Book of the Sad Facts of Life.* il. Jared Lee. New York: Scholastic, 1980.

*Everything You Need to Know to Survive Brothers and Sisters.* With Jane Stine. il. Sal Murdocca. New York: Random House, 1983.

*Everything You Need to Survive First Dates.* With Jane Stine. il. Sal Murdocca. New York: Random House, 1983.

*Everything You Need to Survive Homework.* With Jane Stine. il. Sal Murdocca. New York: Random House, 1983.

*Everything You Need to Survive Money Problems.* With Jane Stine. il. Sal Murdocca. New York: Random House, 1983.

*Gnasty Gnomes.* il. Peter J. Lippman. New York: Random House, 1981.

*Going Out! Going Steady! Going Bananas!* photogs. Dan Nelken. New York: Scholastic, 1980.

*Golden Sword of Dragonwalk.* il. David Febland. New York: Scholastic, 1983.

*The Great Superman Movie Book.* New York: Scholastic, 1984.

*How to Be Funny: An Extremely Silly Guidebook.* il. Carol Nicklaus. New York: Dutton, 1978.

*The Pig's Book of World Records.* il. Peter J. Lippman. New York: Random House, 1980.

*The Sick of Being Sick Book.* With Jane Stine. il. Carol Nicklaus. New York: Dutton, 1980.

*The Time Raider.* New York: Scholastic, 1982.


## AWARDS AND HONORS

*The Sick of Being Sick Book*
        Children's Choice Book


## ADDITIONAL SOURCES

Commire. *Something about the Author.*
*Contemporary Authors.*

Todd Strasser

## BIOGRAPHICAL NOTE

New York City is the hometown of Todd Strasser, who was born there on May 5, 1950. He graduated from Beloit College in Wisconsin in 1974. His writing career began as a reporter for the *Middletown* (New York) *Times Herald-Record* and continued through 1977 as an advertising copywriter. Mr. Strasser and his wife, Pamela Older, have a daughter, Lia. Todd Strasser's pseudonym is Morton Rhue.

## PRELUDE TO THE INTERVIEW

Todd Strasser hit it just right with his first novel, *Angel Dust Blues.* Though the writing took him six years and many versions, the book's publication in 1979 told the world that here was a new writer who intended to stay. Since then his books and readership have grown with him, placing him in a prominent position within young adult literature.

He started his writing career as a newspaperman and an advertising copywriter. But neither position allowed room for the development of his creativity. In journalism and advertising, only time and word count matter; a space must be filled; excess words are cut. Todd prefers the more leisurely book world, where an author is allowed full rein to take as many pages as are needed.

He is a contemporary writer, tapping into today's young adults and their concerns. Offering hope and solutions, Todd also wants to offer good stories with strong options. That is the direction his writing is now taking. He has been able to maintain this, all the while growing in writing strength and ability.

# THE INTERVIEW

J.R.     Let's start your interview talking about your fortune cookie business.

T.S.     Oh, the cookies! Well, I started that business after I got a three thousand dollar advance for my first novel, *Angel Dust Blues,* and realized that it wasn't going to last me very long. Since I come from a business family, I've always felt inclined to do something businesslike as well as be a writer. I just happened to start with fortune cookies.

J.R.     Weren't you an advertising copywriter at some point, too?

T.S.     Yes. I spent a year at it, around 1977. I also worked for a newspaper for two years before that. But I was never happy telling someone else's stories. I wanted to tell my own.

J.R.     How did you come to start writing for a living, then?

T.S.     When I was in college I took a creative writing course and the professor said, "It looks like you have potential." After college I got a job writing in the public relations department at my college. Then I found the job on the newspaper.

I guess I decided I wanted to be a novelist while I was working at the newspaper. There were stories I wanted to tell. Later I moved to advertising to give me more time to work on fiction. When I sold my first novel I quit my advertising job. And then I went the route of the poor struggling novelist. I used to do things like cut my own hair.

Even with the fortune cookie business I was still broke most of the time. You know in New York every penny you make goes toward rent. The first date I ever took Pam on was to a bar in midtown Manhattan. They had a free smorgasbord if you bought a drink. I used to eat there two or three times a week. Buy a beer and get a free dinner.

Even when *Angel Dust Blues* was auctioned for paperback I was still poor. I couldn't believe how much the publisher paid for it, but the hardcover house took half and my agent got her cut and then I didn't see all of my share for almost two years! It took forever.

J.R.     *Angel Dust Blues* was not a bad way to break into writing for young adults. What's the story behind it?

T.S.     It was based on something that happened in high school to people I knew and I felt it was worth writing about. I actually wrote the first draft in college in 1973. Eight drafts later it was published. In 1979, to be precise. The funny thing is, the draft that Ferdinand Monjo[1] bought, his assistant recommended that it be rejected. I only know that because when they gave me the manuscript back, the recommendation not to buy was under the first page!

But Ferdinand decided to take a chance on me. What he bought and what he eventually got were different books. I remember he took me out to lunch and told me, "This is what you've done and this is what I think you really meant to do. Go ahead and do it."

He was amazing because he was able to see what I was trying to do even though I wasn't yet skilled enough to bring it off. He had that kind of vision.

There aren't many editors like that. Whatever that book is would not have been written without him. He was really something. Unfortunately, he died without seeing the final version.

J.R.    Did you grow up thinking—knowing, perhaps—that you were going to be a writer someday?

T.S.    In school I was a terrible writer, a terrible speller and was never given any encouragement at all until I got to college.

For many years after I started writing I never believed I would actually be a writer. I wrote the way some people sing in the shower. In a shower you don't think anyone is going to hear you. I wrote thinking no one was ever going to read me.

I guess my becoming a writer was really a process of elimination. I tried a variety of things in college. Medicine, law. Nothing worked. I tried premed and was afraid of blood. In premed you get to do blood tests on each other. That was the end for me.

My family felt I had to be a business person, or if I was lucky, a doctor or a lawyer. I never really thought I would be a writer. In fact, even today I find it hard to believe that I manage to make most of my living by selling books.

J.R.    After *Angel Dust Blues* you wrote *Friends till the End,* which was followed by *Rock 'n' Roll Nights.* The latter was a distinct departure from the first two. Why?

T.S.    I wanted to do a different kind of book. *Rock 'n' Roll Nights* is a light book, probably more commercial than the first two and not as serious. I had a lot of fun writing it. I had just finished *Friends till the End,* which is about a kid who has leukemia and I wanted to write a fun, happy, up book. There's a sequel, *Turn It Up!*

What I wanted to do is follow this rock-and-roll band from the days when they were playing in the street to the days when they are a supergroup with ten thousand screaming kids in front of them, chronicling their lives, what it means, and how they are affected by their success.

I want it to be an uplifting story. Essentially whatever they come up against, they're going to succeed. I guess that's the difference between being in the business of writing, which is what I am, and being a writer who's strictly writing for posterity.

J.R.    Is there something wrong in writing for posterity? You hint as if you might think so.

T.S.    No, I don't mean that. But I do think there are people who sit down and really don't care if a book will sell as long as the book is great literature. And then there are many more who write what they think is going to get published.

How do we know what's going to last?

I think it's pretty pretentious for any writer alive today to think his or her books are going to be read one hundred years from now.

J.R.    From the sound of what you're saying, you seem to have the attitude that writers are becoming "brand-name" products in the sense the public will buy what writers it recognizes in books, much in the same way they buy coffee and aspirin.

T.S.    I think writers *are* products. Every year the publisher comes out with his line with certain products on it. We are *sold*. When you see a book in a store by Todd Strasser, fifty percent of that book is me. The other fifty percent is the guy on the road doing the selling. It's all for the product. I am as much a piece of that product as my books are. I think that's writing in the future. It's all "star" mentality and publicity and *People Magazine.*

Take John Irving. He wrote one novel, *Garp,*[2] that "worked." I think he is now a product. I don't think that's bad or good. That's the way it is. Judy Blume is a product. I guess it would be nice to be as well known as John Irving or Judy Blume.

J.R.    What about those writers who write just for the sake of writing? Is there any hope for them?

T.S.    We all write for the sake of writing. It's just that some of us have families to support. And there are writers out there who are phenomenally good writers and whose books will never be tremendously popular because the author does not want to become a product. Did you ever hear of a guy named William Wiser? You should read his book, *Disappearances.*[3]

William Wharton, who wrote *Birdy,*[4] would not allow himself to become a product. William Wharton is not even his real name. He stands only on his books alone. I think *Birdy* was probably one of the most interesting pieces of literature to come out of this country in years. It is an extremely original, fascinating novel. Then there's someone like me. I spend a lot of time writing, but I also spend a lot of time on the road, speaking before groups of librarians and teachers. I also visit a lot of schools and do assemblies and speak to students. I really think publishers want writers to go out and sell themselves these days. You almost have to because there are so many writers out there that the only way anyone is going to know who you are is if they've actually met you.

J.R.     How much of your peers' writing do you read?

T.S.     Not as much as I should.

Time is the major problem here. I start writing around 9 in the morning and I usually keep busy with one thing or another until 5 P.M. Then my daughter comes home and a few hours later my wife gets home and by the time we've all eaten and my daughter is in bed it's usually 9:30 or 10. If there's nothing else to do I can read for about an hour.

Also, when it comes to teens, I am always looking for nonfiction articles and stories about them rather than fiction. I want to know what's going on in their lives; I'm looking for information I can use in my own stories about them. *Rolling Stone* and the *New York Times* are two of my best sources of information about teenagers.

Finally, when it comes to fiction, there's almost always some new hot adult novel out that somehow diverts my attention.

J.R.     Do you see yourself continuing with "up" novels rather than returning to the problem novel?

T.S.     This whole idea of problem novels—"let's deal with drug addiction, let's deal with alcoholism"—has been overdone. It seems like every problem has been written about one hundred times already. And how many of these problems does a typical teenager face anyway?

I think it's better to write a real novel, to tell a story about teenagers and not just focus on alcoholism or prostitution or suicide or something that can be delineated in just one word. Problem novels are artificial in that respect. They take a single part of life and try to make it all of life. I think people want to read books that are about all of life, that have problems, that have romance, that have real characters.

J.R.     How involved do you get in the art and design of your book covers?

T.S.     For *Angel Dust Blues* the publisher did the paperback jacket without consulting me. It's a story of two boys and their relationship in terms of trust and friendship. One of the boys also has a strong romance. But the cover had two boys on it and no girl! I really wanted to have a girl because I felt the romantic aspect was very important. So I convinced the publisher to paint a girl and she came out looking like a scarecrow.

Ever since then I make sure early on that I let the publisher know what I hope the cover will look like. After that it's up to them. What they sometimes do is give me a cover before it's done. I point out what I think would be better. They generally make those improvements within the concept of the cover as it is. I can't say, "I don't like this cover, give me a new cover." I can say, "Put in an amplifier, put in a guitar, change her hair," and they'll do that.

One exception to that. In *Workin' for Peanuts* I originally described Jeff in the book as having black hair. On the cover he had brown hair.

When I saw the cover I asked to have the hair changed to black. The publisher said, "Hey, look. It's easier for you to go through the manuscript and change his hair to brown than to change his hair to black on the cover." So I did. It only meant three or four changes. Of course, every other character in the book had brown hair so I changed a few others, too, so everyone wouldn't have brown hair.

J.R.    Have you thought about doing books for adults?

T.S.    Yes! I have three novels for adults and they're all terrible and unpublishable. But I think someday I probably will. As I write I get more confident. Even when I write bad books I gain confidence.

J.R.    Confidence in. . . ?

T.S.    My writing ability. And as a writer. As far as I can tell, it's not a matter of the skills involved. There's enough schlock stuff for adults to prove that.

There is something that bothers me about writing for adults, though. I'm sure you've heard this before. It is, you write an adult book and it's got a couple of months life in hardcover if it's lucky. Maybe it comes out in paperback or maybe it doesn't. If it does, it's on the shelf for a month and then it's gone.

Regardless of the money involved, the idea that something I've put so much work into has two months to live, essentially, is very hard to accept. One of the great things about writing for young adults is that your books stay in print for so long. *Angel Dust Blues* was published in 1979 and still sells, and, of course, the paperback is still in print. All the money in the world can't replace the feeling of walking into a bookstore and seeing all your books on the shelf.

J.R.    Well, money is certainly important, no question about that. But how often—and how long—can a writer sacrifice a life for "art"?

T.S.    I think about that a lot. Especially now that I have a daughter. But I don't believe writers who say they write only for money. I honestly believe that even writers who say they are totally commercial are writing for another reason, too. The biggest advances in the world are not as much as you could make if you were really determined to make money by any means possible.

J.R.    Certainly the one thing that helps any writer further a career is to be optioned for the movies. Has this happened to you?

T.S.    Yes, *Workin' for Peanuts* was sold to Scholastic Productions for a one-hour made-for-cable movie. But the idea that Hollywood has unlimited amounts of money is an oversimplification. It does have a lot of money, but there are a lot of people going after that money. The chances of you having a book made into a major two-hour theatrical release that people will see in a theater is pretty slim.

It took S. E. Hinton[5] fifteen years before anything of hers was made into a movie. Suppose she got one hundred thousand dollars. If you divide that by fifteen, it's about the same as earning minimum wage! It's not that I wouldn't mind writing for television or the movies. Television especially uses up an enormous amount of material and somebody has to keep coming up with it.

J.R.  Why don't you pursue it then?

T.S.  I'm still living in a fool's paradise. I have not faced the need to do it. I would not be motivated to write for TV except out of need. My desire is to write books. The only reason I would like to write for television is because someday I'll have to send my daughter to college. But, right now she's only a few months old.

Another thing is, I spent a long time knocking on doors, trying to get people to read what I wrote, trying to get magazine articles published and trying to get books published. It was fun, an adventure. But it was also degrading. You're being put on hold all the time. You're trying to get your foot in the door.

After I published a couple of books I didn't have to do that anymore. Now my publishers ask me if I'll have a book for next year. I don't have to go on my knees to them. That really makes a difference. And I'm not looking forward to starting over again. But I have a strong suspicion I'm going to have to!

J.R.  You've done one book under a pseudonym. Why?

T.S.  That was for *The Wave.* I was "Morton Rhue."

It was a novelization from a TV script. I spent three weeks on the book and I couldn't tell if it was a good book or bad one. You have no objective view in that short period of time. You have to put it down for six months and come back and then read it. The publisher wanted to put "Todd Strasser" on the cover, but I didn't want that. I didn't want my name on it because the book was not originally my idea. And I didn't want to have my name associated with what *might* be a bad book. Ironically, the book has gone through more than four printings and has been translated into something like six languages.

Why "Morton Rhue?" In German, 'Todd' is very similar to the word 'dead' and 'Strasser' is the word for 'street.' Hence, Mort-du-Rue in French, or "Morton Rhue."

J.R.  What kind of feedback, if any, do you get from your readers?

T.S.  I get fan mail, but I think almost every YA writer knows that a certain amount of their mail comes because a teacher tells her class, "OK, everybody. You are going to write to an author this week." Then there are other letters I can tell were written on the spur of the moment. They're really earnestly-written letters.

Some girls have also sent little gold lockets with their pictures inside. Guys write me poems. I'm really getting fascinated with the idea of how I perceive myself versus how I am perceived by these people.

J.R.    What's the difference?

T.S.    I see myself as a typical person who just happens to sit in this room and pound out books because he's basically unemployable. But other people seem to think if you're a writer you're something special.

I write back to everyone. And sometimes they write back again to me. It's good, a way of researching. They tell me what books they like, what their lives are like.

Just to show you how corny I am, I put the first fan letter I ever got in a scrapbook!

J.R.    Do you ever write fan letters to other authors?

T.S.    Actually, I do. I read books by certain writers that overwhelm me. So I write them fan letters. Sometimes they write back. If they're very famous writers I don't give my return address because I don't want them to feel compelled to send me a letter.

I wrote to a fellow named Robert Merkin who wrote *The South Florida Book of the Dead*,[6] a book about drug smuggling. This guy wrote a book I wish I'd written. It's a terrific book.

J.R.    How have your friends who are not writers handling you? I mean, very often when people get published friendships change, and not always in subtle ways.

T.S.    I can honestly say that my friends haven't changed. I think part of the reason is because there are so many writers around New York that having one for a friend is not a big deal. The other thing is that I doubt many of my friends have read more than one or two of my books and I'm pretty sure a few of them haven't read any. Sure, we talk to each other about our work, but I don't ask them to show me their memos or legal briefs.

But from strangers you do get a lot of funny reactions when they find out you're a writer.

J.R.    In what way?

T.S.    A lot of people don't think you really work. They'll ask, "What do you *really* do?"

The most common question I'm asked is how can I spend all that time alone in a room? And try as I may, I cannot explain how I do it.

I just do. Half the time I don't even know I'm alone in a room because I'm in a book somewhere when I'm writing. Now I'm to the point where I'm starting to wonder how I do this because everybody asks me how can I be doing this?

People always want to know where I get my ideas, too. So I say I get my ideas from life or from the things I wish I'd do that I don't do. But I don't know where I get my ideas. Where does anybody get an idea from?

Another thing. Once I got published, some people I used to know began to come back into my life. And I have the feeling that maybe if I'd gone on to become a dishwasher they may not have come back. A remarkable number of them turn out to have manuscripts which they just happen to be trying to get published.

J.R.  Surprise, surprise!
So, where do you go from here?

T.S.  I try and not think about the future too much because I don't know where I'm going to end up. If you're a doctor you set up your practice. The practice grows and you take on associates so you can play golf four times a week.

If you're a writer, I don't know where you go. I don't know if I'm going to wind up in television or what. I know I'd like to stay in book writing, but sometimes I wonder if there will always be enough to write about or if there will be enough of an audience.

But, for now, I'll just take it book by book.

## Notes

[1] Ferdinand N. Monjo, former editor-in-chief of children's books for Coward, McCann & Geoghegan, was also an author of children's books.

[2] John Irving, *The World According to Garp* (New York: E. P. Dutton, 1978).

[3] William Wiser, *Disappearances* (New York: Atheneum, 1980).

[4] William Wharton, *Birdy* (New York: Alfred A. Knopf, 1979).

[5] S. E. Hinton, author of *The Outsiders* (Viking, 1967), *Rumble Fish* (Delacorte, 1975), *That Was Then, This Is Now* (Viking, 1971), and *Tex* (Delacorte, 1979).

[6] Robert Merkin, *The South Florida Book of the Dead* (New York: William Morrow & Company, 1982).

## BIBLIOGRAPHY

### As Todd Strasser:

*Angel Dust Blues: A Novel.* New York: Coward, McCann & Geoghegan, 1979.

*The Complete Computer Popularity Program.* New York: Delacorte, 1984.

*Friends till the End: A Novel.* New York: Delacorte, 1981.

*Rock 'n' Roll Nights: A Novel.* New York: Delacorte, 1982.

*Turn It Up!* New York: Delacorte, 1984.

*Workin' for Peanuts.* New York: Delacorte, 1983.

### As Morton Rhue:

*The Wave.* New York: Delacorte, 1981.


## AWARDS AND HONORS

*Friends till the End*
> Best Book for Young Adults
> Notable Children's Trade Book
> > in the Field of Social Studies

*Rock 'n' Roll Nights*
> Best Book for Young Adults

_Jane Yolen_ (signature)

Jane Yolen

# BIOGRAPHICAL NOTE

The noted author of _The Girl Who Cried Flowers_ was born in New York City in 1939. In 1960 she received a B.A. from Smith College in Northampton, Massachusetts, and in 1974 she earned a master's degree from the University of Massachusetts in Amherst. From 1960 through 1965 Ms. Yolen worked in publishing, at which time she became a full-time writer. She married David Stemple in 1962 and they have three children, Heidi, Adam, and Jason. The Kerlan Collection holds some of Ms. Yolen's original manuscripts.

# PRELUDE TO THE INTERVIEW

Jane Yolen is, by her own admission, a "middle-aged Turk." Her self-parody on her almost quarter-century involvement with bookmaking refers to the idea that she was only twenty-three when her first book was published, enabling her to be called a "young Turk."

She has, quite literally, lived through the major children's literature currents and undercurrents of the times, and has been a vocal advocate for many of them. A popular and much-in-demand speaker, she is a familiar figure on the children's literature landscape, able to speak to all issues knowlegeably and from all sides. Once an editor, she is familiar with book acquisition and marketing, and for a much longer time, she has been an author. She knows the procedures and pitfalls well and speaks of them here.

Much of her reputation rests on two areas of her multileveled writing: her science fiction and her folk tales. It is in these books where the genius of her talent is seen. Her richly woven stories in either genre have received wide recognition and acclaim. It is in this style of writing where she is most articulate and comfortable.

Jane is an eager speaker. There is much she knows and is comfortable discussing. She is a cooperative and willing participant in a discussion, willing to clarify when it is necessary.

There is a phrase of hers that has become closely aligned with her that is the refrain in _Touch Magic:_ "Pass it on." In her context, "pass it on," pass on the news about children's books. If you don't, who will?

# THE INTERVIEW

J.R.     You have had quite an intensive background in publishing and writing. So let's start at the beginning and see where we go. OK?

J.Y.     OK.

After college I started with *Newsweek* doing mostly mail room, research, and other menial tasks. Then I got a job with *This Week,* again in research, then *The Saturday Review* in the production department. Finally I got a job at Gold Medal paperback books as a first manuscript reader for the bang-bang-shoot-'em-up books.

I was infamous in the trade for a few months for having written the cover line on one book, "She was all things to two men." It was clear I had a future in publishing!

In the meantime I had sold my first two books, *Pirates in Petticoats,* a nonfiction study of women pirates, and the picture book *See This Little Line?* Both are long out of print. But since I had written two children's books and knew nothing about children or children's book publishing, I decided to learn something about at least one of those. So I found a job with a children's book packager, Rutledge Press. There I learned the physical process of putting a book together—writing copy, editing, production work, flap copy writing, writing captions, publicity, et cetera. I was there a year and then got a job as assistant juvenile editor at Knopf, a job I kept for three years.

My last year at Knopf we lived on my husband's salary and banked mine so we could travel in Europe and the Middle East, camping out for almost a year. I got pregnant over there—on a town common outside of Paris! We traveled until I was about eight months pregnant, then returned to the States. My husband got a job as a professor at the University of Massachusetts in the Computer Science Center and we bought our first house in the country. We definitely did not want to raise children in the city.

J.R.     And you were writing at the same time?

J.Y.     When we left for Europe, my fourth book had just been published. By the time we came back, my fifth book, which I had written with a friend, was about to come out. But all the while we were traveling, though I had been writing like crazy, I had not been selling. The day after we landed in New York City, my agent, Marilyn Marlow, sold three books in one day. That was a record sale for me.

Two were sold to Ann Beneduce[1] at World, the first I ever sold to her. When I went to meet Ann, I was so pregnant, my stomach led the way! But those two books, *The Emperor and the Kite* and *The Minstrel and the Mountain,* were the start of a really wonderful publishing relationship. We have done many, many books together. Over twenty-five. She has published almost all of my fairy tales.

J.R.      You have had many editors over your career. Coupled with your own expertise in editing and publishing, what have you come to expect from an editor?

J.Y.      What do I expect or what do I get?

J.R.      Expect.

J.Y.      To begin with, I expect a sympathetic but critical reading. And I hope to get read sooner than an unknown writer. But, alas, that's no longer true.

And it's also no longer true that I can expect editors to trust me to revise my manuscripts or that I can (with all editors) get a contract for a manuscript that still needs hefty revisions.

J.R.      Explain that some more.

J.Y.      Recently I sent a book to an editor I had worked with before, one for whom I have done a number of books. She said she liked the manuscript, but wouldn't give me a contract until I did the revisions. My feeling was that I *could* revise and she knew it. I had certainly demonstrated that ability many times before. I told her that, but she said—in effect—"I can't be sure. You might revise it and make it worse. I might not get a book from you that is publishable." In other words, my years of demonstrated professionalism, my track record, should have counted with her and it didn't. So I said the heck with it and took the book back from her. I have enough editors who trust me and enough books to work on that *are* under contract. I asked for a commitment from that editor and when she didn't trust me enough to give it to me, I took the manuscript back.

J.R.      What else do you expect?

J.Y.      An honest and early reading. But I don't want someone to take a book just because of my name.

J.R.      Has this happened?

J.Y.      Perhaps. I look at some of my books now—even prize winners—and wonder why the editors didn't ask me to rewrite more. I certainly see ways to make the stories better now. Of course, I am older and wiser! Perhaps they are, too!

I also want the truth from an editor.

J.R.      The truth?

J.Y.      I don't try to pass off a book if I don't feel it is good. I may not be totally pleased with a story when I show it because, quite frankly, a book on the page is never as good as the one in your head. Edith Wharton said, "I dream of an eagle, I give birth to a hummingbird." Every book is like that—an eagle in the head, a bright little thing on the page. But still it flies.

And I want an early response. In the first month. I've been an editor and I know it *is* possible to make up one's mind on a manuscript within a month, especially from a known author, one you have worked with before. There are some editors who read my things quickly and I always appreciate that. There are others—no names mentioned—who sit on manuscripts for months and months. And all the kicking and screaming done by my agent and the phone calls from me do no good. I'll never send them another thing.

J.R.    What else do you expect?

J.Y.    When the book is under contract I want a *named* someone working on it with me. Not "the copyeditor," or "our readers think. . . ." I want to work *with* someone I can call by name, someone I can fight with and laugh with and come to terms with. And I don't want an editor to do the revisions for me, thank you. My book is *mine,* not the editor's. It has *my* name on the jacket and the title page and the running heads. I don't want to be *told* what to change. But *ask* me, *suggest.* Then give me time to think about the suggestions.

I have had manuscripts come back with changes I did not make. So I changed things back to my original. It is very wrong for somebody— copyeditor, manuscript reader, editor-in-chief, I don't care—to put words in or take words out without checking with me. (Though to be realistic, as an editor I worked with several writers who did *not* care. One, I remember vividly, said, "Do what you want, just send me my check.") There are editors who are heavy editors and those who are light. I don't mind heavy editing as long as I am the one making the decisions, as long as the marks on the manuscript are in the form of a query, not a directive.

Sometimes copyeditors are the strangest to deal with. They are supposed to be checking spelling, punctuation, and consistency. ("Consistency" means being sure you did not change the hero's eyes from blue to green halfway through a novel.) Publishing house style is also under their aegis—changing "toward" to "towards," punctuating with final commas in a series or not. But sometimes I wonder about them. In a story of mine, "Skule Skerry,"[2] which is set in England in the 1940s, the copyeditor wanted to change "flat" to "apartment" and "too dear" to "too costly" because she was afraid American readers wouldn't know the difference. I changed them back.

J.R.    And artists. How involved do you get with artists? Many of your books are wonderfully illustrated. Do you have much input as to who will illustrate your book?

J.Y.    How involved I get depends upon the editor. Ann Beneduce always invites me into the process. We discuss the mood, the mode, the style of art. Sometimes I even suggest artists, or discover them for her. For example, David Palladini was my suggestion for *The Girl Who Cried Flowers,* Michael Hague for *Dream Weaver,* and I discovered Barbara Berger, who was a student in one of my workshops. I showed her portfolio to Ann who used her as the illustrator for my book *Brothers of the Wind,* which began her illustrating career. But other editors have said, literally, "That's my job," effectively slamming the door in my face.

What I want in an artist is someone who loves my story or poem or idea, who understands the book at its deepest levels, and who draws pictures that are more than just accurate responses to the story. The two words I think that best describe the finest illustrations are *contrapuntal* and *resonantal.*

J.R.     And your agent? What does she do for you?

J.Y.     Very often she does the first screening for me, contacting editors. She also gives me her own responses to my books, and as she is an ex-English teacher and a great lover of literature, her responses are important to me. She tracks down editors, which is a major job. There are some editors who seem to never be in their offices, or are at least never available. One agent friend of mine—not my agent—has a theory that editors are only at work in their offices at three p.m. on April 16! Many writers and illustrators think this may indeed be true!

My agent also deals with all the contractual and money matters for me. The business end of things. Oh, I am certainly conversant with contract clauses and royalty statements, but I always would rather have such "filthy" matters handled by someone else so I can deal with the editor only about Story.

J.R.     What is the most difficult aspect of being a writer?

J.Y.     The begging. There is a lot of begging involved in being an author.

You are always in a position of waiting for someone to *offer* you something. And when an editor decides to take a book, it can seem like a royal acceptance, a gift handed down from above. I don't like the feeling of servitude, indentured slavery, taxation without representation. Book-making should be between two equal parties. Actually, the author should be more equal because without the author there would be no book. Yet too often the suggestion from the editor is, "That's nice, dear. You've done your part, now go away quietly." I even heard an editor seriously suggest that writers were like children—prodigies, perhaps, extremely gifted children, but children nonetheless.

J.R.     That sounds very cynical.

J.Y.     Maybe, but it is also realistic.

And in no other business do the powers-that-be refuse to understand public relations, refuse to understand marketing demands, refuse to understand the need for advertising.

J.R.     That is a common complaint of all authors and illustrators. Certainly you understand the economics of publishing as well as anybody.

J.Y.     Yes, I understand the economics. But we are not talking just about "product." We are talking about literature. And the great hunger of humans for Story.

With some publishers it's like pulling teeth to get them to even agree to send books out for sale. I have gone on tours that have been planned months, even a year, in advance and the books never arrive. Or they arrive three days after I have left. Some publishers refuse to deal with school visits. Some don't even respond to letters. It can be very frustrating.

J.R.     What kind of feedback do you get from your readers?

J.Y.     I get letters every day. Recently I heard about a child who was named Greyling after one of my books. Poor child. I hear from storytellers who have told my stories at weddings, funerals, at old age homes, at schools and libraries. I get adults and children coming up to me and saying, "You changed my life with your story." That is both touching and frightening. An awesome responsibility. I love telling stories, writing stories, and so I am delighted when one of my stories means so much to a reader. But to be honest, that isn't my reason for writing. I write a story out of the hidden recesses of my heart. Personal spelunking—going down into the heart's cavern. And if along the way the story comes to life again for someone else, that is the *extra* gift.

I received a letter once from the head of the Mark Hamill Fan Club[3] who wanted to give Mark an autographed copy of *Commander Toad in Space.* That kind of letter is another gift.

J.R.     You are primarily known for your original fairy tales. What is the ongoing fascination with that genre?

J.Y.     I believe that Story is what distinguishes humans from beasts. The wonder tales, or fairy tales as we sometimes call them, are an important part of Story tradition. In a way I come straight out of the oral tradition. I do a lot of oral storytelling, folk singing, audience participation. These days I have been spending a lot of my time with oral tale tellers. There is a resurgence in this country of oral telling, fueled by NAPPS, the National Association for the Preservation and Perpetuation of Storytelling.[4] Stories are being told again in schools, in libraries, in concerts, at conventions.

J.R.     Are there other storytellers on the family tree?

J.Y.     My family is a family of writers, storytellers, and folk song singers. In fact, all of my father's relatives are wonderful tellers of jokes and stories. Unfortunately most of their stories end in Yiddish. I say unfortunately, because I never learned Yiddish. We're also related to the first family who owned Coca-Cola. Sadly my family never made any money on it; just a great story out of it!

On my husband's side there is a signer of the Constitution and Admiral Peary who traveled to the Pole. David comes from a line of Appalachian storytellers.

So our children are mutts, hybrids. And they are each great punsters and storytellers. Not liars, mind you, though that is another branch of both families!

I see myself as a professional writer and storyteller. I love the taste, the cozy feeling about wonder stories. It is talking about what never was but always is; ourselves but one step away.

I have a great ease with fairy-tale convention. But it has, on occasion, betrayed me.

J.R.    What do you mean?

J.Y.    It happened to me when I wrote a historical novel, my first long YA novel, about the Shakers in the 1850s, *The Gift of Sarah Barker.* The book was originally set in a three-day period. First my husband, then my best friend, then my agent all said, "Why three days?"

Then Linda Zuckerman,[5] my editor at Viking asked the same thing but a little differently, "Tell me, *why* everything must happen in three days?"

I suddenly realized that I was comfortable with the fairy-tale mode that uses the number three as a structuring device. I had forced the novel into that mode to make myself feel safe. But it was not allowing the novel to breathe properly. Once I understood that, I was able to expand the novel's time focus, and at the same time added characterization. The book now takes place over a two-and-a-half week period, much better for the novel though it is not a comfortable formulaic time.

By the way, though I can plan and think about a novel and outline a nonfiction project, I never know what course a fairy tale is going to take. I cannot say, "Today I am going to write a wonder tale." It comes out when it is ready because such stories are usually dealing, in a metaphoric way, with personal problems I am wrestling with.

Of course I may just write those kind of stories because I have this strange point on my head and. . . .

J.R.    Characterize yourself as a writer.

J.Y.    I think my strengths are inventiveness, story, and style. My weakest link is characterization. I tend to take people at face value in life, never looking for that dark underside, the Byzantine motives. That may be why I am so comfortable with fairy tales where the characters tend to be archetypes.

I also wish I could plot more intricately. I love to read murder mysteries and the more intricate the better. But I can't write them because I'm not a good chess player. I can't think two or three moves ahead and I am not convinced other people can either!

J.R.      Do you surprise yourself when you're working on a story?

J.Y.      Always.

Sometimes I work from a strict outline, but not too often. Along the way—serendipity—come wonderful surprises. Like the protagonist in my story "Sleep of Trees."[5] The hero was meant to be a Greek farmer quoting Homer, only when I came to write about him, he turned into Jeansen Forbes, an American actor of the Ryan O'Neal type. Like *Dragon's Blood*, which began as a single book and became a trilogy because *I* wanted to know more about the world of Austar IV and young Jakkin Stewart and his mighty dragon, Heart's Blood. Like the surprising revelation of the faun-boy Gabriel in *The Stone Silenus* who in his first incarnation eighteen years ago *was* a satyr and who slowly over the years of my rewriting changed. Like the nasty girl in the Indian orphanage, Indira, who was never in the original plot outline but who grew into a most important actor in *Children of the Wolf*. She was simply not to be denied.

Sometimes I get to the end of the story or a book and everything suddenly comes together. I look back and I say, "Wow! How did I do that? How did I pull that off? Who gave me the answers?" Or, as one child once wrote to me, "Who helps you? Your mother?"

J.R.      How many stories or books do you work on at one time?

J.Y.      I can't really say. Lots.

I've usually got the start of ten or twelve stories, mostly openings to wonder tales or fantasy books or science fiction novels.

I'll take a folder out of my file drawer, read the pages aloud, maybe change one word or one sentence or noodle with a section, then put it back. There are times I go weeks on end working over and over a single page. Other times I can draft two and three chapters in a day.

If I'm revising I can go for longer stretches at a time. But the first draft of anything is *the* most frustrating time. There is usually a moment in a book or story when the dam breaks, when the thing becomes absolutely clear to me and I know where it is going. And then I write and write all day. Till the fingers are bloody stumps and the brain is mush. Total mush. Or at least it feels that way.

I don't remember which writer said, "I only write when I'm inspired. Fortunately I'm inspired at nine every morning." It may have been Faulkner.

J.R.      What is your day like?

J.Y.      I start every morning by doing my mail. If I had to wait to get my mail til one in the afternoon, I couldn't get going. My day is usually over by one or two. I go down to the post office and pick up my mail. It's one of the advantages of living in a small country town. It's a wonderful way to start the writing day. I try to write until the kids come home from school or my brain is mush, whichever comes first.

J.R.     Have you ever done any other types of writing, screenplays for example?

J.Y.          I was called to see if I would write a screenplay for an "E.T."-clone movie. It had big bucks, but I didn't want to do it. If I don't come up with an idea, it doesn't interest me. I'm not a writer-for-hire.

         I've also been asked to write little fifty-word scenarios for licensed character books. Again a lot of money, but I said no to that, too.

         I am much too involved in writing my novels, fairy tales, and poetry, and I am doing adult fantasy and science fiction now, too. Though I do have two-thirds of an opera liberetto done and have had two musical plays produced. And songs. And essays. And academic papers. And . . .

J.R.     But don't you get tired just sitting at your typewriter every day trying to shape a story?

J.Y.          Right now I'm involved with my kids' homework, the Famous Homework Policeman. I'm tired of that. I'm a coach of a high school team. I get tired of that. I run writers' workshops. Tiring. I teach. Tiring. But no—I don't get tired of writing. Reading and writing for me is one of the . . . it's a most wonderful *release!*

J.R.     So you never suffer from writers' block?

J.Y.          Nope.
         But I did have an epiphany recently.

J.R.     Which was?

J.Y.          "Snow White" is a true story from the mother's point of view. What you really want to do with a sixteen-year-old daughter is to stick her in a glass coffin, pipe rock music in, and let her grow there until the right person or job or college comes along to wake her up.

J.R.     I don't doubt that many people would agree with you! Since you've mentioned your children, how have they managed your persona of writer?

J.Y.          Everyone in the family sees me as writer. Even my children. I was already published and "known" before they were born.

         They've gone through many stages of course—being embarrassed about it ("Oh God, she's going to talk in public"), being proud of it (Jason at age four tried unsuccessfully to convince a woman at the library that his mommy had written *all* those books), asking for help with their own writing (Heidi put a poem up on the mantel and warned me not to look at it and wondered three days later what I had thought of it), and not asking for help.

         And they all write well. Adam has a book of lullabies coming out from Harcourt Brace in 1985. Heidi and Jason have had pieces published in the newspaper for which they were paid.

J.R.    What do you like most, given the spectrum of publishing, writing, bookmaking?

J.Y.    All of it.

I love all the processes involved in the bookmaking. The writing, of course. And the revisions. I love seeing the galleys—my words *in print* the first time! I love seeing the dummies and the picture book folded-and-gathered sheets. And working on the flap copy. And the finished book. And the money and the fame, people passing out in the streets as I pass by!

I also care about bookmaking as a kind of energy. And on the deeper level, the wonderful mystique about language and Story. I care about books as representatives of my labors and my particular gifts. A lot of people work all their lives and they have nothing tangible to show for it. I do. Long after I am gone, my books will live. A child showed me this in a letter. He wrote, "Your stories will live forever. I hope you live to ninety-nine or a hundred, but who cares."

J.R.    You have been involved in publishing for over twenty years now . . .

J.Y.    Yes, my first children's book was published in 1962 when I was just twenty-three. In fact I was given the contract on my twenty-second birthday. It was a wonderful present.

I was one of the so-called Young Turks. Now I'm a Middle-Aged Turk.

Nowadays I find myself astonished when somebody that age sells his or her first book. Like my son Adam who is in his mid-teens! And I think, rather crossly, "How dare he or she? They don't *know* enough!" And then I laugh at myself and remember how I felt at that young age when my first book came out.

J.R.    So how does that make you feel?

J.Y.    Creaky. Cranky. Old. And ever young.

J.R.    Would you recommend—or do you recommend—writing as a way of life to anyone?

J.Y.    Only if that person enjoys working by himself a lot. A writer does work in a vacuum much of the time.

I wouldn't recommend writing to anyone who thinks of it as a career choice, a way to make money. A writer writes because he/she has to write. Because a story is bursting the walls of the heart. A story has to be told. Nobody tells a writer to do or not to do it.

However, if a writer is what someone just *has* to be, then I always suggest that he or she go about it in a professional and organized manner. Don't just flap your wings; crank your typewriter, and pray.

And I ask someone contemplating becoming a writer how much they are willing to give up. Not many writers make a lot of money on their writing alone.

But if the story is begging to be told, and if through hard work and perseverance, and a great helping of directed luck, it is published, and you get that letter from the child reader in the mail, the one signed "Your *fiend*" and smudged all over with erasures then. . . .

## Notes

[1] Ann K. Beneduce, then editor-in-chief of children's books for World Publishing Company, now editorial director of Philomel Books.

[2] "Skule Skerry" is in *Neptune Rising.*

[3] A fan club for Mark Hamill, who played Luke Skywalker in the *Star Wars* movie trilogy. Jane's book, *Commander Toad in Space* and others in the series, enjoyed a minor success as a spoof of the movie and science fiction in general.

[4] For more information on this organization, contact NAPPS, Box 112, Jonesborough, TN 37659.

[5] Linda Zuckerman, then editor of children's books at Viking-Penguin, Inc.

[6] "Sleep of Trees" is in *Tales of Wonder.*

## BIBLIOGRAPHY

*The Acorn Quest.* il. Susanna Natti. New York: Crowell, 1981.

*The Adventures of Eeka Mouse.* Middletown, Conn.: Xerox Education, 1974.

*All in the Woodland Early: An ABC Book.* il. Jane Breskin Zalben. Collins, 1974.

*Bird of Time.* il. Mercer Mayer. New York: Crowell, 1971.

*The Boy Who Had Wings.* il. Helga Aichinger. New York: Crowell, 1974.

*The Boy Who Spoke Chimp.* il. David Wiesner. New York: Knopf, 1981.

*Brothers of the Wind.* il. Barbara Berger. New York: Philomel, 1981.

*Cards of Grief.* New York: Ace, 1984.

*Children of the Wolf.* New York: Viking, 1984.

*Commander Toad and the Big Black Hole.* il. Bruce Degen. New York: Coward, McCann & Geoghegan, 1983.

*Commander Toad and the Planet of the Grapes.* il. Bruce Degen. New York: Coward, McCann & Geoghegan, 1982.

*Commander Toad in Space.* il. Bruce Degen. New York: Coward, McCann & Geoghegan, 1980.

*Dragon Night, and Other Lullabies.* il. Demi. New York: Methuen, 1980.

*Dragon's Blood.* New York: Delacorte, 1982.

*Dream Weaver.* il. Michael Hague. Cleveland: Collins, 1979.

*The Emperor and the Kite.* il. Ed Young. Cleveland: World, 1967.

*The Fireside Song Book of Birds and Beasts.* il. Peter Parnall. New York: Simon and Schuster, 1972.

*Friend: The Story of George Fox and the Quakers.* New York: Seabury, 1972.

*The Giants' Farm.* il. Tomie dePaola. New York: Seabury, 1977.

*The Giants Go Camping.* il. Tomie dePaola. New York: Seabury, 1979.

*The Gift of Sarah Barker.* New York: Viking, 1981.

*The Girl Who Cried Flowers and Other Tales.* il. David Palladini. New York: Crowell, 1974.

*The Girl Who Loved the Wind.* il. Ed Young. New York: Crowell, 1972.

*Greyling.* il. William Stobbs. Cleveland: World, 1968.

*Gwinellen, the Princess Who Could Not Sleep.* il. Ed Renfro. New York: Macmillan, 1965.

*Hannah Dreaming.* Springfield, Mass.: Springfield Museum of Art, 1977.

*Heart's Blood.* New York: Delacorte, 1984.

*Hobo Toad and the Motorcycle Gang.* il. Emily McCully. New York: World, 1970.

*How Beastly! A Menagerie of Nonsense Poems.* il. James Marshall. Cleveland: Collins, 1980.

*The Hundredth Dove and Other Tales.* il. David Palladini. New York: Schocken, 1980.

*Invitation to the Butterfly Ball: A Counting Rhyme.* il. Jane Breskin Zalben. New York: Parents Magazine, 1976.

*The Inway Investigators; or The Mystery at McCracken's Place.* il. Allen Eitzen. New York: Seabury, 1969.

*Isabel's Noel.* il. Arnold Roth. New York: Funk & Wagnalls, 1967.

*It All Depends.* il. Don Bolognese. New York: Funk & Wagnalls, 1969.

*The Little Spotted Fish.* il. Friso Henstra. New York: Seabury, 1975.

*The Longest Name on the Block.* il. Peter Madden. New York: Funk & Wagnalls, 1968.

*The Magic Three of Solatia.* il. Julia Noonan. New York: Crowell, 1974.

*The Mermaid's Three Widoms.* il. Laura Rader. Cleveland: Collins, 1978.

*Mice on Ice.* il. Lawrence DiFiori. New York: Dutton, 1980.

*Milkweed Days.* Photogs. Gabriel Amadeus Cooney. New York: Crowell, 1976.

*The Minstrel and the Mountain: A Tale of Peace.* il. Anne Rockwell. New York: World, 1967.

*The Moon Ribbon and Other Tales.* il. David Palladini. New York: Crowell, 1976.

*Neptune Rising: Songs and Tales of the Undersea Folk.* il. David Wiesner. New York: Philomel, 1982.

*No Bath Tonight.* il. Nancy Winslow Parker. New York: Crowell, 1978.

*Pirates in Petticoats.* il. Leonard Vosburgh. New York: McKay, 1963.

*The Rainbow Rider.* il. Michael Foreman. New York: Crowell, 1974.

*Ring Out! A Book of Bells.* il. Richard Cuffari. New York: Seabury, 1974.

*The Robot and Rebecca and the Missing Owser.* il. Lady McCrady. New York: Knopf, 1981.

*The Robot and Rebecca: The Mystery of the Code-Carrying Kids.* il. Catherine Deeter. New York: Random House, 1980.

*Rounds about Rounds.* il. Gail Gibbons. New York: Watts, 1977.

*See This Little Line?* il. Kathleen Elgin. New York: McKay, 1963.

*The Seeing Stick.* il. Remy Charlip and Demetra Marsalis. New York: Crowell, 1977.

*The Seventh Mandarin.* il. Ed Young. New York: Seabury, 1970.

*Shape Shifters: Fantasy and Science Fiction Tales about Humans Who Can Change Their Shape.* New York: Seabury, 1978.

*Shirlick Holmes and the Case of the Wandering Wardrobe.* il. Anthony Rao. New York: Coward, McCann & Geoghegan, 1981.

*Simple Gifts: The Story of the Shakers.* il. Betty Fraser. New York: Viking, 1976.

*The Simple Prince.* il. Jack Kent. New York: Parents Magazine, 1978.

*Sleeping Ugly.* il. Diane Stanley. New York: Coward, McCann & Geoghegan, 1981.

*Spider Jane.* il. Stefen Bernath. New York: Coward, McCann & Geoghegan, 1978.

*Spider Jane on the Move.* il. Stefan Bernath. New York: Coward, McCann & Geoghegan, 1980.

*The Stone Silenus.* New York: Philomel, 1984.

*The Sultan's Perfect Tree.* il. Barbara Garrison. New York: Parents Magazine, 1977.

*Tales of Wonder.* New York: Schocken, 1983.

*Touch Magic: Fantasy, Faerie, and Folklore in the Literature of Childhood.* New York: Philomel, 1981.

*The Transfigured Hart.* il. Donna Diamond. New York: Crowell, 1975.

*Trust a City Kid.* With Anne Huston. il. C. Kocsis. New York: Lothrop, Lee & Shepard, 1966.

*Uncle Lemon's Spring.* il. Glen Rounds. New York: Dutton, 1981.

*The Witch Who Wasn't.* il. Arnold Roth. New York: Macmillan, 1964.

*The Wizard Islands.* il. Robert Quackenbush. New York: Crowell, 1973.

*The Wizard of Washington Square.* il. Ray Cruz. New York: World, 1969.

*World on a String: The Story of Kites.* Cleveland: World, 1969.

*Writing Books for Children.* Boston: The Writer, 1973; rev. ed., 1983.

*Zoo 2000: Twelve Stories of Science Fiction and Fantasy Beasts.* New York: Seabury, 1973.

## AWARDS AND HONORS

*The Acorn Quest*
> Parents' Choice Award

*All in the Woodland Early*
> Book Show

*The Bird of Time*
> Book Show

*The Boy Who Had Wings*
> Library of Congress list

*Commander Toad in Space*
> Garden State Children's Book Award

*Dragon's Blood*
> Best Book for Young Adults
> Children's Choice Book
> *Parents' Choice* Award

*Dream Weaver*
> Book Show

*The Emperor and the Kite*
> Best Book of the Year
> Book Show
> Randolph Caldecott Medal honor book
> Lewis Carroll Shelf Award
> Notable Children's Book

*The Fireside Song Book of Birds and Beasts*
> Best Illustrated Children's Book
> Library of Congress list

*The Gift of Sarah Barker*
> Best Book for Young Adults
> Best Book of the Year

*The Girl Who Cried Flowers*
> Best Book of the Year
> Best Illustrated Children's Book
> Book Show
> Lewis Carroll Shelf Award
> Golden Kite Award
> National Book Award finalist
> Notable Children's Book

*The Girl Who Loved the Wind*
> Lewis Carroll Shelf Award
> Library of Congress list
> Showcase Book

*The Hundredth Dove*
> Library of Congress list
> Notable Children's Trade Book in the Field of Social Studies

*The Little Spotted Fish*
> Showcase Book

*Mice on Ice*
> Children's Choice Book

*Milkweed Days*
> Notable Children's Trade Book in the Field of Social Studies

*The Minstrel and the Mountain*
> Junior Book Award

*The Moon Ribbon*
> Golden Kite Award honor book

*Ring Out!*
> Library of Congress list

*The Robot and Rebecca*
> Children's Choice Book

*Rounds about Rounds*
> Library of Congress list

*The Seeing Stick*
> Children's Choice Book
> Christopher Award
> Library of Congress list
> Notable Children's Trade Book in the Field of Social Studies

*The Seventh Mandarin*
> Best Book of the Year

*Simple Gifts*
> Notable Children's Trade Book in the Field of Social Studies

*The Transfigured Hart*
> Children's Choice Book
> Golden Kite Award Honor
> > Book

*Trust a City Kid*
> Best Book of the Year

*World on a String*
> Notable Children's Book

## ADDITIONAL SOURCES

Commire. *Something about the Author.*
*Contemporary Authors.*
de Montreville. *Fourth Book of Junior Authors and Illustrators.*
Kirkpatrick. *Twentieth-Century Children's Writers,* 1978 and 1983.
Nicholls. *The Encyclopedia of Science Fiction.*
*Science Fiction and Fantasy Literature.*
Ward. *Authors of Books for Young People.*

# —APPENDIX A—

## Library Collections

The following libraries retain original art and manuscript materials of the interviewees here. To locate the present curator's name consult a recent edition of the *American Library Directory* (Bowker).

Alexander Library
Department of Special Collections and
    Archives
Rutgers, the State University of New
    Jersey
College Avenue
New Brunswick, NJ 08901
        (Gauch, Raskin)

Boston University Libraries
771 Commonwealth Avenue
Boston, MA 02215
        (Asimov)

Cooperative Children's Book Center
600 North Park Street
Rooms 4289-90
Madison, WI 53706
        (Raskin)

de Grummond Collection
McCain Graduate Library
University of Southern Mississippi
P. O. Box 5148 Southern Station
Hattiesburg, MS 39406
        (Holland, Hopkins, Kroll,
        Myller)

Kerlan Collection
Children's Literature Research Collection
University of Minnesota
109 Walter Library
117 Pleasant Street SE
Minneapolis, MN 55455
        (Fritz, Gauch, Greene, Holland,
        Hopkins, Mikolaycak, Ross,
        Yolen)

The Library
Department of Special Collections
University of Oregon
Eugene, OR 97403
        (Fritz)

# —APPENDIX B—

## Awards and Honors

This section provides capsule descriptions of the awards and honors listed in each interview. For more complete information on these, please consult the volumes listed in the Awards Bibliography on page 245 or contact the sponsoring organizations directly.

Entries for annual lists such as the Library of Congress list, *Horn Book's* Fanfare, et cetera, have come directly from the publications themselves. These are often available as brochures or can be found in special issues of the magazines.

Authors and illustrators who are recipients of these honors follow each listing. Awards are listed through the 1984 award year.

*American Book Awards,* children's book category, began in 1980 under the sponsorship of the Association for American Publishers. It succeeded the National Book Award for the same category. The award was suspended following the 1983 award year. (Fritz, Raskin).

*Best Books for Young Adults,* administered by the Young Adult Services Division of the American Library Association, is an annual list of the best books to appeal to teenagers. (Holland, Sleator, Strasser, Yolen).

*Best Books of the Year,* an annual list of children's books prepared by the book review editors of *School Library Journal,* appears each December. The exception is 1979, which appears in the January, 1980 issue. "Best Books of the Spring," which appeared annually in the May issue until 1983, are not listed here. (Alexander, Avi, Crews, Fritz, Hopkins, Raskin, Sleator, Yolen).

*Best Illustrated Children's Books,* an annual listing of the ten best illustrated children's books of the year, is sponsored by the *New York Times Book Review.* The *"New York Times* Choice of Best Illustrated Children's Books of the Year"* listing appears annually in the November children's book issue. (Alexander, Hopkins, Raskin, Yolen).

*Best of the Best Books* is a compilation of reevaluations of the "Best Books" in *School Library Journal.* The list appeared in the December, 1979, issue, the twenty-fifth anniversary issue of the magazine, and reconsiders the best of the "Best Books" in the thirteen-year history of the "Best Books," 1966-1979. (Crews, Fritz, Raskin).

*Best of the Best/YA* was administered by the Young Adult Services Division of the American Library Association in 1984 and reconsiders the previous "Best Books for Young Adults" lists. Overlooked titles from the first publication were added in. The full listing is available in "The Best of the Best Books 1970-1983," published by the American Library Association. (Greene, Holland, Sleator).

*Best Young Adult Books of the Year* is the young adult equivalent of "Best Books of the Year" in *School Library Journal.* (Holland, Singer).

*Bluegrass Award* is chosen by Kentucky school children as their choice of the "best" book of the year. (Alexander).

*Book Show* books mentioned appeared in the American Institute of Graphic Arts Book Shows for books that exhibit excellence in design and manufacture. (Alexander, Crews, Hopkins, Mikolaycak, Raskin, Yolen).

*Boston Globe-Horn Book* Awards, begun in 1967, sponsors awards in three categories, Outstanding Fiction, Outstanding Nonfiction, and Outstanding Illustration. Listings include honor books. (Fritz, Gauch, Raskin, Sleator).

*Brooklyn Art Books for Children* citations were presented by the Brooklyn (NY) Museum and the Brooklyn Public Library; they recognized books that are works of art and literature. It is believed to have been discontinued in 1977. (Crews, Mikolaycak, Raskin).

*Randolph Caldecott Medal,* administered by the Association for Library Service to Children, is presented annually to the most distinguished picture book of the preceeding year. Listings include honor books. (Crews, Sleator, Yolen).

*Lewis Carroll Shelf Awards,* sponsored by the University of Wisconsin, recognize books worthy of consideration to sit on a bookshelf alongside *Alice in Wonderland.* It has been discontinued. (Yolen).

*Child Study Children's Book Committee Award* is presented annually to a book that helps children or young people deal honestly and courageously with world problems. The "Child Study Children's Book Committee of Bank Street College Award" is sponsored by Bank Street College in New York City. (Fritz).

*Children's Choice Books* appear in an annual listing administered by a joint committee of the Children's Book Council and the International Reading Association, and are chosen by children. It was previously known as "Classroom Choices." The list appears in *The Reading Teacher* in the October or November issue. (Alexander, Avi, Crews, Cuyler, Fritz, Gauch, Greene, Hopkins, Kroll, Raskin, Ross, Singer, Sleator, Stine, Yolen).

*Christopher Awards* are presented annually to the best work in nonfiction or fiction by The Christophers, in several age categories. (Alexander, Avi, Fritz, Yolen).

*Fanfare* is an annual list presented by *The Horn Book Magazine* in its June issue, choosing the best books each year. (Fritz, Gauch, Holland, Mikolaycak, Raskin, Sleator).

*Garden State Children's Book Awards,* sponsored by the New Jersey Library Association, are awards in fiction and nonfiction for children in early and middle grades. (Yolen).

*Golden Kite Awards* are presented annually to members of the Society of Children's Book Writers. Listings include honor books. (Greene, Yolen).

*Junior Book Awards,* sponsored by the Boys' Clubs of America, were designed to encourage wider reading among its membership. They have been discontinued. (Yolen).

*Library of Congress list* books appear on an annual list prepared by the staff and associates of the Children's Literature Center at the Library. The list, "A List of Books for Preschool Through Junior High Age," is generally available in the early spring. (Alexander, Crews, Demi, Fritz, Gauch, Greene, Holland, Mikolaycak, Myller, Raskin, Sleator, Yolen).

*Maud Hart Lovelace Award* is sponsored by the Friends of the Minnesota Valley Regional Library System in Mankato, Minnesota, and is named after the prominent children's author. (Singer).

*Massachusetts Children's Book Awards* are annual awards chosen by children in the middle and junior-high grades and is administered by Salem State College. (Greene).

*National Book Award* has been superceded by the American Book Award. (Greene, Yolen).

*John Newbery Medal,* administered by the Association for Library Service to Children of the American Library Association, is presented annually to the author of the most distinguished contribution to literature for children, for the preceding year. Listings include honor books. (Fritz, Greene, Raskin).

*Notable Children's Books,* administered by the Association for Library Service to Children of the American Library Association, are chosen annually and the list is available in the spring. (Crews, Fritz, Greene, Hopkins, Mikolaycak, Raskin, Sleator, Yolen).

*Notable Children's Books, 1940-1970* are reevaluated titles of the Notable Children's Books chosen in those years mentioned. The full listings are published in *Notable Children's Books 1940-1970,* published by the American Library Association in 1977. (Fritz, Raskin, Sleator).

*Notable Children's Books, 1971-1975* is a continuation of the above. The full listings are published in *Notable Children's Books 1971-1975,* published by the American Library Association in 1981.

*Notable Children's Trade Books in the Field of Social Studies* is an annual list administered by a joint committee of the Children's Book Council and the National Council for the Social Studies. The list appears in *Social Education* in April. (Crews, Demi, Fritz, Gauch, Hopkins, Myller, Ross, Strasser, Yolen).

*Helen Keating Ott Award* is presented by the Church and Synagogue Library Association in recognition of a significant contribution to those libraries. (Holland).

*Outstanding Science Trade Books for Children* is an annual list administered by a joint committee of the Children's Book Council and the National Science Teachers Association. The list appears in *Science and Children* in March. (Myller).

*Parents' Choice Awards* are sponsored annually by the Parents' Choice Foundation and the newspaper of the same name. Listings include honor books. (Fritz, Greene, Mikolaycak, Singer, Yolen).

*Regina Medal,* begun in 1959, is awarded by the Catholic Library Association for continuing distinguished contributions to children's literature. (Fritz).

*Reviewers' Choice* is an annual selection of the best books of the year by the editors of *Booklist.* It appears in the January 15 issue. (Fritz, Hopkins).

*Showcase Books* appeared in an annual exhibit of the best illustrated and/or designed books of the year. Sponsored by the Children's Book Council, the exhibit has been discontinued. (Alexander, Crews, Mikolaycak, Raskin, Yolen).

*Spring Book Festival Awards,* originally sponsored by the *New York Herald Tribune* and later by *Book World,* were given to the "best" books of the season. They have been discontinued. (Alexander, Raskin).

*Teacher's Choice Award,* established in 1981 and administered by the National Council of Teachers of English, cites books that need to be brought to the attention of children and that otherwise may be overlooked. (Fritz, Hopkins).

# —BIBLIOGRAPHY OF AWARDS INFORMATION—

Children's Book Council, Inc., comp. and ed. *Children's Books: Awards and Prizes.* New York: Children's Book Council, 1981.

Claire, Walter. *Winners: The Blue Ribbon Encyclopedia of Awards.* New York: Facts on File, 1978.

Jones, Dolores Blythe. *Children's Literature Awards and Winners: A Directory of Prizes, Authors, and Illustrators.* Detroit: Gale in association with Neal-Schuman, 1983.

*Literary and Library Prizes.* 10th ed. revised and edited by Olga S. Weber and Stephen J. Calvert. New York: Bowker, 1980.

Moransee, Jess R., ed. *Children's Prize Books: An International Listing of 193 Children's Literature Prizes.* New York: K. G. Saur, 1983.

# —BIBLIOGRAPHY OF BIOGRAPHICAL SOURCES—

This section of the bibliography is to be used with the lists of additional sources which follow the interviews.

Bader, Barbara. *American Picturebooks from "Noah's Ark" to "The Beast Within."* New York: Macmillan, 1976.

Bleiler, E. F., ed. *Science Fiction Writers: Critical Studies of the Major Authors from the Early Nineteenth Century to the Present Day.* New York: Scribner's, 1982.

Commire, Anne D., ed. *Something about the Author: Facts and Pictures about Contemporary Authors and Illustrators of Books for Young People.* 36 vols. Detroit: Gale, 1971-1984.

*Contemporary Authors: A Bio-Bibliographical Guide to Current Authors and Their Works.* 112 vols. Detroit: Gale, 1962-1984. This listing includes *Contemporary Authors: Permanent Series* (vols. 1-2) and *New Revised Series* (vols. 1-12).

*Contemporary Literary Criticism: Excerpts from Criticism of the Works of Today's Novelists, Poets, Playwrights, and Other Creative Writers.* 29 vols. Detroit: Gale, 1973-1984.

de Montreville, Doris, and Elizabeth D. Crawford, eds. *Fourth Book of Junior Authors and Illustrators.* New York: H. W. Wilson Company, 1978.

de Montreville, Doris, and Donna Hill, eds. *Third Book of Junior Authors.* New York: H. W. Wilson Company, 1972.

Hopkins, Lee Bennett. *More Books by More People: Interviews with Sixty-Five Authors of Books for Children.* New York: Citation Press, 1974.

Kingman, Lee, Joanna Foster, and Ruth Giles Lontoft, eds. *Illustrators of Children's Books: 1957-1966.* Boston: Horn Book, 1968.

Kingman, Lee, Grace Allen Hogarth, and Harriet Quimby, eds. *Illustrators of Children's Books, 1967-1976.* Boston: Horn Book, 1978.

Kirkpatrick, D. L., ed. *Twentieth-Century Children's Writers.* New York: St. Martin's Press, 1978.

Kirkpatrick, D. L. *Twentieth-Century Children's Writers.* 2d ed. New York: St. Martin's Press, 1983.

Nicholls, Peter. *The Encyclopedia of Science Fiction, an Illustrated A to Z.* London: Grenada Publishing, 1979.

Reginald, R., comp. *Contemporary Science Fiction Authors.* New York: Arno Books, 1975. (Also issued as *Stella Nova: The Contemporary Science Fiction Authors.* Los Angeles: Unicorn, 1970).

*Science Fiction and Fantasy Literature: A Checklist, 1700-1974 with Contemporary Science Fiction Authors II.* Detroit: Gale, 1979.

Smith, Curtis C., ed. *Twentieth-Century Science Fiction Writers.* New York: St. Martin's Press, 1981.

Steinbrunner, Chris, Otto Penzler, Marvin Lachman and Charles Shibuk, eds. *Encyclopedia of Mystery and Detection.* New York: McGraw-Hill, 1976.

Vinson, James, ed. *Contemporary Novelists.* New York: St. Martin's Press, 1972.

Vinson, James, and D. L. Kirkpatrick, eds. *Contemporary Novelists.* 2d ed. New York: St. Martin's Press, 1976.

Vinson, James, and D. L. Kirkpatrick, eds. *Contemporary Novelists.* 3d ed. New York: St. Martin's Press, 1982.

Wakeman, John, ed. *World Authors, 1950-1970: A Companion Volume to Twentieth-Century Authors.* New York: H. W. Wilson Company, 1975.

Ward, Martha E. and Dorothy A. Marquardt. *Authors of Books for Young People.* 2d ed. Metuchen, N.J.: Scarecrow Press, 1971.

Ward, Martha E. and Dorothy A. Marquardt. *Authors of Books for Young People.* Supplement to the second edition. Metuchen, N.J.: Scarecrow Press, 1979.

Ward, Martha E. and Dorothy A. Marquardt. *Illustrators of Books for Young People.* 2d ed. Metuchen, N.J.: Scarecrow Press, 1975.

# —BIBLIOGRAPHY OF BIBLIOGRAPHIC SOURCES—

*Books in Print.* 36 vols. New York: Bowker, 1948-1984.

Commire, Anne D., ed. *Something about the Author: Facts and Pictures about Contemporary Authors and Illustrators of Books for Young People.* 36 vols. Detroit: Gale, 1971-1984.

*Contemporary Authors: A Bio-Bibliographical Guide to Current Authors and Their Works.* 112 vols. Detroit: Gale, 1962-1984. This listing includes *Contemporary Authors, Permanent Series* (vols. 1-2) and *New Revised Series* (vols. 1-12).

*The Cumulative Book Index: A World List of Books in the English Language, Supplementing the United States Catalog Fourth Edition.* 29 vols. New York: H. W. Wilson, 1933-1983.

de Montreville, Doris, and Elizabeth D. Crawford, eds. *Fourth Book of Junior Authors and Illustrators.* New York: H. W. Wilson, 1978.

de Montreville, Doris, and Donna Hill, eds. *Third Book of Junior Authors.* New York: H. W. Wilson, 1972.

Fuller, Muriel, ed. *More Junior Authors.* New York: H. W. Wilson, 1963.

Kingman, Lee, Joanna Foster, and Ruth Giles Lontoft, eds. *Illustrators of Children's Books: 1957-1966.* Boston: Horn Book, 1968.

Kingman, Lee, Grace Allen Hogarth, and Harriet Quimby, eds. *Illustrators of Children's Books: 1967-1976.* Boston: Horn Book, 1978.

Kirkpatrick, D. L., ed. *Twentieth-Century Children's Writers.* New York: St. Martin's Press, 1978.

Kunitz, Stanley, and Howard Haycraft, eds. *The Junior Book of Authors.* 2d ed. New York: H. W. Wilson, 1951.

*Library of Congress and National Union Catalog Author Lists, 1942-1962; A Master Cumulation: A Cumulative List Representing Entries in the Library of Congress-National Union Catalog Supplements to Catalog of Books Represented by Library of Congress Printed Cards.* Vols. 136-152. Detroit: Gale, 1967-1971.

Miller, Bertha Mahony, Ruth Hill Viguers, and Marcia Dalphin, eds. *Illustrators of Children's Books: 1946-1956.* Boston: Horn Book, 1958.

*The National Union Catalog: A Cumulative Author List Representing Library of Congress Printed Cards and Titles Reported by Other American Libraries.* 104 vols. Ann Arbor, Mich.: J. W. Edwards, 1973.

*The National Union Catalog, 1956-1967: A Cumulative Author List Representing Library of Congress Printed Cards and Titles Reported by Other American Libraries: A New and Augmented Twelve Year Catalog Being a Compilation into One Alphabet the Fourth & Fifth Supplements of the National Union Catalog with a Key to Additional Locations through 1967 and with a Unique Identifying Number Allocated to Each Title.* Totowa, N.J.: Rowman and Littlefield, 1970-1972.

*The National Union Catalog, Pre-1956 Imprints: A Cumulative Author List Representing Library of Congress Printed Cards and Titles Reported by Other American Libraries.* 754 vols. London: Mansell, 1968-1981.

Roginski, Jim, comp. *Newbery and Caldecott Medalists and Honor Book Winners: Bibliographies and Resource Material through 1977.* Littleton, Colo.: Libraries Unlimited, 1982.